VISIT:
WWW.PRISONPROFESSORS.COM/BOOK

EARNING FREEDOM / PAPERBACK

Readers see 9,500-day journey through federal prisons of every security level. From arrest, on August 11, 1987, through release, on August 12, 2013, we see a continuous focus on earning higher levels of liberty at the soonest possible time. Readers see and understand the challenges that surface while serving a lengthy prison term. They also learn how a deliberate adjustment strategy can lead to earning freedom.

PRISON: MY 8,344TH DAY / WORKBOOK

Ten module course begins by building trust with participants, showing how a values-based, goal-oriented adjustment prepared the author for success. While serving 26 years in federal prisons of every security level, the author adhered to lessons he learned from leaders such as Nelson Mandela, Viktor Frankl, and Malcolm X to use his time inside to prepare for a life of meaning, relevance, and dignity after his release.

SUCCESS AFTER PRISON / WORKBOOK

This self-directed workbook helps participants understand the relationship between adjustment decisions and prospects for success upon release. While crossing through 9,500 days in prison, the author developed credentials and a release plan. He leveraged that plan to launch a life of meaning, relevance, and dignity upon release. Each chapter concludes with open-ended questions, challenging participants to prepare for success.

PERSEVERANCE, 2023 / WORKBOOK

The Perseverance self-directed workbook offers daily lessons for people to memorialize their preparations for success. Daily lessons challenge participants to make intentional decisions. By documenting their pathway to success, participants can influence case managers, wardens, probation officers, and others who have discretion over their lives. Use this workbook to document preparations for success.

RELEASE PLAN, 2023 / WORKBOOK

Building a pathway to success begins with an effective release plan that shows how a person prepares for success upon release. An effective strategy will show that a person understands the same terminology that stakeholders will use, including "criminogenic needs, triggers, and risk factors." More importantly, the release plan should document behavior goals to address such needs. Use this self-directed course as a guide.

WE PUBLISH
BOOKS/COURSES/VIDEOS
TO HELP PEOPLE IN PRISON HELP THEMSELVES

FORWARD

My name is Michael Santos, and I am writing this personal letter to welcome every participant to our course:

» Preparing for Success after Prison.

In the 30-hour, First-Step-Act-approved course, participants will learn the value of self-directed efforts to improve:

» Communication skills,
» Critical thinking,
» Self-directed learning,
» Release Planning,
» Prioritizing,
» Creation of tools, tactics, and resources,
» Progress on the execution of the plan, and
» Documentation of progress.

Those tactics help to restore confidence and advance prospects for success. They worked for me. I am confident they will lead to a higher level of liberty for anyone who adheres to a values-based, goal-oriented adjustment.

Although I concluded my obligation to the Bureau of Prisons in 2013, I continue using this course's lessons. They are an integral part of the advocacy strategies our team believes will improve outcomes for all justice-impacted people.

INCENTIVIZING A PURSUIT OF EXCELLENCE:

Our team at Prison Professors uses this course to persuade stakeholders to support reforms that will empower the Bureau of Prisons to incentivize the pursuit of excellence. Those arguments led to Earned Time Credits in federal prison and Milestone Credits in state systems. We're continuing to advance those initiatives.

We must collect data to persuade stakeholders, including business owners, citizens, and administrators to join our coalition. Those influencers can show legislators why reforms that allow people to earn increasing levels of liberty through merit can improve the culture of confinement and contribute to community safety.

I began making those arguments more than 20 years ago while working through the depths of a 45-year sentence. I began serving that sentence during a different era. Legislators had passed laws that removed incentives, calling for truth-in-sentencing. If a judge imposed a lengthy sentence, lawmakers wanted people to serve the entire sentence.

Those legislative changes resulted in a larger prison population. As high recidivism rates show, they did not result in safer communities.

COALITIONS:

With our new course, we can present evidence that shows the positive results when people start sowing seeds early to prepare for success upon release. A researcher from UCLA is helping us collect data and publish findings in peer-reviewed journals. We hope those findings will lead to broader coalitions that will include:

- » Prison administrators,
- » Judges,
- » Prosecutors,
- » Probation officers, and
- » Business leaders.

Together, we should work toward bringing changes in policies and laws that will empower administrators to incentivize the pursuit of excellence. Those incentives may include:

- » Broader use of furloughs,
- » Work release programs,
- » Access to compassionate release and commutations.

We can only succeed in our work if imprisoned people invest in themselves. When people prepare for success upon release, we can show that we're working to make prisons safer and lowering recidivism rates.

To broaden the initiative, we've launched PrisonProfessorsTalent.com. This website is part of our nonprofit enterprise. It allows people with access to email, directly or indirectly, to document the systematic steps they're taking to build effective release plans. The website encourages people to memorialize their journey by:

- » Engineering release plans,
- » Showing the courses they complete, and
- » Demonstrate the value they can add to prospective employers and stakeholders.

For more information, please send an email to our interns:

» Interns@PrisonProfessorsTalent.com.

We hope all participants will become a part of the change we want to see in the world.

Respectfully,

Michael Santos,
Founder

Other Books by
Michael G. Santos / Prison Professors

Earning Freedom:
Conquering a 45-Year Prison Term
PrisonProfessors.com
(Shows strategies to build strength and discipline through long term)

Prison! My 8,344th Day: Workbook
PrisonProfessors.com
(Shows strategies to be productive through single day in prison)

Success After Prison: Workbook
PrisonProfessors.com
(Shows outcomes for people who use time in prison to prepare for success)

Perseverance Workbook
(Annual Edition)
PrisonProfessors.com
(Self-directed course to help people in jail or prison)

Release Plan Workbook
PrisonProfessors.com
(Self-directed course to help people in jail or prison)

Inside: Life Behind Bars in America
St. Martin's Press
(Insight to high-security prisons in America)

Preparing for Success after Prison—
FSA-Approved Course (SENTRY code PSAP)

ISBN: 9798399552026

Version: June 30, 2023

To Contact us, please visit:
www.PrisonProfessors.com
Books@PrisonProfessors.com

To get our newsletter: Send invite to
Interns@PrisonProfessorsTalent.com
32565 Golden Lantern Street, B-1026
Dana Point, CA 92629

Contents

Section I
Preparing for Success after Prison

Welcome to our course: Preparing for Success after Prison.

As readers will find in this course, it's never too early, and it's never too late to begin preparing for success after prison.

Why?

Lots of reasons, including recidivism rates.

No one believes that they will return to prison after release. Unfortunately, statistics show that many people going into the system face enormous hurdles when they get out. From the time of an initial arrest, a person's life changes in unanticipated ways:

» They must interact with criminal defense lawyers, prosecutors, and a judicial system they don't understand.
» If a prison term follows, people get separated from those they love. Friends and family move on, which causes anxiety.
» While living in the system, constant challenges can complicate an adjustment—regardless of security level.
» Upon release, people face challenges finding housing, securing credit, or keeping up with an ever-changing society.

On the other hand, some people leave prison and thrive. Take the case of Weldon Long. His struggles with addiction influenced his behavior as a young man. Weldon participated in armed robberies that led to three separate prison terms. During his first two terms, he adjusted to the culture of confinement. Decisions inside led to further problems outside. After his third conviction, Weldon decided to transform his life. Now he leads a company that provides sales training to major corporations, such as Wells Fargo, Federal Express, Home Depot, and others.

What made the difference?

During his third term, Weldon decided he didn't want to live a criminal lifestyle any longer. He chose to prepare for success after prison. Regardless of what went on inside the penitentiary, he could always work toward improving himself by:

» Enhancing his vocabulary,
» Improving his writing skills,
» Becoming a better verbal communicator,

>> Evolving his critical-thinking skills,
>> Developing a self-directed work ethic.

Like many other people in prison, Weldon eventually learned that regardless of what went on around him, he bore the responsibility to prepare for success upon release.

Many people in prison believe that while living inside, they should focus on the culture of confinement and forget about the world outside. People who succeed upon release understand that an urgency exists. The sooner they start sowing seeds for success, the more effective they become at opening opportunities.

Our course on Preparing for Success after Prison urges participants to pursue a self-directed strategy. We offer the course in three sections:

Section 1:
>> Lessons 1 through 5 offer an introduction, showing the power that comes from leading a values-based, goal-oriented adjustment.

Section 2:
>> Lessons 6 through 15 provides guidance on how any person in prison can use this strategy to begin sowing seeds for a better outcome.

Section 3:
>> Lessons 16 through 30 offer stand-alone lessons on personal development.

Each lesson should require about one hour to compete. Participants who work through the 30-hour course should engineer a personal release plan that will allow them to:

>> Define the best possible outcome,
>> Create a release plan that will lead to success,
>> Put priorities in place,
>> Develop their tools, tactics, and resources,
>> Create personal accountability metrics, and
>> Motivate them to work relentlessly at executing the plan.

Our entire team at Prison Professors believes that anyone can work toward becoming extraordinary and compelling. It all starts with a personal release plan. Iterate the plan over time and document the incremental steps necessary to prepare for success.

For people in federal prison who want ongoing support, please send us a Corrlinks invite to get our newsletters.

We believe in you.

LESSON 1: VALUES AND GOALS.
DEFINE SUCCESS

Annotations: Values and Goals

Regardless of what stage in the journey we're in, we can begin sowing seeds for success by looking back and looking forward. In this introductory lesson, we'll get started on what it means to define values and goals—with a reflection on thoughts we could consider (or should have considered) before sentencing.

My name is Michael Santos and I'm the founder of Prison Professors. I'm grateful to introduce our series on Preparing for Success after Prison.

For full disclosure, I'm a person who served a lengthy prison term. Since concluding my sentence, in 2013, I've advocated for reforms that would lead to more incentives for people in prison. As participants in this course will find, I'll never ask anyone to do anything I didn't do while going through 9,500 days in prison, and that I'm not still doing today.

Leaders taught me lessons on how to prepare for success upon release. Since those lessons worked for me, others may want to learn from them.

Regardless of what stage of the ***journey*** a person may be in, we know that it's never too early and it's never too late to begin sowing seeds for success. At any time, we can look back on the decisions we made. If we ***introspect***, we can see how our early decisions led to where we are today.

Likewise, if we ***project*** into how we want to live in one year, five years, or ten years, we can reverse engineer a plan. That plan can lead us to the success we want to become.

Course design / Time Requirements / Resources:

A participant should complete each lesson in 50 to 90 minutes using this self-contained workbook. The time ***variable*** depends on whether participants watch the optional DVD video profiles or engage in interactive exercises—we make the video files optional because not all institutions have the capacity to offer such resources.

With each lesson, participants will have opportunities to show how they're engineering a pathway to success.

Objective:

Through our Preparing for Success after Prison series, participants will develop skills. Those skills contribute to each participant's success—regardless of the stage in the journey or place of confinement. For example, the lessons will help people if they're:

» Contemplating their response to a criminal charge,
» Preparing before sentencing,
» Engineering an adjustment strategy that leads to the best outcomes,
» Preparing for a career after release.

Lessons in the Preparing for Success after Prison series assist people who want to help themselves. And the ***self-contained*** lesson plan includes everything a person needs to complete the personal-development exercises. Those exercises will lead to:

» Expanding a vocabulary,
» Improving writing skills,
» Developing reading skills,
» More confidence when communicating verbally,
» Critical thinking skills,
» Commitment to self-directed learning, and
» Advanced networking skills to find mentors.

Personal Exercises:

We're ***purposely*** writing this course at a basic level, using short sentences and simple analogies. Mostly, we write from the ***plural*** voice with ***gender-neutral pronouns***. We will occasionally use "he" or "she" because we want to be inclusive. The lessons apply to all justice-impacted people, regardless of age, ***ethnicity***, or gender.

We minimize labels such as "inmate," "convict," or "prisoner" because we want participants to identify as people or citizens of the broader community. Our entire team at Prison Professors ***strives*** to help people ***emerge*** from prison with their dignity intact and with opportunities to thrive as the individual defines "thriving" or "succeeding."

Note on Vocabulary Building:

The end of this booklet includes a ***lexicon***. That's another word for dictionary. If we ***highlight*** a word in ***bold italics***, we cite that word in the back of the book. The back-of-the-booklet lexicon includes a definition. We encourage participants to learn any words they do not know as part of a self-directed vocabulary-building exercise. Participants who make a commitment will not need a teacher, a classroom, a video player, or any resource other than this simple workbook (or collection of printed lesson plans) to build a more ***robust vocabulary***.

Note on Developing Writing Skills:

Each lesson includes a series of open-ended questions. Participants may write as little or as much as they would like. Questions do not have a single right or wrong answer. Instead, each answer should align with how a person thinks. And people think differently. If a person chooses to develop better writing skills, that person will become more valuable in the marketplace. People can develop better writing skills and thinking skills if they use this self-directed learning strategy.

Note on DVD Supplement:

Each lesson includes an optional DVD video. We burned *captions* into the bottom of each video. Participants may read the captions while listening to *enhance* their reading skills. The DVDs include interviews with *justice-impacted* men and women from different backgrounds. Those people either built successful careers after their release from prison or triumphed over other adversity. The videos also include ideas that justice-impacted people can use to prepare for income-generating opportunities upon release. When we listen to successful people share their stories, we find clues or takeaways we can use to become more successful.

Section one covers five lessons:

- » Defining Success with Values and Goals,
- » Attitude and Aspiration,
- » Action and Accountability,
- » Awareness and Authenticity,
- » Achievement and Appreciation.

As a *virtual* instructor, let me start by sharing the backstory. To earn trust, participants will learn that I never ask anyone to do anything I did not do while going through a personal journey that included multiple decades in prison.

I'd like to earn your trust.

History of the Course:

Our Preparing for Success after Prison series is part of a larger project, a lifelong commitment to advocating for justice-impacted people. To succeed, I rely upon the same lessons I'm offering in this course. To advocate effectively, we need to build *coalitions* with many moving parts, including:

- » Legislators that influence laws,
- » Administrators that influence policies,
- » Justice-impacted people that go through the system,
- » University scholars who assess the effectiveness of our programs,
- » Business owners that may work with justice-impacted people,
- » Financial institutions that influence *collateral consequences* for justice-impacted people,

» Community organizations that welcome justice-impacted people into society, and
» Citizens that vote.

As this course teaches, succeeding as an advocate requires us to ***influence*** authority figures. We must begin with a plan. To influence authority figures, we must develop more skill at turning letters into words, words into sentences, sentences into paragraphs, and paragraphs into persuasive arguments. We learned that lesson in advocacy from authority figures, such as Frederick Douglass.

Frederick Douglas and the Power of Advocacy:

Some participants may know the story of Frederick Douglass, who began his life as an enslaved person. That struggle brought enormous adversity. In time, an opportunity opened for him to escape to freedom. Rather than moving on to enjoy his liberty, Mr. Douglass devoted his life to advocacy, working tirelessly as a force for the ***abolition*** of slavery.

To succeed in getting the outcome he wanted, Frederick Douglass understood that he would need to develop new skills:

» He had to learn how to read.
» He had to learn how to write.
» He had to learn how to speak persuasively.
» He had to learn how to build a coalition of influential people.
» He had to work with those influential people to change laws that would lead to the abolition of slavery.

The story of Frederick Douglass gives us an example of excellence. Despite being born into slavery, he ***adhered*** to a values-based, goal-oriented strategy to live for good. Millions of other people benefited. Knowing it would be a long walk to freedom, as another great advocate advised us, Frederick Douglas advanced the cause by turning words into sentences and sentences into paragraphs.

To use his life's story as a tool that would persuade more people to believe in his vision, he authored three ***autobiographies***:

» *Narrative of the Life of Frederick Douglass, an American Slave,*
» *My Bondage and My Freedom,* and
» *Life and Times of Frederick Douglass*

By writing his life story, Frederick Douglass developed the power to influence people he would never meet. Readers began to see a different perspective as they read about his experiences and the ***resilience*** of his life. They invited him to participate in public forums, where he would deliver ***orations*** and respond to questions from the audience. Through his story, he changed the minds of ***adversaries***.

Some people criticized Frederick Douglass because he spent time with people who supported slavery, including those who enslaved others. Those critics wanted to know why he would **converse** with anyone supporting slavery. Mr. Douglass said he did not need to **convert** people who knew the evil of slavery; he lived by the motto: "I would unite with anybody to do right and with nobody to do wrong."

By changing minds, Frederick Douglass influenced how people voted. He persuaded people to see that slavery was wrong and convinced them to **elect** candidates who would vote to **abolish** slavery.

Take Ten Minutes (1-1):

Write responses to the following three questions in approximately ten minutes. If participating in a class setting, discuss verbally.

> » 1-1: What takeaways can you gather from this abbreviated lesson on Frederick Douglass?

_____

_____

_____

_____

_____

_____

_____

> » 1-2: In what ways can this brief synopsis on Frederick Douglass influence a strategy you create to prepare before you face an authority figure that will judge you?

_____

_____

_____

_____

_____

_____

_____

_____

» 1-3: In what ways would you say that slavery influenced Frederick Douglass' understanding of the world?

_____

_____

_____

_____

_____

_____

Personal Story:

Unfortunately, I didn't begin to learn from leaders like Frederick Douglass until after prosecutors convinced members of a grand jury to **_indict_** me. DEA agents arrested me on August 11, 1987, when I was 23. I'd never been incarcerated before that arrest and didn't know what to expect. At that stage in my life, I only wanted liberty.

With that mindset, I willingly listened to people around me who told me what I wanted to hear rather than what I needed to hear. Then, I made more bad decisions.

Since my charges carried a potential life sentence, I spent most of my pre-trial detention in **_solitary_** confinement. Because of that time in solitary, I didn't learn much about how the criminal justice system operated. Without knowledge of the legal system, I left myself **_vulnerable_** to the messages other people in the detention center tried to **_convey_**. Those people gave me a variety of messages:

» There was a big difference between an indictment and a conviction.
» The best way to serve time would be to forget about the world outside and focus on my time inside.
» The government only wins cases because most people plead guilty; prosecutors rarely prove cases when people go to trial.

By listening to viewpoints of questionable value, I made a **_series_** of **_catastrophic_** decisions. Following the trial, members of the jury convicted me of every count. My choices exposed me to a harsher sentence than I would have received if I had acted differently. Following the first trial, prosecutors brought new charges of perjury against me.

Take Ten Minutes (1-2):

Write responses to the following questions in approximately ten minutes. If participating in a class setting, discuss verbally.

» 1-4: In what ways would you say the author's preparation before sentencing differed from the leadership of Frederick Douglass?

_____

_____

_____

_____

_____

_____

» 1-5: In what ways would you say the author's conviction influence possibilities for him to become an advocate?

_____

_____

_____

_____

_____

_____

» 1-6: How would you predict that authority figures in society would respond to the author's conviction?

_____

_____

_____

_____

_____

_____

Retrospect:

Looking back, I see how my lack of preparation before sentencing hurt me. Instead of responding deliberately, with an intentional strategy during a *pivotal* moment, I *abdicated* all responsibility to prepare.

I effectively gave up by allowing myself to *succumb* to guidance from others. Rather than being *intentional* about my decisions, I hoped that someone else could solve problems *spawned* by my previous decisions.

Frederick Douglas took a different approach. He didn't only think about what he wanted or what would benefit his life. He thought about society and figured out ways he could influence the making of a better community for all. Then, he **embarked** upon a **methodical**, deliberate plan. To abolish slavery, he understood that he would have to:

» Define success as the abolition of slavery,
» Put a plan together that would advance prospects of abolishing slavery,
» Put priorities in place,
» Execute the plan, and
» Hold himself accountable.

Preparing for success at any phase in life requires that we begin by defining success. Then, we must set clear and SMART goals that align with our definition of success. If we value success, we need to take the incremental steps that will lead to success.

Whether we like it or not, we must live in the world as it exists and not as we want it to be.

Frederick Douglass understood that slavery existed. He couldn't wish it out of existence. Instead, he had to take a series of **systematic** steps that moved closer to success as he wanted to experience success—living in a world that did not allow anyone to enslave another person. He had already solved his problem by escaping from slavery. But he also wanted to solve problems that were far bigger than his own.

I didn't have that **presence** of mind when I began serving my sentence. I simply wanted to get out of detention and avoid prison. I didn't think about anything other than what I wanted.

That mindset would not work out so well for me.

I would have been far better off thinking about stakeholders in the system. As Zig Zigler, an influential sales leader, is famous for having said:

"If we can help others get what they want, we can get everything we want."

I didn't learn those lessons until long after a judge sentenced me. Reflecting on those months before sentencing, I see that I made many mistakes by not thinking about stakeholders. Had I considered the questions below, I would have used these strategies to prepare before sentencing.

Take Ten Minutes (1-3):

Write responses to the following questions in approximately ten minutes. If participating in a class setting, discuss verbally.

» 1-7: What motivates a prosecutor?

_____

_____

_____

_____

_____

_____

_____

_____

_____

_____

_____

_____

_____

_____

_____

_____

» 1-8: What motivates a judge?

_____

_____

_____

_____

_____

_____

_____

_____

_____

_____

_____

_____

» 1-9: What motivates the people who will influence prospects for liberty going forward?

LESSON 2—ATTITUDE AND ASPIRATION
100% COMMITMENT

Annotation: Attitude and Aspiration

Once we define success and set clear goals, we need to pursue success with the right attitude. For our course, we define the "right" attitude as a 100% commitment to success—as the individual defines it. That strategy works for people who anticipate a sentencing hearing, and for people after sentencing. Aspire to the best possible outcome.

Halim Flowers:

Halim Flowers is now one of our nation's most celebrated artists, writers, and activists. But that isn't how he started his life.

Like many people who go through the criminal justice system, Halim began his life in struggle. Street gangs influenced his ***adolescent*** years. Before he turned 10, he walked across puddles of blood that oozed from a dead person. Neither gunshots nor seeing death ***fazed*** him. His father became addicted to crack cocaine.

Conditioned by his environment, Halim started selling crack at 12, ***adapting*** to life on the streets and housing projects of Washington, DC. Most children his age have positive role models and learn in school, preparing them to live as productive adults. Their lives reflect what they see around them. Unlike other teenagers, Halim didn't grow up with the opportunities and privileges that so many people take for granted. His behavior mirrored what he saw, and by the time he turned 16, he had to start preparing for sentencing and prison.

Authorities charged him with gang-related crimes. After ***judicial*** proceedings concluded, Halim had to cope with the ***plight*** of two life sentences.

What does it even mean to serve double life?

Since a judge sentenced him to serve a term with letters rather than numbers, authorities sent Halim into high-security penitentiaries. He stepped inside the walls before being old enough to vote.

While incarcerated, Halim made a commitment. Despite starting his sentence at 16, he had the wisdom to know that he didn't like his environment. People convicted of crimes surrounded him. Those people tried to influence his adjustment, giving him a message that ***permeates*** every jail and prison in America:

"The best way to serve time is to forget about the world outside, and to focus on time inside."

It's tough to start serving a sentence under those conditions. Prison can **obliterate** hope. Few people know what it's like to live with the following challenges:

» Being born into an environment that doesn't **abound** with positive role models,
» Being influenced by gangs and crime before knowing how to **decipher** the consequences of decisions,
» Being separated from a mother at 16,
» Learning that a federal judge imposed two life sentences,
» Hearing that the system doesn't offer any way out.

Take Ten Minutes (2-1):

Write responses to the following questions in approximately ten minutes. If participating in a class setting, discuss verbally.

» 2-1: How would you expect a person with Halim's background to adjust inside the penitentiary?

_____

_____

_____

_____

_____

_____

_____

» 2-2: In what ways would you expect his life to be different after 20 years in prison?

_____

_____

_____

_____

_____

_____

_____

» 2-3: What would you say would be the best possible outcome for a person with Halim's background?

_____

_____

_____

_____

_____

_____

_____

_____

_____

Despite the challenges of Halim's backstory, he had an attitude of ***self-empowerment***. He didn't like the backstory of illiteracy, poverty, drug abuse, and a pipeline that would carry children from school playgrounds to the penitentiary. Rather than complain, he found a way to write a new chapter in his life story. He wanted to make a difference that would lead to a better community.

Halim coined a phrase:

"Love is the antidote."

As he moved through his sentence, he developed his mind and understanding of the world by reading. Through reading, he trained himself to become a better communicator. He learned to put words into sentences, and sentences into paragraphs. Over time, he ***authored*** several books, including:

1. *A Reason to Breathe*
2. *Mind Over Matter*
3. *What our Fathers Never Told Us*
4. *Makings of a Menace*
5. *Buried Alive*
6. *Time: How to Do it and Not Let it Do You*
7. *For Young Offenders*
8. *Be Great Wherever You Are*
9. *Niggernomics: What Blacks Must Know about Money*
10. *A Reason to Breathe*

Knowing the importance of using many mediums to communicate, he also taught himself how to paint.

With words and pictures, Halim worked to help others see the pain that comes when society shackles a boy's soul in chains. Despite living in cages, as years turned into decades, knowing that he did not have a release date, he learned to master the use of words and pictures. By communicating, he could take steps that would lead to liberty. He wrote books and converted ideas into images, ***transcending*** prison boundaries, influencing others to believe in him.

Mechanisms didn't exist to change his life sentence. Yet Halim's attitude gave him the fuel to keep working toward his aspirations. In time, he wanted to make a difference. Through his work, he could contribute to ending ***intergenerational*** cycles of poverty.

Like Mahatma Gandhi, Halim Flowers **aspired** to live as the change that he wanted to see. He gives us an example of what it means to live with the **audacity** of hope, believing that with the right attitude, he could be more than the label of "super **predator**" that society had **bestowed** upon him when he was only a boy.

He made a 100% commitment to that end.

Leaders inspired him.

But inspiration without actions is fantasy. Halim gives us an example of excellence. If a person has the right attitude, and if a person aspires toward the best outcome, **perseverance** and commitment can bend the arc toward justice.

By the time that Halim served 22 years, the law changed. Those changes allowed a federal judge to take another look at injustice. The judge agreed that, based on Halim's extraordinary and compelling adjustment, a double-life sentence no longer served the interests of justice.

In 2019, after 22 years in prison, Halim returned to court. During the second hearing, he walked out of the courtroom to begin his life as a successful artist, writer, and activist.

Take Ten Minutes (2-2):

Write responses to the following questions in approximately ten minutes. If participating in a class setting, discuss verbally.

» 2-4: What role would you say that Halim's attitude at the start of his sentence had on his eventual release?

_____

_____

_____

_____

_____

_____

_____

_____

_____

_____

_____

» 2-5: In what ways would you say that Halim's aspiration fueled his adjustment?

_____

_____

_____

_____

_____

_____

_____

_____

_____

_____

_____

_____

» 2-6: In what ways could a story like Halim's influence your preparation for sentencing?

_____

_____

_____

_____

_____

_____

_____

_____

_____

_____

_____

_____

_____

Attitudes, Aspirations, and Sentencings:

Halim is a special kind of human being. Intuitively, soon after authorities locked him in prison as a teenager, he had an idea of what success should look like for him. Then, he set clear goals that would lead him to become a better communicator. Over time, he trained himself to write books, to launch a publishing company, and to paint pictures that would help others see what they did not see previously.

By the time an opportunity opened for him to go through a new sentencing hearing, Halim had a new story. The judge responded by releasing him from the injustice of a double-life sentence.

Few people go into a sentencing hearing with the preparations that Halim made during the 22 years that he served. Taking the long view requires patience, commitment, and the right attitude. Even people who face relatively short sentences (and anything is short compared to a life sentence) tend to think about themselves in the immediate moment rather than what they can become over time.

That's understandable. They're about to lose their liberty.

The **concept** of being separated from all that a person loves can feel **surreal**. Yet even people facing short sentences can learn a great deal from Halim's story. They can think about the different people that they're going to **encounter** and figure out a strategy to influence perceptions.

We tend to view our lives from the limited **perspective** of how we see ourselves. Yet others may see us differently from the way that we see ourselves.

When I went through the criminal justice process, I had the wrong attitude because I didn't know how to think differently. Instead of thinking about the realities that follow for people facing sentencing, I should have been thinking about the people I would face in the future. Many people would have enormous discretion over my future. Rather than coming up with a deliberate, intentional plan to influence those decision makers, I thought about how the sentence would influence my life.

Later, by reading influential books, I began to see a different perspective. For example, I remember a book that changed my perspective. I don't recall the book's name, but I remember it taught me the concept of "The Johari Window."

With the "Johari Window," people learn to understand their relationship with themselves and others. Psychologists use the concept of the Johari Window in self-help groups. Anyone preparing for sentencing may want to consider lessons from the Johari Window teachings.

Start by thinking of a **quadrant** with two columns and two rows, as follows:

	Known to Self	Unknown to Self
Known to Others	**(open area)** The open quadrant is that part of our conscious self that we're aware of, and that is known to others. Anyone can assess our attitude, behavior, motivations, values, and way of life. In preparing for sentencing, we can be certain that prosecutors and the judge are assessing us.	**(blind)** This quadrant represents what others perceive in us but that we do not think about when thinking of ourselves. Although we may see ourselves as being good people, when authorities charge us with crimes, we should consider the likelihood that they're looking at us as being bad people.
Not Known to Others	**(façade)** In this quadrant, despite what we know about ourselves, others do not see it. For example, we may think of ourselves as being remorseful. Yet prosecutors or the judge may not see it.	**(unknown)** This quadrant includes all that neither others know about us, nor that we know about ourselves. Who knows what we will be in the days, months, years, or decades ahead? For example, who could have predicted what Halim would become when he went into prison at 16?

Using this framework before sentencing can influence a person's attitude and aspirations. Instead of living with *delusions*, we can prepare for reality. Those who love us may know the "real" us, but we would be *naïve* to believe that our adversaries will see us in the same way.

If we want to prepare for the best possible outcome at sentencing, we need to go into the proceeding with the right attitude, and with the right aspiration. We need to think about the obstacles we face today, and the strategies we can create to prepare for a better tomorrow.

If a person does not take appropriate steps before sentencing, the only record that will exist will be the documents that describe our crime. To influence a better outcome, we can use Johari's Window to consider questions that will help us prepare.

Take Ten Minutes (2-3):

Write responses to any of the following questions in approximately 20 minutes. If participating in a class setting, discuss verbally.

Open questions:

» In what ways do you see yourself?

_____

_____

_____

_____

_____

_____

» How or why would the prosecutor or judge know this about you?

_____

_____

_____

_____

_____

_____

_____

» What steps can you take to help the prosecutor or judge know this about you?

_____

_____

_____

_____

_____

_____

_____

_____

Blind questions:

» What motivated the prosecutor or judge to pursue his position?

_____

_____

» How does the prosecutor or judge define success?

» In what ways does the prosecutor or judge view you?

Façade questions:

» When the prosecutor or judge meets with others in his profession, how do they think about people like you?

» What common traits do you have with other people the prosecutor or judge must assess?

_____

_____

_____

_____

_____

_____

_____

» In what ways does the prosecutor or judge believe you are unaware or unrealistic about how you see yourself?

_____

_____

_____

_____

_____

_____

_____

Unknown questions:

» What influences in your future are neither you nor your prosecutor or judge considering?

_____

_____

_____

_____

_____

_____

_____

» In what ways does your behavior show that you're contemplating such unknowns?

_____

_____

_____

_____

_____

_____

_____

_____

_____

What motivates your prosecutor or judge to want to deny your request for special consideration?

_____

_____

_____

_____

_____

_____

_____

_____

These kinds of questions should help us build the right attitude and aspiration as we face a sentencing hearing. We don't only want to think about consequences we must face for the decisions we made.

We also want to think about how others will perceive us. Then we need to create a strategy that will put us in a better position to succeed.

Regardless of what stage we're in on the journey through the criminal justice system, we will encounter people who do not know us. Yet they will judge us based on what government officials or media reports have written to describe us.

To the extent we can think about our challenges, we can put ourselves on pathways toward better outcomes. The sooner a person starts to contemplate these realities, the more effective the person becomes in preparing for success.

Personal Story:

While locked inside a solitary cell, I awaited my sentencing date. After a year of trial proceedings, a jury found me guilty on every count. Anticipating a lengthy sentence, I needed to make sense of all the ways my life had gone wrong.

When DEA agents arrested me in 1987, I didn't know how to think from the perspective of others. I'd never heard of Johari's Window. All I knew was that I hated being in confinement and I wanted out. I had a natural ***inclination*** to think about myself and all I was losing. Everyone in law enforcement, on the other hand, thought about the crimes I committed and the victims of my crime.

In that early frame of mind, I had the wrong attitude. I argued that my crime didn't have any victims. A group of ***consenting*** adults paid to purchase cocaine from a group of people that I influenced. I hoped for the lowest possible sentence, but I didn't do the work to prepare for the lowest possible sentence.

While I ***languished*** in the solitary cell, a correctional officer began bringing books that he said would change my thoughts.

I knew him as "Officer Wilson," one of the kindest officers in the detention center. He could see something in me that I could not see in myself. Besides passing me books on Frederick Douglass, he gave me an ***anthology*** on philosophy. I didn't know the meaning of ***philosophy*** at the time. But he assured me that I could learn from reading the lessons in the books he brought.

To create meaning in my life from prison, I needed to learn how to think differently. Instead of ***perseverating*** on how I could get out early, I needed to change my attitude and aspiration. That books Officer Wilson provided opened my eyes to a different way of thinking.

I read about Socrates, a man who lived more than 2,500 years ago. ***Ordinarily,*** such a story wouldn't have interested me. In reading the first paragraph of the story on Socrates, I learned that he was in a jail cell awaiting the day when authorities would carry out a death sentence for a crime he committed.

I wouldn't have read the book, or the story about Socrates previously because I neither identified with the concept of philosophy nor did I have any interest in history. Sometimes, we get the message we need at the right time. The story spoke to me because I faced life in prison. Facing life in prison felt as if I faced a death sentence—because I could potentially die in prison. I needed a better attitude, and I needed to aspire to something bigger than my life. That story about Socrates helped me to learn that I had been living by a bad philosophy.

Fortunately, it's never too early, and it's never too late to begin making better decisions.

After reading that story, I began to **contemplate** the different ways that I could make sense of my journey. I realized that I could not change the past:

- » I broke the law,
- » A jury convicted me,
- » A judge would sentence me,
- » I would go to prison.

Like Halim Flowers, I would have to **confront** the challenges ahead. My attitude would influence whether I wasted time in prison, or whether I used that time to **reconcile** with society and make amends. In preparing before sentencing, I needed to convey a message. I wanted stakeholders to know that, going forward, I would make **disparate** decisions than I had made before my arrest. I intended to work toward something bigger than my own life.

The prosecutor responded to my **proclamations** of **remorse,** by telling the judge:

"If Michael Santos spends every day of his life in an all-consuming effort to repay society, and if he lives to be 300 years old, our society will still be at a significant net loss."

The federal judge **presiding** over my case sentenced me to 45 years. Fortunately, reading the story about Socrates helped me to process the sentence **imposed.**

I'll **paraphrase** an ancient fable that can help us come to terms with the challenges we face.

A scorpion asks a frog to carry him over the river. The frog initially refuses, claiming its fear of being stung. The scorpion argues that if it stung the frog, they both would die because the frog would sink, drowning the scorpion.

The frog then agrees.

Midway across the river, the scorpion stings the frog, dooming them both.

As they started to drown, the frog asked the scorpion why he stung him. The scorpion replied that it's in its nature to sting.

The prosecutor's nature is to ask for a lengthy sentence. The judge's nature is to impose a term that will protect the interests of society—not to make things easier on the person who broke the law.

Like Halim, I could choose how to respond to the sentence. My attitude going forward would determine my aspirations.

LESSON 3-ACTION AND ACCOUNTABILITY
INCREMENTAL STEPS

Annotation: Action and Accountability

We may know what we want, and we may commit verbally to preparing for success. We also must act. Each decision we make should align with our commitment to success. If we know what we're striving to achieve, our personal accountability tools will help us measure the incremental progress we make.

Taking Action:

We prepare ourselves for a better outcome when we take time to learn from others. The earlier lessons of our course profiled leaders such as Frederick Douglass, Halim Flowers, and Socrates. Those leaders show us the *relevance* of:

» Defining success,
» Setting goals,
» Moving forward with the right attitude, and
» Aspiring to the outcomes we want for our life.

Yet unless we take *incremental* action steps, we never open opportunities. Without opening opportunities, we fail to position ourselves for the success we want.

An old proverb teaches us that if we want to know the journey ahead, we should ask people who have walked back. I remember getting that message from reading a story written during *medieval* times. The *trilogy,* known as *The Divine Comedy*, begins in a scary forest, which is a *metaphor* for darkness—or a *predicament* beyond what we take as being familiar.

While trying to escape that forest, Dante, the author and *protagonist* in the story, looks for safety. He fears a lion, a leopard, and a wolf that want to *devour* him. Those beasts represent the sins of pride, lust, and greed. If a person doesn't exercise discipline, those sins can lead to a person's *demise*.

Dante knows his death is *imminent*, as those animals present an *existential* threat.

In Dante's pursuit of safety, he encounters the spirit of Virgil, a man who could save him. To get to safety, however, Virgil had to take him from the forest and through the nine *concentric* circles of hell. Each ring holds people who lived a life of gradually increasing wickedness. By telling Dante the stories that *condemned* those people to suffer through *eternity* provided Dante with knowledge, or the wisdom he needed to escape hell and *transcend* to paradise.

The story, Dante wrote, is not about his life—but about the entire human experience. If we know more about the punishment that follows our wickedness, we can avoid behavior that brings consequences we do not want.

Like Dante, we all must act to prepare for a better life. It's never too early, and it's never too late, to start sowing seeds for something better.

Any person going into a prison term can learn great lessons about action and accountability from others who have gone through the journey before us.

Participants who have access to DVD videos that our team at Prison Professors produces will find examples of people's experiences. The justice-impacted men and women come from different backgrounds, and authorities convicted them of various crimes. All those people have stories to tell. Each of us has a responsibility to listen to the stories of others.

We should strive to *decipher* lessons that will help us make better decisions; we should act in ways that lead to better outcomes. When we create *accountability metrics*, we develop resources that can keep us on track.

Watching the videos that accompany this course may prove helpful because we can always learn from people who've gone through challenging times—especially if they've overcome those challenging times.

We also should learn from the people around us. By *conversing* with people serving time, we can learn a great deal—especially if those people describe previous experiences of going through the system, and challenges they faced upon release. If people try to *perpetuate* the *myth* that the best way to serve time is to forget about the world outside and focus on time inside, we should work through the following exercises, which we can start right now:

Take Ten Minutes (3-1):

Write responses to the following questions in approximately ten minutes. If participating in a class setting, discuss verbally.

» 3-1: Describe a justice-impacted person who did well after release.

_____

_____

_____

_____

_____

_____

» 3-2: Describe a justice-impacted person who failed after release.

_____

_____

_____

_____

_____

_____

» 3-3: In what ways would you say those people's actions in prison put them on a pathway for success or failure?

_____

_____

_____

_____

_____

_____

_____

Tommy Walker's Story:

While preparing our course on Preparing for Success after Prison, I had a conversation with Tommy Walker, III. Authorities arrested Tommy and sentenced him to three life sentences. He served more than two decades inside the walls of the United States Penitentiary in Lewisburg before the First Step Act opened an opportunity for release.

With a reputation for holding some of the most volatile people in federal prison, Lewisburg could darken a person's spirits. Tommy understood the **bleakness** of his sentence. The US Parole Commission did not have authority to release him. He would spend the rest of his life in prison unless:

» An appeals court **vacated** his sentence,
» The President **commuted** his sentence, or
» Congress **legislated** a new law that the President signed.

Despite those complications, Tommy chose to live productively. Living productively requires a person to have a plan, and to execute the plan with **incremental** action steps. Even

if he had to spend his life inside of a federal prison, he could live with meaning, *relevance,* and dignity.

How?

He could live for something bigger than his life. Instead of complaining about the sentence *imposed,* Tommy decided to become useful to others. He became a better:

» reader,
» researcher, and
» writer.

Over time, Tommy developed skills in learning how to use *esoteric* resources in the prison's law library. He learned about the legal process, including decisions by District Court Judges, Circuit Court Judges, and Supreme Court Justices. He read about *statutes*, citations, and Court rules for Civil or Criminal procedure. Tommy became a master of the Prison Reform Litigation Act, administrative remedy process, and habeas corpus.

With those skills, Tommy served his community and he also served himself. Every day he could hold himself accountable, *devoting* hours to learning. Those actions kept him focused on becoming more useful to people in his community.

Through his work, Tommy helped many people file *pro se* motions that advanced prospects for their liberty. Although he didn't know whether opportunities would open for him to walk out of prison, he created meaning by becoming more useful by helping others.

By studying law, Tommy understood the importance of keeping a *pristine* disciplinary record—free of any infractions. Since he had a purpose to work toward, he avoided behavior that could lead to problems with other people in prison, either staff or others serving time.

In 2018, after 25 years inside, Tommy Walker, III had built an "extraordinary and compelling" record.

When sentencing Tommy to serve three life sentences, the judge considered the prosecutors' arguments. They focused on his past behavior. Tommy couldn't do anything to change his past decisions, and the judge sentenced him for those crimes. Yet Tommy's actions in prison, and his commitment to hold himself accountable, *differentiated* him from others.

When President Trump signed the First Step Act, a mechanism opened for Tommy to argue for liberty. Since he served a triple-life sentence for crimes that included violence, he did not complain that Earned Time Credits did not apply to him. Instead, he *seized* upon other opportunities that the law opened, such as compassionate release.

The First Step Act empowers every person in prison to make an argument for compassionate release. Before President Trump signed that law, people in federal prison had fewer

opportunities to **self-advocate** for liberty. To become a better **candidate** for relief, however, the person should show an "extraordinary and compelling" adjustment record. People will advance their **prospects** for success with compassionate release if they can show that they've used their time to prepare for success after prison.

Tommy Walker III provides us with an example of excellence. He understood that he could not change the past. Yet through his behavior, he could build a compelling record that would persuade others to view him through a different **lens**.

Skilled defense attorneys told Tommy that **immutable** laws would block him from ever getting relief.

Despite those **admonishments**, Tommy believed in himself. He acted in ways that would reframe the narrative of his life. When a federal judge reviewed Tommy's petition for compassionate relief, he didn't only consider the history of violence or criminal behavior that led Tommy to prison. The judge also considered Tommy's extraordinary and compelling prison adjustment. She granted his petition, allowing him to walk out of prison as a free man.

Besides developing skills while in prison, Tommy also earned credentials to become a certified paralegal. To live productively in society, he launched his own business: Second Chance 4 R.E.A.L, a paralegal service to help people in prison get relief from their sentences. Through his work, many people have gotten relief through administrative remedy, habeas corpus, and filings related to the First Step Act.

Personal Story:
Like Tommy and Halim, I would have to live with a lengthy sentence. People like them, who had overcome severe hardship and injustice, taught me the importance of being deliberate and intentional. Although I didn't know Tommy or Halim when I began serving my sentence, I could learn from other leaders by reading. For example, I learned a great by reading about Nelson Mandela.

Authorities in South Africa released Nelson Mandela around the same time that I transferred from the detention center to the penitentiary. Despite serving 27 years for the injustice of **apartheid**, Nelson Mandela lived without bitterness or anger toward anyone. He only wanted to use his life as a **catalyst** to help others. Like Halim Flowers wrote decades later, Nelson Mandela showed that love is the **antidote** to pain and suffering.

Other examples of excellence inspired me. The life stories of inspiring people **manifested** lessons I learned from reading about Nelson Mandela, Viktor Frankl, and Malcolm X. Their actions in prison led to massive contributions.

To find my path, I began with the end in mind, following the lessons that Stephen Covey taught in his **opus**, *The Seven Habits of Highly Effective People*.

I could not change that:

> » I violated laws that prohibit people from selling cocaine,
> » A jury convicted me,
> » A judge sentenced me to 45 years, or
> » Prison administrators sent me to a high-security penitentiary.

To begin with the end in mind, I could think about how I wanted to emerge. Regardless of how much time I served, when I got out, I wanted to live meaningfully. I didn't want to struggle through the *trauma* of homelessness, poverty, unemployment, or further problems with the criminal justice system. Like Halim and Tommy, I would have to take actions to prepare.

I began by thinking about the people I anticipated meeting:

> » Future case managers,
> » Future wardens,
> » Future probation officers,
> » Future employers,
> » Future business partners or sponsors,
> » Future legislators or prison administrators.

Take Ten Minutes (3-2):

Write responses to the following questions in approximately ten minutes. If participating in a class setting, discuss verbally.

> » 3-4: In what ways have you thought about the people who currently have influence over your liberty?

_____

_____

_____

_____

_____

_____

_____

_____

_____

» 3-5: What action plans have you set to influence people who will influence your success in the years to come?

_____
_____
_____
_____
_____
_____
_____
_____

» 3-6: Describe accountability resources you created to stay on track with your action plans.

_____
_____
_____
_____
_____
_____
_____
_____

As Virgil advised Dante, today's actions influence the life we lead in the weeks, months, and decades ahead. Leaders taught me that instead of *dwelling* on the *predicament* I created, I should *contemplate* the future.

What would people who had influence over my life expect of me?

Those kinds of questions do not have a right or wrong answer. At any time, we can *meditate* on such questions. While staring at the wall of a solitary cell, I had to think of the decisions that put me there.

No one would care that I hated living in confinement.

If I wanted to lead a meaningful life, regardless of my location, I had to take steps like any other person who overcame struggle. I had to build a record that would convince others to *advocate* on my *behalf*.

By ***introspecting***, I realized the importance of using time inside wisely. If I didn't make changes, people would always see me for the crimes that led me to prison. Every decision would come with an opportunity cost. If I chose to ease the pains of confinement by watching daytime soap operas, playing table games, or acting in ways that could lead to disciplinary infractions, I could ***prolong*** rather than shorten the time that I would spend in prison.

On the other hand, if I thought about the people I would meet in the future, I could create an effective action plan. To the extent that I created accountability metrics to measure progress, I may succeed in overcoming the ***stigma*** of being a convicted felon.

The ***tripart*** plan would require me to focus on:

» Earning academic credentials,
» Contributing to society, and
» Building a support network of positive mentors.

In his book, *Good to Great,* author Jim Collins wrote about the ways that good companies could become great companies. Readers may find similarities in how they could use the same ***principles*** from that *Good to Great* to reach a higher potential.

A memorable ***metaphor*** from that book invites readers to consider the difficulty of starting a new plan. He wrote about a ***spindle*** or ***axis*** mounted to the ground. On top of the axis, sat a heavy ***disk*** made of stone. Mr. Collins wrote that, because of the disk's weight, it would take an enormous amount of energy or force to spin the disk. But once the disk started to spin, it would require less force or energy to keep spinning.

The metaphor helped me realize that I would have to get started if I wanted to become better at anything. To get started, I must *apply* myself with commitment, energy, and discipline. Getting started would be difficult, as I had been a terrible student before my imprisonment. I didn't read well or write well, and as evidenced by the decisions I made that led me to prison, I wasn't too good at critical thinking.

Yet just as Jim Collins wrote in his book about building great businesses, we could take small actions that would be part of a ***methodical*** plan to build a better life. Although difficult to get into the habit of daily study at first, the more I read, the better I became at reading. The better I became at reading, the better I became at thinking and writing.

Those self-directed efforts changed my life. They helped me to prepare for success through prison and beyond.

While going through that phase of getting started, I remember reading *The Autobiography of Malcolm X.* That story showed how hard Malcolm work to develop his vocabulary. From inside a solitary cell, Malcolm made a commitment to improve his vocabulary. By learning to put words into sentences, and sentences into paragraphs, he became a powerful ***orator*** and a leader for his people. He ***embodied*** the ***maxim*** that the pen was mightier than the sword.

Another influential message from *Good to Great* influenced my actions and accountability in prison. He wrote about the importance of setting a BHAG—an *acronym* for a big, hairy, audacious goal. Leaders of great companies, he wrote, always had something gigantic that they wanted to solve. As human beings, we all could follow the model of setting a BHAG.

Prison and Sentence Reform:

Another *mentor* who inspired me, Mahatma Gandhi, advised people to work toward being the change they wanted to see. I wanted to live in a world that measured justice differently. People in our society measured justice by waiting for calendar pages to turn. Yet leaders like Jim Collins convinced me that we could work toward big, hairy, audacious goals—such as changing the way that society measured justice.

Instead of waiting for calendar pages to turn, we could start with the end in mind. If society wanted people to emerge from prison successfully, we should *reconfigure* the goals of confinement. If we want people to *emerge* as good neighbors rather than *recidivists*, we should open opportunities that would incentivize them to work toward earning freedom, through incremental steps.

To work toward that end, I would have to consider all my strengths, weaknesses, opportunities, and threats. Business leaders used an *acronym* to refer to this exercise. They called it a "SWOT" analysis.

Strengths:

My greatest strength was that I had defined success. I knew that I wanted to emerge from prison with my dignity intact, and with opportunities to live a life of meaning and relevance and dignity. Since I hated being in prison, I made a commitment to engineering a plan. I would have to take *intentional* steps that would allow me to make an *impact* on society. Like Socrates taught, success wasn't only about what was happening to me, but also the role I could play in making society better for all.

Weaknesses:

Despite wanting to get out of prison, and wanting to see *systemic* change, I had many weaknesses. During my first 23 years on the planet, I hadn't accomplished much of anything. As an adolescent, I lived *recklessly*. I sold cocaine, and a jury convicted me of crimes that led to a 45-year sentence. I graduated high school with *mediocre* grades, and I didn't learn much. I didn't read well, write well, and I hadn't produced much of anything that would cause people to see me as being anything other than a criminal.

Opportunities:

I considered our nation's pathway that led to mass incarceration as being the greatest social injustice of our time. It led to ***intergenerational cycles*** of failure. People learned how to live in prison. By focusing on their time inside rather than preparing for success after prison, many people ***emerged*** from prison to experience homelessness, unemployment, under employment, or further problems with the law. An opportunity existed to change the system and introduce the concept of earning freedom through merit.

Threats:

The culture of confinement did not ***foster*** an environment for learning. In a high-security penitentiary, I felt the ***pervasive*** threat of violence and disruption. Although I could control my behavior, I could not control other people's behavior. Legislators and administrators that I would never meet created laws and policies that ***governed*** my life. They supported an ***ecosystem*** that did not value the voice or the mindset of a person with my background. Although I wanted to change laws and open opportunities for people to work toward earning freedom, they wanted to protect the security of the institution.

In my view, that system ***perpetuated*** cycles of failure. Trying to change that system could lead to problems with other people serving time, and with people that supported the system as it existed.

To work toward prison reform, I would have to consider the strengths, weaknesses, opportunities, and threats. I didn't like being in prison, and I wanted to get to the other side, becoming the change that I wanted to see. I felt as if I would have to walk across a high wire, with ***incremental*** steps. The wrong step could lead to my ***demise***, but if I held myself accountable, and made the commitment, I hoped to contribute to the changes I wanted to see. They may not lead to my liberty, but those changes could lead to a better society. And working toward that end could bring meaning to my life while I served the sentence.

Since I was only in my early 20s, I didn't know how to contemplate the ***implications*** of a 45-year sentence. I hadn't been alive that long. With credit for good behavior, I understood that I could complete the term within 26 years—but I didn't have a frame of reference to put that time into ***context***.

Instead, I focused on the first 10 years. To reach the goals I wanted to achieve, I would have to hold myself accountable. During those first 10 years, I pledged to work toward making myself a more ***potent*** voice for prison reform. First, I would need to overcome the weaknesses that I perceived in my backstory. I would need to develop ***credentials*** that would lead influential people to consider ideas I would propose. I had to overcome weaknesses that included:

- » A lack of academic credentials,
- » Poor writing skills,
- » Low confidence in verbal communications,

» A felony conviction for drug trafficking at the start of the war on drugs,
» A lack of influence with leaders in society.

Within ten years, I intended to change those weaknesses. Since I knew what I wanted to accomplish within ten years, I could craft a pathway to work through the first five years. And since I knew what I wanted to achieve in five years, I could chart a course that would lead to incremental stages of success within three years. Knowing what I wanted to achieve during my first three years of imprisonment helped me to make better decisions during my first year, my first months, and my first days of confinement. I could develop accountability metrics to keep me on track.

Take Ten Minutes (3-3):

Write responses to the following questions in approximately ten minutes. If participating in a class setting, discuss verbally.

» 3-7: What weaknesses could you overcome from prison?

_____
_____
_____
_____
_____
_____
_____
_____
_____
_____
_____
_____
_____
_____
_____
_____
_____
_____
_____

» 3-8: If you worked toward overcoming those weaknesses, what opportunities would open for you?

_____

_____

_____

_____

_____

_____

_____

_____

_____

_____

_____

_____

_____

_____

» 3-9: In what ways could you create accountability metrics to ensure that you're making incremental progress?

_____

_____

_____

_____

_____

_____

_____

_____

_____

_____

_____

_____

_____

_____

_____

Lesson 4-Awareness and Authenticity
Keep Your Head in the Game

Annotation: Awareness and Authenticity

Opportunities exist all around us, but we don't see them if we don't open our eyes. When we're aware, we keep our eyes open for the possibility of seizing or creating opportunities. They become more abundant when we're authentic, keeping everything we think, say, and do in harmony. Staying aware of how our daily actions relate to how we define success leads others to appreciate our authenticity.

Awareness:

As human beings, sometimes we fall off track. If we're living according to the principles of the Straight-A Guide, we can ***recalibrate***. That means we stop ***perpetuating*** the problem and start working toward the solution.

Nurse Tina is a great example of someone who understood the importance of getting back on track.

I spoke with Tina during a time of crisis. She is a wife and a mother of five but also faced challenges that would complicate her life.

Tina told me that, as a child, she lived in Southern New Jersey, not even knowing that she was poor. Her grandmother played a ***pivotal*** role in her life. As a teenager, she moved into an area she described as a ghetto of Trenton. Tina's grandmother ***reared*** her in the Christian faith, emphasizing the importance of education. With that guidance, Tina could avoid complications ***derailing*** opportunities for many other people who spent their ***formative*** years in poverty.

Tina attended a Bible college and earned an ***undergraduate*** degree. She began earning a living in her chosen ***career***. Since her grandmother had played such a pivotal role in her life, Tina wanted to comfort her and provide the best quality of life for her grandmother's end-of-life experience. Later, her grandmother needed 24-hour care. Tina wanted to provide comfort and care for everyone in the ***convalescent*** home, so she understood that she would have to learn more.

It would be one thing to say that she wanted to provide the best care, but it's quite another to prepare in ways that would allow her to give the best care. Aware of what it would take to reach her highest potential as a caregiver, Tina made a commitment. She enrolled in nursing school.

What did it mean for her to become a nurse?

It meant that Tina would have to return to school. Many people find it challenging to study math and science as adults. But Tina thrived in an academic environment because she had a purpose: she knew that by earning a bachelor's degree in nursing, other healthcare professionals would see her authenticity.

To be authentic, a person had to:

- » Define success,
- » Develop an awareness that would help her create a plan,
- » Put priorities in place, and
- » Execute the plan.

By applying herself, Tina worked through courses that included microbiology, anatomy and physiology, and other coursework that would prepare her to pass exams necessary to work as a board-certified registered nurse. With those credentials, Tina could do more than comfort patients in need. As a licensed healthcare provider, she could also treat them within her ***scope*** of nursing practice.

Tina became a role model for her five children and anyone wanting to see a model of excellence. To succeed, she had to stay aware of opportunities and be authentic in her commitment.

As a registered nurse, Tina had the skills to serve her community during the COVID pandemic. Administrators frequently needed her to work in the hospital for 18-hour shifts, trying to save people's lives. The stress from being in such ***constant proximity*** to death, without time for her family, took a toll on her.

During the ***duress*** of the COVID crisis, she became ***susceptible*** to a pitch by a conman. When he promised her an easier life during that unusual phase of her career, she made an ***aberrational*** decision that violated the law.

To save the economy, the Small Business Administration began offering loans to support businesses that struggled because of the COVID crisis. The conman ***pitched*** Tina, promising that the government supported a transfer of wealth. That idea sounded good to Tina. She needed hope for something better than the long hours she worked and the proximity to so many people dying. He told her that he could do the following:

- » Set businesses up for her,
- » Operate those businesses,
- » Create jobs with those businesses, and
- » Generate profits for Tina.

When she asked him what it would cost, the ***charlatan*** told her it wouldn't cost her anything. She would simply need to sign documents that he prepared. Those documents, he said, would qualify her to receive loans from the government. Once the Small Business Administration

funded the loans, Tina would turn the resources over to the conman so that he could use them to build the businesses that they would own together. He promised to *structure* the loans so that Tina's business would not need to make payments for two years. By then, he *pledged* that the businesses would *generate sufficient* income to repay the *debt*.

He misled her into believing that she could own businesses without using her own money—only her credit. But all that glitters is not gold. The conman *deluded* Tina, and in her *fragile* state of mind from work *exhaustion*, she agreed to sign the documents he prepared, hoping they would help her escape the stress of caring for COVID patients at a hospital in Jersey City.

The *swindler* had *duped* Tina. Based on the documents he submitted, the government *funded* the loans, *obligating* Tina to repay them. The government's Small Business Administration deposited approximately $300,000 into bank accounts that Tina controlled.

As soon as the resources came in, Tina turned the money over to the *fraudster*, believing he would execute the plan. After a few weeks, she realized he had *entangled* her into a mess. She began to worry that she had broken the law.

Tina began reading the documents he prepared. When she read that the documents included fraudulent information about employees and past revenues, she felt as if she had walked into a *labyrinth*, but she didn't know how to get out.

Tina pleaded with the swindler to return the funds so that she could send them back to the government. He refused, telling her that he had already used the money to start the businesses.

For months, Tina tried to believe the problem would go away. She lost sleep. She felt anxious. She knew that she had done wrong, and she wanted to make things right.

As many people have done before, Tina had fallen off track. She *reverted* to the pathway that led to her earlier success in getting back on track. She began reading to become aware of the steps to surrender voluntarily.

The government had not charged her with a crime, yet she couldn't stand living with the guilt of what she had done. Being authentic, to her, meant accepting responsibility and moving forward with her life—even though she understood that she would have to endure some pain to make things right. To *recalibrate*, Tina contacted the Department of Justice, offering to surrender, cooperate, and create a plan to demonstrate her *remorse*.

Take Ten Minutes (4-1):

Write responses to the following questions in approximately ten minutes. If participating in a class setting, discuss verbally.

» 4-1: How do you stay aware of opportunities to transform your life?

_____

_____

_____

_____

_____

_____

_____

_____

» 4-2: How do you think prosecutors responded to Tina's unsolicited admission of guilt?

_____

_____

_____

_____

_____

_____

_____

_____

_____

» 4-3: Describe steps a person could take to demonstrate authenticity when it comes to remorse.

_____

_____

_____

_____

_____

_____

_____

_____

_____

_____

The U-Shaped Curve:

As people go through the prison system, **_perspectives_** change. Like Tina, anyone who faces a criminal charge instantly becomes a "justice-impacted" person. That means the person should become aware of opportunities to seize or create. When a person shows commitment to learning, growing, and making things right, others become aware of the individual's character and **_integrity_**. People may try to fake authenticity, like the person who defrauded Tina. Yet as the Bible tells us, castles built on sand cannot stand.

Knowing that in time, I wanted to advocate for reforms that would improve outcomes for all stakeholders in the prison system, I began reading. I had to become more aware of how the system operated to change the system. I wanted to learn more about different **_theories_**. One of those theories used the metaphor of the U-Shaped curve.

Regardless of sentence length, or phase, the theory held people's adjustment would follow through three phases that would trace the pattern of a U. At the top of the U, in the first phase, we could imagine the culture of the broader society. At the bottom of the U, we had the middle phase, the prison culture. And on the upside of the U, we moved into the third phase.

In the first phase, when authorities first bring people into the system, they experience a high degree of separation from family, friends, and everything they take for granted. As time passes, they move into the middle phase. They develop routines and grow more accustomed to the prison experience. By the time a person gets to the mid-way point of the sentence, the person knows prison well. He is more at ease with the circumstances. Then, the person begins climbing toward the other side of the U, the third phase. As release dates get closer and they know they're getting back to the broader community, the anxiety comes back. They wonder how they will adjust.

Similarly, Tina went through phases. Once she realized that she had signed her name to documents that included fraudulent information, she suffered from anxiety and unbearable guilt, expecting that she would need to answer for her crime in time. Wanting to make things right, she took action by first becoming more aware of steps she could take to recalibrate. As she anticipated various stages of the criminal justice system, she began to **_restore_** confidence. Authenticity meant going through the pains of a U-shaped curve that would likely bring her into the judicial and prison experience.

As a young man, I didn't have the same good-character traits as Tina. I never considered turning myself in or admitting that I had broken the law. It wasn't until Officer Wilson began passing me books about Socrates and others that I began to see the world differently. I had already made a series of very bad decisions, including:

» Organizing a group that would sell cocaine,
» Denying my **_culpability_** after my arrest,
» Going through trial and **_perjuring_** myself with lies about not being guilty.

Those decisions would have consequences, including a sentence requiring me to serve 26 years. While going through the first phase of my U, reading about Socrates, Frederick Douglass, and Malcolm X, I developed more *insight* into what authenticity would mean. They inspired me to want to learn more so that, in time, I could build *credibility* so that people I admired me would see my commitment and authenticity.

I needed to go through a long adjustment. I wouldn't reach the midway point until I served 13 years. Yet I knew precisely how I wanted to emerge once I exited prison. Like Frederick Douglass, I tried to use my time inside to make a difference or improve system outcomes. The SWOT analysis helped me realize the importance of making *intentional* decisions.

While working through the down leg of my U, I intended to strengthen my weaknesses. To become an effective advocate for reform, I would first need to develop skills and earn credentials.

As Tina's example shows us, a person shouldn't simply talk about wanting to succeed. A person must become aware of opportunities and be authentic in pursuing those growth opportunities.

Preparations for success after prison resembles preparations for success everywhere. We must be aware of what it takes and be authentic with our commitment to preparations. For example, when Tina aspired to become the best caregiver for her grandmother and others, she sought information on becoming a nurse. Making herself aware of nursing school led to her earning such credentials.

Knowing that I wanted to learn, I began writing to universities. Not knowing the names of people to write, I created a *template* letter that I could send to any university. In essence, the letter said:

Dear Admissions Officer,

My name is Michael Santos. I am in prison. I write with a request to attend your university so that I can earn academic credentials. I am serving a lengthy term in federal prison. While incarcerated, I hope to learn. By learning, I believe that I can prepare to live as a contributing citizen upon release.

If opportunities open for me to study with your university, please advise.

By sending a version of that letter to *scores* of universities, I made administrators aware of me. Although some of those administrators may have dismissed a letter from a person in prison, I found others who offered to help. Through those efforts, I became a university student. Once the university sent books and courses that I could complete through *correspondence*, I felt as if my life had changed. In an instant, I wasn't only a person in prison. I was a student.

Before prison, as a teenager, I hadn't prepared well to **matriculate** through university studies. That lack of earlier preparation meant that I had to complete some **remedial** studies and work extra hard to grasp basic concepts.

I found an example of excellence by reading *The Autobiography of Malcolm X*. Although the first part of that **biography** profiled the influences that led to his life as a criminal, the second part showed how he used time in solitary **cells** to become a better student. Knowing he wanted to become a better communicator, Malcolm became **autodidactic**, studying the dictionary. By learning new words, he realized that he could **empower** himself.

In the example of Malcolm X, we learn the importance of being aware of opportunities. If we don't open our eyes, we cannot see. But if we open our eyes, we may see pathways that will take us from where we are today to all we want to experience. Leaders leave us clues on how they prepare for success. We must choose whether we want to be authentic in that **pursuit**.

Take Ten Minutes (4-2):

Write responses to the following questions in approximately ten minutes. If participating in a class setting, discuss verbally.

» 4-4: In what ways do you anticipate your adjustment changing as you move through the U-shaped curve?

_____

_____

_____

_____

_____

_____

_____

_____

» 4-5: In what way would expanding your vocabulary, or fluency with language, influence how **others perceive you?**

_____

_____

_____

_____
_____
_____
_____
_____
_____
_____

> » 4-6: In what way would the accumulation of credentials help or hinder authenticity?

_____
_____
_____
_____
_____
_____
_____

Regardless of what bad decisions we may have made in the past, at any time, we can begin making good decisions. Yet we must always anticipate that people will question our authenticity. Therefore, we must always keep our heads in the game, knowing the opportunity costs that **_accompany_** every decision we make.

As a young man, I used to listen to classical rock, and I remember the lyrics from a song by the Rolling Stones: "You can't always get what you want, but if you try sometimes, you just might find, you get what you need."

Like every other person in prison, I wanted to get out. After my judge sentenced me to serve a 45-year prison term, the US Marshalls transferred me to a high-security penitentiary. I had been locked in solitary cells, incarcerated for about a year in pre-trial proceedings before I walked on the penitentiary's yard. While going through transit, I became more aware of the inner workings of the federal prison system.

The more I learned about the system, the more I wanted to engineer an adjustment plan. In time, I hoped the adjustment plan would lead to a more successful release. More importantly, I hoped that plan would help me **_emulate_** the leadership of Frederick Douglass—making me an authentic voice for prison and sentence reform.

Although other people in prison advised that the best way to serve time would be to forget about the world outside and focus on a prison reputation, I hated being in prison. If I spent all my time trying to fit into the prison system, I would learn skills that might help me fit in with

the prison society. Yet those skills seemed unlikely to advance me as a candidate for the success I wanted to experience on the other side of the journey. By the time I would move into the latter phase of my prison experience, I hoped that others would view me as being authentic in my *quest* to advocate for a better prison experience.

In the mid-1980s, the prison system was in a ***transitional*** stage. For decades, judges had used an ***indeterminate*** sentencing system. In other words, a judge would impose a sentence after a jury convicted a person, or a person pled guilty. Yet the system had a series of mechanisms that would serve as release valves. For example, people could file motions allowing them to ask a judge to reconsider the sentence. If the judge agreed that the sentence no longer served the interests of justice, he would have ***jurisdiction*** to reconsider.

Besides filing judicial motions seeking relief from the sentence, people could get relief through administrative mechanisms from either the prison system or from the US Parole Commission. The prison system incentivized people to avoid disciplinary infractions with credit for "good time." By avoiding disciplinary infractions, people could complete the sentence much sooner than the time a judge imposed. For example, my judge sentenced me to 45 years. If I did not lose any good time for violating disciplinary rules, I could complete that sentence in 26 years—or 9,500 days. Every person in federal prison could earn credit for good behavior—or receive credit for avoiding bad behavior.

The US Parole Commission provided another release mechanism under the indeterminate sentencing system. It operated as a separate body from the Bureau of Prisons. When I began serving my sentence, members of the Parole Board would visit the prison. Typically, a person who qualified would meet with the Board after he completed one-third of the sentence imposed. During that time, he could work to build a personal case showing why he was a worthy candidate for release on parole. If members of the Board agreed, they would allow him to return home. If he abided by the conditions of release, he would be able to live in society, go to work, and in many ways, resume his life.

If a person's ***statutory*** conviction did not render him ineligible for release on parole, the person could expect to serve a third of the sentence in prison and the remainder on parole in the community. If a person had a sentence of longer than 30 years, even a life sentence, the US Parole Commission could consider the person for release on parole after ten years.

That sentencing law changed for anyone convicted after November 1, 1987. After that cutoff date, people would serve ***determinate*** sentences, also known as "truth-in-sentencing" laws. If a judge imposed a sentence, the person could expect to serve at least 85% of the sentence. Those sentences became known as the "guideline" era, one contributor to America's movement to mass incarceration.

While I advanced through different stages of my sentence, I hoped to build credentials that would lead to improvements of the system. As Jim Collins wrote about in his book *Good to Great*, advocacy for prison and sentence reform would become my BHAG—Big, Hairy, ***Audacious*** Goal.

Take Ten Minutes (4-3):

Write responses to the following questions in approximately ten minutes. If participating in a class setting, discuss verbally.

» 4-7: In what way could awareness influence preparations before sentencing?

_____

_____

_____

_____

_____

_____

_____

» 4-8: What steps could a person take to shape perceptions of stakeholders?

_____

_____

_____

_____

_____

_____

_____

» 4-9: How are the interests of stakeholders similar or different from the interests of people going through the system?

_____

_____

_____

_____

_____

_____

_____

LESSON 5-ACHIEVEMENT AND APPRECIATION
CELEBRATE SUCCESS

Annotation: Achievement and Appreciation

To stay motivated as days turn into weeks, weeks turn into months, and months turn into years, we must learn to celebrate the small achievements. Daily achievements put us into a position of new opportunities that we can seize or create. Simultaneously, we must learn to appreciate the blessings that come our way. Even after a lengthy prison term, we can appreciate opportunities to contribute to society.

Purple Cow:

Seth Godin ***authors*** books for people who want to ***market*** goods and services to ***consumers***. One of his books encourages people to think different—and to think differently—about how they message.

Incidentally, since developing communication skills is an ***integral*** component of this self-directed course, write the phrase "thinking different" and "thinking differently" in two separate sentences.

He used an ***analogy*** of cows in a ***pasture***.

People don't pay much attention when they drive down the road and see cows ***grazing*** in a pasture. Yet they would pause for a second look if they saw a purple cow in the field. The purple cow might ***captivate*** their attention.

Marketing, according to Seth Godin, is about grabbing people's attention.

That book gave me a new perspective on how I fit into a prison setting from the perspective of many staff members. Like everyone serving time in the penitentiary, I wore khaki clothing. In their eyes, every person in prison merited about as much thought as a cow in a pasture.

Instead of recognizing our common humanity, many staff members viewed me as registration number 16377-004. Unless I did something to ***differentiate*** myself, my past bad decisions would always define my life.

I may have considered myself an individual, but to stakeholders, there wasn't anything remarkable about me or my ***predicament***. People in my inner circle may have cared about the sentence I served, but people ***tasked*** with carrying out my sentence wouldn't care about my future. To them, I was a ***cog*** in a ***bureaucratic*** machine that they had to keep going.

The transfer from detention centers in Seattle took me through a transit center in Oklahoma, followed by a few weeks as a holdover in an Alabama federal prison.

When I got to the penitentiary where I would serve my sentence, I heard **dubious** advice from hundreds of people who had served time. From coast to coast, people with experience living in jails and prisons told me that forgetting about the world outside and focusing on time inside would be the best adjustment strategy.

After a month in the penitentiary, a Case Manager scheduled me for my Initial Classification—also known as a team meeting. The staff members reviewed my file and advised that my projected release date would be August 2013, so long as I did not lose any credit for disciplinary infractions. I would have to serve another 25 years before the system would release me.

When the Unit Manager asked if I had any questions, I inquired whether it would be possible to transfer to one of the lower-security Federal Correctional Institutions that I had heard about from others.

"You have a greatest-severity drug offense, and a 45-year sentence," he said. "You should expect to serve your entire term inside high-security penitentiaries."

To members of my Unit Team, the bad decisions that put me in prison defined me. Similarly, other people in prison had their views on how a person should serve a sentence. Fortunately, Socrates, Frederick Douglass, and Nelson Mandela inspired me to engineer a personal release plan. They convinced me to **emulate** the adjustment strategies of people that transformed their lives while living in struggle.

I **detested** every part of living in prison. Reading about leaders such as Mahatma Gandhi taught me that I should "strive to be the change that I want to see in the world." In his commitment to liberating India from **tyranny,** he pledged to keep everything he said, thought, and did in harmony. That guidance seemed far more **prudent** than the messages I received inside the penitentiary.

If I wanted others to look beyond my criminal past and **perceive** me as being different from the **herd**, I needed to adjust differently. I would need to become the change that I wanted to see in the world. I could find a path by reading about leaders from all segments in society. Since those leaders taught me, I feel responsible for passing that message to others.

Some participants may have read the biography of Elon Musk, a remarkable businessman who has created jobs for more than 100,000 people. People know him as the founder of successful companies, including Tesla, PayPal, Space X, and many others.

Yet Elon Musk didn't begin his life as a **titan** of industry.

As a young and impoverished college student, Mr. Musk **immigrated** to North America from South Africa. Wanting to accelerate his pathway to success, he wrote **unsolicited** letters to

leaders from whom he believed he could learn. That *tactic* of *writing* opened opportunities for him to build relationships with business leaders, including the CEO of one of the largest banks in the world. The banker became so impressed with the teenage Musk that he offered him a summer internship.

That same strategy of writing unsolicited letters helped me *transcend* prison boundaries to build relationships with leaders who would become mentors that *catapulted* my journey to advocacy.

Take Ten Minutes (5-1):

Write responses to the following questions in approximately ten minutes. If participating in a class setting, discuss verbally.

» 5-1: In what ways would staff view you differently from other people in prison?

_____

_____

_____

_____

_____

_____

_____

_____

» 5-2: How can you bring mentors into your orbit?

_____

_____

_____

_____

_____

_____

_____

_____

_____

_____

PRISON PROFESSORS
Talent

» 5-3: In what way would finding mentors lead to greater achievements in your life?

_____

_____

_____

_____

_____

_____

_____

_____

_____

Incremental Achievements and the Other Side:

What does the other side of a prison term look like?

Participants working through this course serve sentences in detention centers, jails, or prisons. As someone who spent his 20s, 30s, and 40s in those environments, I encourage participants to remember a **_maxim_** of this introductory course:

It's never too early and never too late to begin preparing for success after prison.

Start by thinking about the other side. Statistics show that most justice-impacted people face **_monumental_** challenges when they leave prison. The **_irony_** of corrections is that **_recidivism_** rates in many jurisdictions show that seven out of every ten people in jail or prison return to custody after release. As people spend more time in a "correctional" setting, they become less likely to function as law-abiding, contributing citizens.

People can **_speculate_** and draw **_conclusions_** about the reasons behind those **_dismal_** success rates. Rather than **_dwelling_** on the reasons behind failure, I always encourage participants to think about success. Regardless of where participants begin working through this course, I hope they will architect a release plan. That plan should lead them to where they want to go, and the **_legacy_** they want to leave society after they're gone.

For example:

Socrates lived more than 2,500 years ago—yet his leadership and teachings still influence people today.

Frederick Douglass died in 1891, but through the books he wrote, and others wrote about him, we see an example of excellence in advocacy for good.

Viktor Frankl did not allow the losses he suffered in a concentration camp to stop him from bringing change to the world, even though he died decades ago.

Nelson Mandela died in 2013, and others have written *volumes* about his leadership, despite the 27 years he served in prison.

Those people left legacies that people *revere,* despite the time they spent in *bondage*.

My life is different today because of the *incremental* achievements that began inside of that high-security penitentiary, back in 1987. I can still trace the steps:

While I *languished* in a solitary cell, Officer Wilson gave me a series of books that taught me about Socrates, Frederick Douglass, Nelson Mandela, and others. From those books I learned to stop thinking about my problems and to start thinking about how I could reconcile with society from inside of a prison cell.

Frederick Douglass' story inspired me to develop communication skills. If I worked to become a better writer and better speaker, I hoped to persuade leaders that we should reform opportunities for people in prison to earn freedom.

Mahatma Gandhi, Nelson Mandela, Viktor Frankl, and many other leaders showed the path to succeed as an advocate. Besides developing skills, a person had to develop relationships.

Every achievement begins with incremental steps. Some of those steps will be harder than others, but people who commit know that each step should lead to an *intended* destination.

When I started my path inside a solitary cell before my judge *inflicted* a lengthy sentence, I visualized the life I'm leading right now—working to improve outcomes for all justice-impacted people.

A conversation with Lynn Stephens helped me along that path. She supervised the business office of the prison's factory. When I applied for a job, she asked why I wanted to work in the business office. The *initial* meeting with the Unit Team convinced me that I needed a plan to write the next chapter of my life. I told Lynn that I wanted to find a quiet spot where I could avoid the *volatility* of the penitentiary and work on a release plan that I could use to pry open opportunities and prepare for success upon release from prison.

The more I spoke with her about my release plan and preparing for success after release, even though I had only begun to serve a sentence that would keep me confined for multiple decades, the more I could see her perceptions of me change. From the release plan, she could question me and see the deliberateness of every step I took.

Engineering that release plan became the first step toward becoming a purple cow.

Lynn authorized me to work as her clerk. She *tacitly* allowed me to complete my schoolwork after I finished my office duties. Because of her support, I earned an *undergraduate* degree. Independent study and correspondence courses taught lessons that opened new opportunities.

As Jim Collins wrote in *Good to Great*, the most **onerous** part of success is getting started. But **momentum** builds.

With Lynn's trust, new opportunities for growth opened. Looking for **sanctuary** from the **asylum**, I found a niche by volunteering for a suicide-watch program through the psychology department. When the shift in the business office **concluded,** I sat in a quiet area of the prison's mental health unit. In that **niche**, I had the **solitude** I would need to concentrate on my studies. While on the suicide-watch shift, I could write to prospective mentors.

I began writing letters using the same strategy that persuaded a university to admit me as a **correspondence** student and the same approach that Elon Musk used to **network** when he **immigrated** to North America. If an article or a book inspired me, I'd introduce myself by writing a letter. **Typically**, at that early stage of my journey, I wrote to professors who published books or articles about the prison system.

Those **scholars** didn't know me from anyone else, but I doubt they received many letters from people serving time in prison. **Ironically**, being in prison may have been an advantage in my efforts to connect with them. Through those efforts, I connected me with professors at Princeton, Harvard, Stanford, Yale, Hofstra, and other great universities. I considered each new relationship a **monumental** achievement and an incremental step in my release plan.

Those professors visited me in prison. As they got to know me, they invited me to publish articles in their books about prison. Some invited me to write chapters for them. As time passed, they introduced me to their publishers, which led to publishing contracts to publish books I wrote.

The takeaway?

Had I not taken incremental steps during the earliest stages of my confinement, I would not have been able to **seize** or create opportunities that advanced my release plan.

Take Ten Minutes (5-2):

Write responses to the following questions in approximately ten minutes. If participating in a class setting, discuss verbally.

» 5-4: In what ways will the incremental step of completing this introductory course influence your adjustment?

_____

_____

_____

_____

_____

» 5-5: In what ways would finding mentors that align with your release plan lead to new opportunities and achievements?

» 5-6: How can you show appreciation for the opportunities that others are opening for you?

Along the way, relationships opened that directly related to the reasons I'm now able to bring courses into state and federal prison systems. The next **phase** of our course will include more details that show the **trajectory.** *For the complete story, participants might consider reading* the following books:

Earning Freedom: Conquering a 45-Year Prison Term
» Details showing the pathway from an arrest on August 11, 1987 to a release date on August 12, 2013.

Prison my 8,344th Day
» Details on the deliberate, intentional decisions during a typical day in prison.

Success after Prison
» Opportunities that opened after release, largely because of the deliberate release plan.

Perseverance
» Strategies to build momentum while working through a lengthy prison term.

Release Plan
» Best practices for creating an initial release plan and working to develop the plan over time.

DVD video series
» Video profiles of others who built pathways to success after prison. Each video shows the relationship between prison decisions and success after release. Staff members may offer those DVD videos in libraries, reentry centers, or broadcast them over institutional televisions.

Creating those **assets** contributed to contracting opportunities with different prison systems, including the Federal Bureau of Prisons, the California Department of Corrections, and other institutions.

The arc included an **apex**, like my marriage inside a prison visiting room during my 16th year, and **nadirs**, like transfers to prisons across state lines and many **stints** in the Special Housing Unit of prisons where I served time. Each step along the way represented a part of my release plan.

On a path of preparing for success after prison, I learned the power of **alchemy**—converting adversaries into advocates. Indeed, while locked in a cell the Special Housing Unit at the federal prison in Lompoc, I met Captain Matevousian. An officer cited me with a disciplinary infraction for publishing a manuscript, which brought me to the attention the prison's head of security.

Since I'd already served longer than 20 years and had created an elaborate release plan, I knew the system well—perhaps too well. Despite prevailing over the incident report, Captain Matevousian told me that he didn't want a person on the compound who about the need for prison reform. Based on his recommendation, administrators shipped me to another federal prison.

Publishing books represented an **integral** component of my release plan. Each time I held a book in my hand, I felt like I was taking another step toward my eventual career in advo-

cacy. I believed those books would advance my commitment to being the change I wanted to see. Despite my goals, administrators viewed my publishing as a potential threat to the institution's security.

Socrates taught me that, to succeed, I had to understand the world in which I lived. Like anyone else who wanted to overcome a challenge, I had to introspect on questions:

- » What strengths did I have?
- » What weaknesses?
- » What opportunities existed?
- » What threatened my progress?

Since my release plan showed what I wanted, I expected to face obstacles. Preparing for success means learning to be comfortable with being uncomfortable.

Working toward prison reform required resources I could ***leverage*** to build an ***ecosystem*** for change. Leaders helped me along the way. To show my appreciation for what they taught, I had to live in gratitude—passing along the lessons that had made a difference in my adjustment.

Those incremental steps across the highwire of imprisonment opened new opportunities when I transitioned to a halfway house on August 13, 2012. Within days, I closed a deal with a real estate developer to acquire my first property, and San Francisco State University invited me to teach as an ***adjunct*** professor. I created "The Architecture of Incarceration," a course for students who wanted to build a career in the corrections ***sector***.

A tri-part adjustment pattern of focusing on earning academic credentials, contributing to society, and building a support network carried me through prison. Similarly, I would need a tri-part plan to succeed upon release.

Despite feeling passionate about prison reform, I also had to cover living expenses and prepare for retirement. Those needs influenced the intentional, three-***pronged*** career in business, investments, and academia that I launched. Each component of the plan related to the other:

- » By building or accumulating appreciating assets, in appreciating ***markets***, I could prepare for my retirement.
- » By building businesses, I could earn a living that would fund my ***ministry*** to improve outcomes for all justice-impacted people.
- » By working in ***academia***, I could ***infuse*** future prison leaders with new ideas that, I believed, would improve outcomes. We could change the way leaders measured justice in America. Instead of waiting for calendar pages to turn, my ***scholarship*** advanced ideas for reforms that would ***incentivize*** people to work toward earning freedom through ***merit***.

As a professor, I expanded my platform, publishing articles like "Incentivizing Excellence" in the UC Hastings Law Review. By publishing in a law review, I took an incremental step toward building a speaking career that would **spawn innovative** ideas to a **cynical** crowd. I spread ideas on the need to empower the Bureau of Prisons with incentives. If we want people to leave prison as productive citizens, we should **empower** administrators to reward people who pursue that path.

Those writings led to an invitation to **keynote** an event that the Ninth Circuit Court of Appeals sponsored. For 40 minutes, while a group of several hundred judges and correctional **practitioners** ate lunch, I promoted the idea of reforms that would include incentives to produce the outcomes we wanted from America's criminal justice system.

Following my presentation, a well-dressed man in a blue suit approached. He extended his hand and asked if I remembered him.

"Of course I remember you," I smiled. "You're Captain Matevousian. Five years ago, when I was in Lompoc, you locked me in the SHU for advancing the ideas I spoke about today."

While we shook hands, Mr. Matevousian told me his career had advanced. The agency promoted him to Warden, and he **presided** over the penitentiary in Atwater. He invited me to give a presentation in his institution.

Instead of making a motivational speech, I proposed to create a course that would show people in prison how they could begin making decisions that prepare them for success upon release.

That conversation spread the program through the Bureau of Prisons and several state prison systems. It led to the birth of Prison Professors, a website I created to help all stakeholders of the system, including all justice-impacted people. More importantly, it allowed me to work with many leaders, influencing their ideas on reforms that included the First Step Act—the most comprehensive and innovative prison-reform legislation since the 1984 Comprehensive Crime Control Act.

The First Step Act passed Congress with **bipartisan** support, beginning a transition from an indeterminate to a determinate sentencing system. It's an incremental step toward more reforms that our team at Prison Professors will continue working to advance.

Our advocacy pushes to advance ideas such as:

» Broader application of incentives with the First Step Act, so that all people in federal prison would qualify for Earned Time Credits.
» Use of additional incentives, such as extended furloughs and **quasi** work-release programs for people who have built release plans showing their commitment to earning incrementally higher levels of freedom.

» Clear pathways to work toward consideration for commutations of sentence, or compassionate release.
» Reinstatement of the U.S. Parole Commission.

Some people may believe such changes will never happen. I urge those people to consider stories like Halim Flowers, or Tommy Walker. Those people worked hard to build extraordinary and compelling records long before the First Step Act became law.

Other people get discouraged because they will finish serving their sentence before Congress or the agency *implements* changes for which we advocate.

We must celebrate each small, incremental achievement along the way. We grow stronger when we live in gratitude, showing appreciation for the blessings that come our way.

I appreciate each participant in this course. Through their work, I open more opportunities to convince *cynical* people on the need for reforms that will improve outcomes of our nation's prison system.

Take Ten Minutes (5-3):

Write responses to the following questions in approximately ten minutes. If participating in a class setting, discuss verbally.

» 5-7: How does the release plan you're creating show a series of incremental steps to prepare for success after prison?

_____

_____

_____

_____

_____

_____

_____

_____

_____

_____

_____

» 5-8: In what way would a small achievement open opportunity in your life?

_____

_____

_____

_____

_____

_____

_____

_____

_____

_____

_____

_____

_____

» 5-9: How would living in gratitude influence your adversaries?

_____

_____

_____

_____

_____

_____

_____

_____

_____

_____

_____

_____

_____

_____

SECTION II

In the first five lessons of our course, we offered an introduction to the Preparing for Success after Prison Course.

We hope participants see the value of pursuing a values-based, goal oriented adjustment strategy.

As participants advance into the second section, they'll see a more practical application of these concepts. As the author of the course, I will offer historical context, and I'll also show how living by these principles influenced my journey inside and upon release. In my view, the lessons in this course will help participants, regardless of:

- » Gender,
- » Age,
- » Sentence length,
- » Type of crime,
- » Socio-economic status.

Those who want to join our advocacy efforts and memorialize how they're using time in prison to prepare for success upon release may send a Corrlinks invite to our interns:

Prison Professors Talent
32565 Golden Lantern Street, B-1026
Dana Point, CA 92629

Corrlinks:
Interns@PrisonProfessorsTalent.com
Subject line: Requesting a Scholarship

Our interns will accept all invite requests. Once approved, send us the following information:

- » Name
- » Prison Name
- » Registration Number
- » Mailing Address
- » City, State Zip
- » Sentence Length (months)
- » Surrender Date
- » Projected Release Date
- » Security Level

We've built a website to profile people who are working to prepare for success upon release. Provided that the institutions authorize, and we have resources available, we'll create individual profiles that allow participants to memorialize their preparations for success and build resumes so that others can see how hard they're working to prepare for success.

We want to show that people who build self-directed release plans are more likely to succeed upon release. The data we collect will advance our efforts at advocacy, as we'll be able to show administrators, legislators, and citizens how many people are memorializing their efforts to prepare for success upon release.

We encourage all people in prison to work toward earning freedom. Those who choose to profile their work may participate in this transparent program with us. We'll work outside to persuade business leaders to provide sponsorship for more scholarships, and to provide job opportunities for people who build effective release plans.

As someone who went through the journey, I learned that the more a person works to memorialize preparations for success, the more opportunities open.

We're striving to show others why it makes sense to incentivize a pursuit of excellence and prepare people to live as good neighbors.

Whether you choose to document your journey with PrisonProfessorsTalent.com or not, we hope that you find value in working through the lessons in Section 2 of our course.

LESSON 6: MASTERMIND

Merriam-Webster dictionary defines a mastermind as "A person who supplies the directing or creative intelligence for a project."

Where would you turn if you're looking for a "mastermind"?

I suppose your answer would depend on your current situation.

If you're a young man who aspires to become a professional athlete, you might consider someone who has proven himself in the athletic arena.

If you're looking to create wealth, you may search for someone who has succeeded in building businesses and creating a sustainable enterprise that generates cash flow and monthly profits.

If you're struggling, you may want to learn from someone who has endured similar challenges—but emerged more potent than ever.

Perhaps that person recovered from an illness. Maybe the person overcame an ***abusive*** relationship. The person may have gone through a lengthy prison term. Yet rather than allowing the prison term to define his life, he responded to the sentence in ways that allowed him to grow. Perhaps he learned lessons that would translate into new opportunities in prison and upon release.

When searching for guidance from an expert, we may want to follow a multi-step process:

> » Step 1: Assess the status of our life at a given stage,
> » Step 2: Assess the merits or the qualifications of the person from whom we want to learn, and
> » Step 3: Create a plan that will help us make incremental progress,
> » Step 4: Put priorities in place,
> » Step 5: Built tools, tactics, and resources that will advance our progress,
> » Step 6: Craft an accountability tool to keep us on track, and
> » Step 7: Execute our multi-step process every day.

I learned those lessons at the start of my journey, when Officer Wilson began bringing a series of books that I could read. I was in the Special Housing Unit, facing a life sentence. Since those leaders had gone through challenges much larger than I would face, I knew that I could learn from them.

From their lessons, I learned that I would need to ***introspect***—getting real with the predicament I had put myself in

Who am I?

As described in the earlier sections, I made terrible decisions as a young man. I didn't listen to my parents, teachers, or guidance counselors. After finishing high school with mediocre grades, I got into trouble with the law. The friends I chose were also violating the law.

> » I began selling drugs when I was 20.
> » Authorities arrested me when I was 23.
> » Prosecutors charged me with violating drug laws.
> » Despite knowing that I was guilty, I refused to accept responsibility.
> » After a lengthy trial, a jury convicted me.

While *languishing* in solitary confinement, I read books that helped question the decisions that put me my predicament. I considered the authors of those books to be masterminds. Had I learned from their valuable lessons earlier, I would have made different decisions. I would have paid more attention to guidance counselors or mentors in school, I likely would have made better decisions. Masterminds could have helped me avoid problems with the criminal justice system.

Fortunately, it's never too early and it's never too late to begin making better decisions.

Masterminds taught lessons that helped me through prison. Those lessons made all the difference in my life. Through this self-directed course, I'd like to share what I learned. Truthfully, I can sum up those lessons in one sentence: The decisions we make today directly influence our prospects for success tomorrow.

> » In what ways does the system bear responsibility for our success upon release?
> » In what ways we bear responsibility for our success upon release?

There isn't any correct answer or wrong answer to such questions. Yet if we mediate on such questions, we can develop better critical thinking. We can develop responses to help guide us to better decisions. Our deliberateness can lead to better discretion when choosing friends and how we spend our time.

When we're living amid struggle, it's sometimes hard to accept the importance of all our decisions. Reflecting on lessons I learned while serving time brings back memories of the many types of pressure I felt.

> » Prison separates people from our families and communities.
> » We live in an environment where other people watch us all the time.
> » Some people want to build or protect reputations.
> » Others want to run away or hide from their past.

Each person adjusts differently. But each person's adjustment influences the life ahead. Sadly, many people leave prison to experience:

>> Further complications with law enforcement,
>> Unemployment or employment in dead-end jobs,
>> Homelessness.

Good preparations can lead to success after prison. And I'm very passionate about sharing the lessons leaders taught me. Since I served more than 26 years inside, I hope to build credibility with my audience. Throughout this self-directed course on Preparing for Success after Prison—and through all the courses I create—I pledge honesty and promise never to pursue any path I did not follow.

In August of 2013, I completed 9,500 days of imprisonment. Since returning to society, I've been committed to sharing strategies that masterminds taught me. I want people to make the connection between better decisions at the start of their journey and a better chance of building lives of meaning and success.

Since my release, I've worked consistently to improve outcomes for all justice-impacted people. To succeed at a higher level, I will need to influence legislators, persuading them why we need ***mechanisms*** and incentives that encourage more people to work toward earning freedom. Those lawmakers and prison executives will want to see ***data***. To persuade them to change laws or policies, our team will need to prove that people who work through the courses we create at Prison Professors have:

>> Lower levels of violence or disruptive activities,
>> Higher levels of participation in educational programs,
>> Fewer disciplinary infractions,
>> Self-directed growth strategies,
>> Better prospects for higher levels of income upon release,
>> Lower levels of recidivism.

I invite participants to collaborate with me in making this case to improve the outcomes of our nation's criminal justice system. To succeed, we will need to work together. I'll share how this concept of building a self-directed, values-based, goal-oriented adjustment strategy influenced my time in prison and led to massive opportunities once I got out.

If participants want family members to follow along, they can always steer people to our websites:

>> www.PrisonProfessors.com,

Those who choose may open a profile to document their pathway to success by visiting:

>> www.PrisonProfessorsTalent.com or sending an invite to:
>> Interns@PrisonProfessorsTalent.com.

We're 100% *transparent* and 100% committed to improving outcomes for all justice-impacted people.

The Path:

I'm grateful for every *dialogue* I have with leaders who work in corrections. It takes a lot of courage for administrative leaders from a prison system to interact with me. After all, I'm a man that served time in prisons of every security level. When those leaders open opportunities for us to bring educational content into prisons, they're fulfilling a dream that started for me when I was locked inside a solitary cell, facing life without the possibility of parole.

Since I began serving my sentence, I've worked toward reforms that would empower administrators to incentivize excellence. In my book: *Earning Freedom: Conquering a 45-Year Prison Term*, I describe how the multi-step strategy I learned from masterminds guided my path. They helped me persuade legislators understand the power of incentives. In the California prison system, we have milestone credits; in the federal prison system, we have First Step Act credits.

The political climate is far more conducive to meaningful reform than when I served my sentence. Many people in leadership positions believe that we need to teach and inspire people at the start of the journey; *opposing* forces want to take us backwards, and repeal laws that incentivize people to earn freedom through merit.

We need to continue efforts to help more people grasp the importance of motivating people as the days turn into weeks, the weeks turn into months, and the months turn into years.

As participants work the lessons of our course, I'll present what I learned from masterminds. They inspired and motivated me, teaching me to introspect and think about the decisions that brought me to prison. Through those reflections, I learned how to engineer a pathway that would lead me home, with my dignity intact and opportunities to prosper.

We're always making choices. Those choices are like sowing seeds. We can choose to *sow* seeds that produce gardens of *abundance*; we can also sow seeds that lead to thorns of misery. Regardless of where a person may be, I encourage people to think about the seeds they're planting. The seeds we're sowing today will undoubtedly influence the future we create going forward.

While incarcerated, I changed the way I think. Those changes put me on a different path from the one I followed during my reckless youth.

Since being released from prison, I feel obligated to pass along lessons that allowed me to be "the change that I want to see in the world," as Mahatma Gandhi advised. I'll share the strategies that empowered me through prison that I've continued using since I returned to society. In sharing these stories and lessons, I hope to teach and inspire others like leaders taught and inspired me.

Through this course, participants will see that I began working to prepare for success back in 1987—at the very start of my imprisonment. After a jury convicted me of every count in my indictment, I decided to change. I still remember the day that I started looking for lessons from leaders. I wanted to find people that could give me the strength to grow. I found those leaders in a philosophy book.

At that time, I didn't even know how to spell philosophy. I didn't know what the word meant. In flipping through the pages of a book I came across in the jail's book cart, I found true masterminds. Reading their stories taught me lessons. Those lessons helped me adjust in high-security penitentiaries, medium, low, and minimum-security prisons. I finished 26 years with the Bureau of Prisons in August of 2013. The adjustment in prison opened opportunities to succeed upon release.

Lessons from leaders helped me to understand how and why I should use time effectively and deliberately. To grasp the influence of every decision, we need to connect the dots from struggle to success.

Let me provide a brief background.

If you're holding this workbook in your hand, you have tangible proof that a person can build a life of meaning and relevance after release from prison. Administrators expose people inside to many courses and programs. But it takes a lot of courage for them to allow books and courses from an author who served decades inside.

I strive to earn their trust and the trust of participants who work through our self-directed courses.

Let me begin by sharing more details of the story that led me through prison and back to society. I'm not like another course creator that didn't experience what participants are going through. I went through every stage of the journey, including:

- » Initial arrest,
- » Pretrial detention,
- » Criminal trial and conviction by a jury,
- » Presentence investigation,
- » Sentencing,
- » Designation to a high-security United States Penitentiary,
- » Transition to a medium-security Federal Correctional Institution,
- » Transition to a low-security Federal Correctional Institution,
- » Transition to minimum-security camps,
- » Transition to a halfway house and home confinement,
- » Early termination of Supervised Release,
- » Success after prison.

For these reasons, I'm more of a tour guide than a travel agent. I've gone through similar experiences, and I know the pain of confinement. I won't be a travel agent who tells a person where to go or what to do.

Through these self-directed lessons, people will see how adjustment strategies transformed my life while serving decades inside.

Decisions that Led me to Prison:

Despite having every opportunity to build a life of relevance and meaning as a younger man, I made one wrong decision after another. In 1982, Shorecrest High School in North Seattle awarded me my diploma. I wouldn't say that I earned my diploma. Looking back, I freely admit that I was a lousy student.

Following high school, I made undisciplined decisions. When I was 20, I watched the movie *Scarface*. The lead character, Tony Montana, made an impression on me. After seeing the movie, I started inquiring about how much dealers would pay for cocaine. I'd never sold cocaine before, but I wanted to learn.

Once I understood more about the market, I traveled to Miami, searching for a supplier. After finding one, I calculated that I could earn a profit while shielding myself from prosecution. Quickly, I began to recruit others to join a distribution network. Not understanding the criminal justice system, I made more bad decisions. If I didn't handle the cocaine directly—I ***deluded*** myself—I'd never get caught. I'd pay people to retrieve the cocaine in Miami, drive it to Seattle, and distribute the cocaine to customers.

For 18 months, trafficking in cocaine became a way of life. I lied to my family and anyone else who asked about what I was doing. On August 11, 1987, the drug-dealing phase of my life ended.

Three men stood close by when I stepped out of an elevator. As I approached, they asked my name. When I responded, the men each drew a handgun. In an instant, I saw the barrels of three different pistols, each pointing at my head. I didn't resist when they ordered me to raise my hands.

The agents frisked me. Then they slammed cuffs around my wrists. That started my institutional routines. The agents locked me in a holding center in Miami, Florida. While being processed inside, I learned that a grand jury indicted me for operating a continuing criminal enterprise and other drug-related charges. The indictment charged that I'd been selling cocaine in Seattle and other cities for about 18 months before the DEA caught me.

The charges carried a possible sentence of life without parole.

At the time of my arrest, I only cared about getting out. Although I knew I was guilty of every charge, my defense attorney told me what I wanted to hear rather than what I needed to hear. He said:

There's a big difference between an indictment and a conviction.

Instead of using good critical thinking, I agreed to let the attorney navigate my way through the judicial process. That strategy didn't work out so well.

My attorney admonished me, telling me not to talk with anyone else in jail. He told me to leave everything in his hands. Foolishly, I held on to a belief that I could win. I would walk out if my attorney could persuade a jury that I wasn't guilty. He coached me on how I should present myself. By lying when I took the witness stand, denying my criminal behavior, I committed the crime of perjury.

My lies didn't fool the jury. The ***foreman*** read the jury's verdict that convicted me on every count. After hearing the guilty ***verdict***, I began to understand the depths of my trouble. Later, I realized much more.

The guilty verdict would change my life forever. United States Marshals locked me in chains and led me out of the courtroom. They returned me to the Pierce County Jail. Suddenly, I was a convicted felon rather than a pretrial detainee. Jailers locked me in solitary. The pressure weighed on me, crushing my spirit, extinguishing hope.

I didn't know what type of sentence my judge would impose, but the conviction exposed me to a life sentence without the possibility of parole. Since I'd never been in prison, the prospects of such a sentence didn't make sense.

Confined to a solitary cell, I remember lying on the rack. Although I wasn't religious, I started to pray, asking God for strength. It didn't make sense to pray for release. By then, I accepted that prison would become a big part of my life. Since I couldn't change the past, I had to deal with reality. Instead of asking for release, I prayed for strength and guidance. Challenges would come as I made the switch from jail to prison. I felt determined to prevail.

Philosophy:
While locked in confinement, I prayed for guidance. In response to those prayers, I got a philosophy book. Lessons in that book helped me to think differently, and by learning to think differently, I started to restore confidence. By restoring confidence, I began to feel better.

Some readers who live in challenge circumstances may find it strange that I would turn to philosophy, and I understand.

Until authorities locked me in jail, I hardly read at all. I hadn't read a single book since finishing high school five years earlier, in 1982. In a jail cell, I didn't have anything besides read-

ing to occupy my mind, and I wanted to change. I remember looking through the stacks of books on a book cart. I saw an abundance of Westerns and romance novels.

Fiction and storybooks would pass the time, but ignoring the problems created by my earlier decisions would not help me. Instead, I needed to solve problems. I needed guidance.

With proper guidance, I believed that I would grow stronger. I would need that strength to cross through years or decades of prison. I'm grateful to an officer who brought me a two-volume book called *A Treasury of Philosophy*. The books were part of an "anthology," which included submissions from many authors who wrote about their "philosophy."

The more I read, the more I understood that I had lived by bad philosophy.

Holding the book of masters in my hand made me feel as if I had the key to begin building a better life.

Socrates:
When I flipped through the pages, I found a story about Socrates. I knew that other people considered Socrates, a man of great wisdom. He lived more than 2,000 years ago, but I didn't know much about him.

As I read the first paragraphs of that chapter, I wholly identified with Socrates because Socrates was locked in a prison cell. His imprisonment caught my attention. I learned that judges sentenced Socrates to death. He waited in that jail cell for his execution date.

Socrates received a visit from his friend Crito. During the visit, Crito told Socrates that others had arranged for him to escape. With the foolproof plot, the jailer agreed to unlock the gate. Socrates could walk out, escaping his execution. Besides that, friends would support Socrates in exile. He could live the rest of his life in peace.

In my mind, Socrates should have *seized* the initiative. I remember lying on that rack and fantasizing that someone would come and open my cell. If I could escape my punishment, I would leave in an instant. More than anything, I wanted to get out of jail or avoid the long-term that the judge ordered.

Socrates responded differently, declining the offer from Crito. He said he would remain in his cell and let the system kill him. When Crito asked why he would make such a choice, Socrates responded.

He said that he lived in a democracy. As a citizen, he had to accept the good with the bad. He had accepted the good of society. He disagreed with the laws that resulted in his conviction and punishment. But Socrates wanted to be a man of principle. He considered himself a citizen of a democracy. As such, he said that he had the right to work toward changing laws he disagreed with, but not to break laws.

Influence on my Adjustment:

Socrates' message influenced my time in solitary. I remember setting the book on my chest while I stared at the ceiling. Although the judge hadn't sentenced me yet, I had more clarity. I knew that I wanted to change. Regardless of how many years my judge would impose, I wanted to grow. I wanted to come out of prison differently from how I went in.

Like Socrates, I wanted to serve my sentence with dignity. I created my problems and would be responsible for creating my solutions.

Yet I didn't know how to define "serving a sentence with dignity." The jail didn't provide much in the way of guidance that I could see. Instead, I felt the walls and ceiling closing in, suffocating my spirit and hope.

What, if anything, could I do to live a life of meaning and relevance?

This course shows what I learned from masterminds like Socrates and how I came to answer that question. As participants work through the course, I encourage them to consider the same types of questions. Mediating on such questions changed my life.

Take 30 Minutes

Use this time to begin building your story. Take time to write your story on a separate page. To prime your story, consider writing your biography in a way that responds to the following four questions:

» 6-1: Intro: What's your name and what's your background?

_____

_____

_____

_____

_____

_____

» 6-2: Supporting Body 1: In what ways did your background influence the decisions that led you to prison?

_____

_____

_____

_____

» 6-3: Supporting body 2: In what ways did your behavior influence the broader community?

_____

_____

_____

_____

_____

_____

» 6-5: Supporting body 3: In what ways are you working to reconcile, or make amends?

_____

_____

_____

_____

_____

_____

» 6-6: Conclusion: In what ways will stakeholders consider your adjustment as being extraordinary and compelling?

_____

_____

_____

_____

_____

_____

With hopes that course participants find me a worthy guide, I'll share strategies that anyone can use time inside to prepare for success outside. Each lesson offers strategies that leaders taught me, and I used them while crossing through 9,500 days in prison.

I'm convinced that anyone can use time in prison to prepare for success. If participants are willing to learn from the same masterminds who taught me, I believe they can open new opportunities.

Our country incarcerates millions of people. By learning how to think differently and applying what they know, participants in this self-directed course may create opportunities that allow them to return to society strong, with their dignity intact. They will learn how to seize opportunities and how to create opportunities.

The decisions we make influence our prospects for success.

Toward the end of my time in prison, I wrote *Earning Freedom: Conquering a 45-Year Prison Term*. In that book, I provide much more detail about my journey through prison. If a participant doesn't have access to *Earning Freedom* in the prison's library, consider requesting it from a friend. If you don't have a friend to send the book, consider writing to the following address to request a copy:

Earning Freedom
32565 Golden Lantern Street, Suite B-1026
Dana Point, CA 92629

Email: Interns@PrisonProfessorsTalent.com

If we have resources available, we will send the book without charge. It's one way of showing our commitment to helping people in prison prepare for success.

Those who read *Earning Freedom* may follow along the entire journey, starting with the day of my arrest, on August 11, 1987. The story takes readers through jails and prisons. It shows the relationship between decisions in prison and opportunities after release.

As a companion to *Earning Freedom*, I wrote *Prison: My 8,344th Day*. This self-directed workbook shows how to maintain discipline and the importance of daily decisions.

On August 13, 2012, after 25 years inside, I transferred from the federal prison camp in Atwater to a halfway house in San Francisco. Then I served the final six months of my sentence in home confinement—in a newly constructed house I purchased during my first weeks in the halfway house.

After getting some traction in the career I was building, I wrote another self-directed workbook, *Success After Prison*. I wrote that workbook with hopes of providing pathways people in prison could use to prepare for success. I wanted them to see the relationship between a person's decisions in prison and prospects for success upon release.

Masterminds taught me those lessons, and I intend to pass them along through the courses we create through Prison Professors. Make a commitment to lifelong learning.

Regardless of where we may be, we always have opportunities to change. When we change how we think, we may alter how we act. If we start sowing seeds for a better future, we simultaneously begin to restore our confidence and build self-esteem—even if we're locked in prison. Remember, today's decisions directly influence our prospects for success in the months, years, and decades ahead.

If we build a stronger mindset, we can adjust to prison in ways that put us on a pathway for more opportunities. A strong mindset helped me commit to positive programs while I served my sentence. It influenced the friends I chose, and my attitude influenced every step I took along my journey.

In my 16th year of the sentence, I got married. I nurtured that marriage through the final decade that I served. When my wife would visit me, I'd tell her about the career I wanted to build when I got out. Besides becoming successful in business, I pledged to pay tribute to the master-minds that influenced my adjustment. I intended to:

> » Create resources that people could use to adjust well as they went into prison.
> » Build bridges that would connect people who served time with employers.
> » Help more Americans understand steps we could take to improve prison systems across America.

To build credibility, I knew that I would need to become successful in society. For that reason, I pledged to my wife that within five years of being released from prison, I would build assets worth $1,000,000. If I could achieve that goal, I believed others would be more inclined to believe in the lessons I offered.

Experience convinces me that anyone can sow seeds for success, even if that person starts inside a solitary cell. The key would be to help people believe that it's never too early (and never too late) to prepare for a *triumphant* return to society.

Below I offer a summary of what I experienced after leaving the Federal Prison in Atwater, California.

August 13, 2012:
> » My wife picked me up from the Atwater prison and drove me to the halfway house in San Francisco.

August 14, 2012:
> » My case manager in the halfway house gave me a pass to the DMV to take the driver's license exam.

August 15, 2012:
> » I had my first day of work at a job I coordinated before I left prison.

August 30, 2012
> » Despite having a 0-0-0 credit score, I persuaded a real estate developer to finance a new house that his company would build for me.

November 24, 2012
> » The San Francisco Chronicle published a front-page story about my journey through prison and returned to society.

February 12, 2013
> » I transitioned from the halfway house to home confinement.

June 14, 2013
> » While still in the halfway house, I traveled to San Diego to speak for a panel of federal judges about the prison experience.

August 12, 2013
> » I finished my obligation to the Bureau of Prisons after 9,500 days.

August 28, 2013
> » I began teaching as an adjunct professor at San Francisco State University.

October 17, 2013
> » NBC news profiled me as I taught in a San Francisco jail, at San Francisco State University, and UC Berkeley.

February 11, 2014
> » I gave a TED talk for a Silicon Valley Joint Venture Conference in front of more than 1,500 business leaders.

April 2, 2014
> » The PBS NewsHour profiled me on a news segment about efforts to bring positive reforms to the prison system.

May 29, 2014
> » I moved from San Francisco Bay to Newport Beach to expand my career with real estate investments.

July 1, 2014
> » The Robina Institute invited me to serve as an advisory council member for a panel to assess probation and parole procedures in 50 states.

August 12, 2014
> » Federal Judge Susan Illston granted early termination of my Supervised Release with support from the AUSA and my Probation Officer.

January 15, 2015
> » I launched PrisonProfessor.com, which became PrisonProfessors.com when I partnered with Shon Hopwood in 2017.

February 13, 2015
> » I keynoted a symposium on Federal Sentence reform at UC Hastings Law School.

March 23, 2015
> » I launched the Earning Freedom podcast on iTunes and MichaelSantos.com.

April 30, 2015
> » I purchased my second rental property.

September 30, 2015
> » I purchased my third rental property.

October 20, 2015
> » I purchased my fourth rental property.

January 20, 2016
> » I purchased my fifth rental property.

June 20, 2016
> » I purchased my family residence, then later turned the house into a rental property.

June 24, 2016
> » I traveled to Guam and Saipan to deliver Earning Freedom products that I sold to the US Attorney and the Federal Court System.

January 25, 2017
> » I launched Earning Freedom, Inc.

May 2018
> » I launched PrisonToParadise.com and Alternative Investment Properties, LLC.

July 31, 2018
> » My wife and I invested $1.4 million to become a limited partner in a property development in Costa Rica.

December 30, 2018
> » I became entangled in civil litigation that exposed me to more than $100 million in civil liability, risking all the assets I accumulated after my release from prison.

January 13, 2019
» I settled the civil litigation, agreeing to walk away from $5 million in assets I'd built since leaving prison in 2013.

January 15, 2019
» I launched Compliance Mitigation, a new company to help small- and medium-sized businesses minimize their exposure to litigation, investigations, or charges for white-collar crime.

January 4, 2021
» I signed a contract with the television network CNBC to film a new reality-based television show that profiles how to use time in prison to prepare for success.

February 1, 2021
» I received confirmation from the California Department of Corrections for a new purchase order to bring the Preparing for Success After Prison Program to people serving sentences in California.

September 1, 2022
» I visited the North Central Regional Office of the Bureau of Prisons to present ideas to the Regional Director and the Wardens presiding over 20 federal prisons in 12 states.

Fall, 2022
» I began introducing our Preparing for Success after Prison course in federal prisons across the North Central Region of the federal Bureau of Prisons.

Summer, 2023
» I hired a researcher from UCLA to begin collecting data that would allow us to show more people the value of incentivizing excellence. The research we collect will further our goals of bringing reforms such as:
  ◊ Broader use of incentives for all,
  ◊ Reinstatement of parole boards,
  ◊ Meaningful access to commutations and compassionate release

If I could emerge successfully after 26 years as a federal prisoner, any other participant could do the same.

Take 10 Minutes

» 6-7: What methodical steps can you begin taking today that will influence the career you lead upon release?

LESSON 7: DEFINING SUCCESS

Your beliefs become your thoughts, Your thoughts become your words, Your words become your actions, Your actions become your habits, Your habits become your values, Your values become your destiny.
—Mahatma Gandhi

If you would like to influence how other people perceive you, this lesson on values will help. Participants will learn the value of questions. By asking good questions, we can start laying the groundwork that will take us from where we are to where we want to go.

The children's book Alice in Wonderland *dispensed* this wisdom from a character known as the Cheshire Cat. The Cheshire Cat said:

"If we don't know where we're going, any road will take us there."

Sadly, many begin a prison term without considering how earlier decisions influenced current struggles. Similarly, they don't connect how today's decisions will influence their future. If we want a better future, we've got to ask better questions. We should think about the *implications* of how we answer those questions.

Any of us can choose to learn how to build a stronger mindset. While incarcerated, I learned two tactics from masterminds that would influence my *prospects* for success while in prison and beyond.

> » Developing strong critical-thinking skills, and
> » Developing more potent communication skills.

As we advance, I'll *reveal* more about *tactics* and *strategies*. For example, notice the words and phrases in bold italics—such as tactics and strategies.

Some participants may have more advanced vocabularies than I had when I entered the prison system. I didn't know how to define either of those words when I started. From a mastermind, I learned that we could *empower* ourselves if we built more *robust* vocabularies.

Regardless of what level of restrictions a prison *imposes,* anyone can work toward building a more robust vocabulary and more *vital* critical-thinking skills.

Before entering the prison system, I would not have taken the time to learn new words or develop critical-thinking skills. I was lazy. If I read words I didn't understand, I would simply skip over the words and move on. Later, I'll *reveal* more about a mastermind that helped me to appreciate the power that comes from developing more *extensive* communication skills and better critical-thinking skills.

Each participant in this course may want to grow stronger and more capable of success upon release.

Building a vocabulary represents one self-directed tactic that any person could ***pursue***. To help, I use bold and ***italics*** to highlight each word that would have been new to me at the start of my sentence. If a participant doesn't know how to define the bold and italicized words or doesn't understand the phrase, then a good personal-development tactic toward the strategy of self-improvement would be to:

» Write down the word,
» Look up the word,
» Write the definition of the word,
» Learn how the word is categorized—a verb, a noun, or adjective,
» And use the word in a sentence.

Take 10 Minutes

» 7-1: How would this exercise of vocabulary building and personal development influence a person's prospects for future success?

_____

_____

_____

_____

_____

_____

_____

» 7-2: How do officials define you?

_____

_____

_____

_____

_____

_____

_____

_____

» 7-3: How do you define yourself?

_____

_____

_____

_____

_____

_____

_____

_____

Reflecting on open-ended questions helped me immensely. By asking good questions, we develop our critical-thinking skills. Notice that there are no "wrong" or "right" answers to the open-ended questions. We can't answer "yes" or "no." We must think. The more time we spend contemplating challenging questions, the more skills we develop.

We succeed by training our minds on how to think differently. We can choose to develop better critical-thinking skills. When we make such a choice, we learn how to think in ways that improve the outcomes of our lives.

Questions help us define our values or what we consider central to who we are as individuals. When we identify values, we can begin to make more deliberate choices that lead to success—as we define success.

Getting Started:

In previous lessons, I wrote about my bad decisions as a young man and how those decisions led to my 45-year sentence. Since those lessons didn't come easily to me, I'll offer the backstory, hoping that participants can follow along. Future modules and supplementary video lessons will show how early preparations influenced the career I began to build upon release. The sooner we begin preparing for success upon release, the stronger we become.

Any person searching for a pathway to personal development from prison may find examples of strategies and tactics helpful.

While I sat in my jail cell, I knew I wanted to change. My crimes exposed me to a possible life sentence. When authorities arrested me in 1987, I understood that a conviction would mean I wouldn't be eligible for parole. The jury's verdict meant I would serve at least a decade and probably much longer.

Since I hadn't been to prison previously, I didn't know what to expect.

Regardless of my sentence length, as I sat in various holding cells, I knew I wanted to leave prison differently. I tried to influence the way others thought about me. A jury convicted me, and a judge sentenced me. I wouldn't be able to reverse that reality. Still, I believed I could create meaning or a positive life if I could influence my future.

When Officer Wilson from the detention center passed me *A Treasury of Philosophy*, I didn't know what I'd learn. After I began reading, I felt as if I had come across a treasure map. If I could follow the teachings in the book, I would build a brighter future. Each chapter brought a new lesson, teaching me how to build strength out of weakness.

The story of Socrates gave me a character with whom I could identify. When I read that Socrates awaited his death while in a jail cell, I felt we had something in common. For that reason, I wanted to learn about his life. As I read more about his inspiring life, I saw that Socrates thought differently from me. In his story, I could **ascertain** that he placed high importance on living responsibly as a good citizen. While in my early 20s, such concepts didn't occur to me.

Socrates' thought process influenced my **perceptions**. Before reading his story, I didn't consider the relationship between my actions and the broader community. Neither did I think about how choices I made would influence others. Instead, I thought about myself.

Before reading that story of Socrates—during my first year of imprisonment—I only wanted to get out. My attorney led me to believe a big difference existed between an indictment and a conviction, and I wanted to believe him. I lacked the maturity to **contemplate** my crimes or what I would do if authorities released me. I simply wanted out of my jail cell.

Socrates changed my thinking. While lying on that concrete rack in the detention center, I stared at the ceiling of my cell. I needed to prepare, to make sure each day felt productive. In search of answers, or a roadmap that would help me **navigate** the pathway to success, I read deeper into that philosophy book.

While reading, I needed a dictionary. Before prison, I felt drawn to a fast lifestyle, not books, learning, or studying. School never held my attention. Reading through that philosophy book made me realize how poorly I had prepared for life's challenges. As a prisoner, I knew I would confront many challenges.

By reading philosophy, I learned the importance of **introspecting** as the first step toward change.

Introspection:

When I looked up "introspection" in the dictionary, I developed a better understanding. Philosophers said that wise men considered the motives that drove them. They took **deliberate** action in pursuit of success—as they defined success. Not every person would define success in the same way. Each person had to define success for himself.

That advice made sense. If people could define what success meant to them, they would have a better chance of advancing along the journey of success.

The more I thought or introspected, the more I realized I had to change. Before prison, my thoughts were **shallow**. I never gave any consideration to what it would mean to define success. Instead, I thought about what I wanted in the immediate moment—material objects, like cars, places to live, or clothes. I didn't comprehend how daily decisions would influence the rest of my life. Like the friends I chose, I lived for the moment.

Introspection brought more clarity. I reflected on my years in school. From my earliest memories, I looked for the easy way, ignoring the teachers that invested so much time trying to teach me. I didn't discipline myself. Whenever I saw opportunities, I acted quickly, without thinking about what would follow. I didn't **hesitate** to lie or cheat if I felt lying or cheating would serve my interest.

The more I introspected, the more disgusted I became with my earlier decisions. Those thoughts and decisions led to the young man I had become—a person locked inside a cell on his way to prison. As I began to develop my thought process, I concluded that I wasn't in jail because I sold cocaine. Instead, the system confined me because I lacked discipline since I was a young boy. I chose the easy route instead of preparing for success. Rather than surrounding myself with good role models, I befriended people with character flaws like mine. As I reflected, I could see how all those earlier decisions put me on a pathway that influenced the person I became.

While alone in that solitary cell, I thought about people I admired. Instead of being driven by greed or the pursuit of immediate gratification, those people aspired to become people of good character. They didn't act in ways that would harm their reputation.

The more I thought about my life in the past, the more I realized how my earlier decisions would influence the future I would build. Although I didn't know what sentence my judge would impose, I understood that I would have to serve many years.

When I finished serving my sentence and returned to society, I surmised that people would always judge me. They would denounce me as a convicted felon or a man who spent decades in prison. Their perceptions of me would influence opportunities or present barriers to opportunities.

As I thought about success, I wondered what steps I could take to influence the perception of people I would meet in the future. I wanted to be positive.

Take Ten Minutes

>> 7-4: In what ways does introspection influence your release plan?

_____

_____

_____

_____

_____

_____

_____

Advice from Confinement

By introspecting, I began to question whether I could do anything to change the course of my future. I considered past decisions and projected into the future. From staff members in the detention centers, I heard two messages:

>> You've got nothing comin'.
>> Don't do the crime if you can't do the time.

From the other people serving time, I heard a variety of messages:

>> The best way to serve time is to forget about the outside world.
>> Focus on your reputation inside.
>> Survival in prison requires hate.

That advice didn't inspire much hope. I needed to believe I could accomplish something during my imprisonment. Accomplishments could redeem the bad decisions from my early 20s. I wanted to reconcile with society and open opportunities for a better life.

From reading Socrates, I learned that if I wanted to change the course of my future, I had to start by looking at my past. I had to contemplate the choices I made in the past. I learned to question all my choices.

>> How did earlier decisions influence my predicament?
>> What effect would those decisions have on my future?
>> Could I take steps during my imprisonment to influence people I would meet in the future?
>> Was it possible to influence how others would perceive me?
>> Could I reconcile in ways that would induce leaders to join my support group?

Those were yes or no questions. While locked in the cell, I questioned whether I could do anything to influence the people I would meet in the months, years, and decades ahead.

Either I had the power within to transform my life, or I didn't. The more I introspected on questions, the more hope I developed. Decisions I made while serving time could influence the life that I would lead upon release. Still, I wanted more clarity. The path ahead wasn't so apparent during those early stages of my journey.

- » I didn't know what sentence my judge would impose.
- » I didn't know where prison administrators would send me.
- » I didn't know the people with whom I would have to serve time.
- » I didn't know anything about prison.
- » I didn't know how I would support myself.
- » And I didn't know what else I didn't know.

There were a lot of unknowns. But I knew what I wanted: return to society ***unscathed*** from prison.

- » How could someone serving decades in prison prepare for a triumphant return to society?

The sooner a person starts asking such questions, the more it becomes possible to engineer a strategy that will lead to success.

Asking good questions led me to further thoughts. The more I ***stared*** at the concrete block walls, the more questions I had. The questions brought clarity. For me, the exercise in personal development began with "Socratic questioning."

We can define Socratic questioning as an exercise in asking questions that may help us come up with better answers. I learned how introspection could empower me.

We all have the power to ask better questions. Masterminds defined insanity as doing the same thing repeatedly but expecting a different result.

As I lay in my cell, I knew I wanted a different life. It dawned on me that if I continued to associate with people who broke the law, I would always have problems with the law. I began to think of what I could do to build a better life—a life where I wouldn't be running from the law or running from anyone else.

Restoring Strength:
Thinking about my past helped. First, I thought about all the decisions that led to my troubles with the law. Then I thought about what I could do to build a life of meaning and relevance.

» What could I do to influence people I would meet in the future?
  ◊ I didn't know who those people would be, but I knew that others would influence my ability to lead a full life after prison.

» A probation officer would supervise me after release.
  ◊ Could I take steps to influence that future probation officer?

» I didn't have much in the way of work experience before prison. Yet I would have to persuade an employer to hire me.
  ◊ Could I influence the ways that future employers would judge me?

» I didn't have any financial resources and would need people or companies to extend credit.
  ◊ Could I take steps while in prison to make it easier to obtain credit when I got out?

» How could I use the time inside to solve problems I would face after release?

Take Ten Minutes

» 7-5: What steps are you taking to convert adversaries into advocates?

_____
_____
_____
_____
_____
_____
_____

Avatars:

My questions turned to the people I would meet in the future. I referred to those people as my "***Avatars***." I considered an avatar as the ideal type of person I would want to support me.

» Could my adjustment in prison influence my avatars? That was another yes or no question.

That led to a new question:

» What would law-abiding citizens expect from me?

Participants should recognize that each question leads to more questions. I had to think about my responses. And I had to assess whether my responses, decisions, and actions would bring me closer to success upon release.

If people were going to open opportunities in the future, they would expect me to show that I'm different. They would want me to do more than serve time. Calendar pages turn without any influence on my part.

You may have heard of the judge who sentenced a man to serve 20 years. The defendant felt weak.
»   *"But judge, I can't do all that time."*
»   *"Well, do what you can," the judge responded.*

I knew my judge would sentence me to a lengthy term. My conviction carried a mandatory minimum sentence of 10 years. But the law allowed my judge to sentence me to life without parole. My judge would have total discretion on sentence length. But I could make choices to **affect** prospects for success. My adjustment in prison could put me on the pathway of opportunities. Or my adjustment could threaten progress.

Crafting a Plan:

The judge would impose a sentence, but there would be more to the process. I could wait for my sentence to end. Yet waiting for calendar pages to turn wouldn't prepare me to overcome challenges, and I anticipated that I would face many difficulties in prison and upon release.

As mentioned above, I thought about:

»   My future probation officer and how I could persuade him to grant me a higher degree of liberty,
»   My prospective employer and how I could persuade him to look beyond my criminal record and allow me to work toward a career,
»   Future lenders and what they would expect me to achieve for them to do business with me.

Those questions made me think more about the people I'd meet. They led me to flesh out my avatars.

»   Who were they?
»   What kinds of friends did they have?
»   What perceptions would they have about someone who served a lengthy term in prison?
»   How could I persuade those people to see me differently from what my criminal convictions suggested?

Thinking about the future brought clarity.

Successful people think about problems and how to find or create solutions. Then they could develop plans that would lead to a successful outcome. By learning from them, anyone could plan. People in prison could create adjustment strategies.

That new "philosophy" helped me believe I could do more than serve time. I could take measurable steps to improve the outcome of my prison experience. Anyone could choose the same strategy.

If I wanted a second chance at life, I would need to do my part. People would always judge me if I didn't work hard to build an **extraordinary** and **compelling** record of accomplishments. I wanted to show how I matured into something more than the 20-year-old kid who sold cocaine. I couldn't keep blaming others for problems I created. To build a better future, I had to solve problems.

First, I had to anticipate what problems I would face in the future. If I didn't make changes:

>   »   I knew that I'd leave prison without any clothes.
>   »   I knew that I'd leave prison without any money.
>   »   I knew that I'd leave prison without a vehicle.
>   »   I knew that I'd leave prison without any credit.
>   »   I knew that I'd leave prison without any work history.
>   »   I knew I'd leave prison without much in the way of resources other people took for granted.

>   ◊   How could a person in prison overcome those hurdles?

If I didn't take steps to solve those problems, my return to society would present many, many challenges. Those challenges, I realized, could complicate my future.

This questioning, introspection, or self-examination led to the values that would define my life. In time, I came away with an answer.

If I were going to emerge from prison with my dignity intact, **unscathed** by the prison experience, I needed to live a values-based, principled life. My values would reflect my commitment to success. As Gandhi said, habits become values, and values become destiny.

Even though I would serve a lengthy term, I could define value categories. I could pledge to live by those value categories. Those value categories could influence every decision I made going forward.

Before learning about values, I didn't have any direction. Although I hated being in prison, and wanted out, I didn't know how to create a path that would lead to a better life. I felt like a **marionette**. The prosecutor, my judge, and the prison system pulled the strings of my life. If I served multiple decades, I anticipated new challenges would await me once I got out.

From masterminds, I learned that I could seize control. I could define values. Then I could make decisions and take steps to show others that I was worthy of a second chance. I wanted to influence the way that others perceived me. I didn't try to fit in with the prison culture or with the expectations of others. Instead, I set my values in accordance with the people I expected to influence later. I didn't know those people by name, but I had an idea of what they would expect. Those ideas influenced the value categories by which I would live.

Those people became my avatars, and I'll write more about how they inspired me in future lessons. The *salient* point of this lesson, I think, is that at any time, we can start making decisions to influence what we become in the future. Regardless of what bad decisions we've made in the past, it's never too early, and it's never too late to start becoming good.

Once I committed to living a values-based life, I took the first step toward a *deliberate* course of action. I knew that I was locked in prison. And I knew that I wanted to return to society strong. To accomplish that goal, I charted the course that would put me in the best possible position upon release.

I committed to living by the same value categories that governed the lives of law-abiding citizens—my avatars.

» What would law-abiding citizens—my avatars—expect from me?

Masterminds convinced me that people would be more receptive to working with me if they believed I lived a values-based life. Instead of "giving" me a second chance, those people may consider my accomplishments and conclude I earned a second chance.

Those thoughts led me to identify three value categories that would be consistent with the values of my avatars. They included commitments:

» To pursue an education
» To contribute to society
» To build a support network

A person may *endure* the struggle of confinement, yet anyone could take time to introspect. By introspecting, a person could look at past decisions. Looking at past decisions, a person could think about the relationship between the choices made and the life created.

Take 30 Minutes

Consider the following questions to prompt your critical thinking.

» 7-6: What past experiences influenced your thoughts?

_____
_____
_____
_____
_____
_____
_____
_____
_____

» 7-7: How did those thoughts influence the way you communicated?

_____
_____
_____
_____
_____
_____
_____
_____
_____

» 7-8: In what ways did your communications lead to your actions?

_____
_____
_____
_____
_____
_____
_____
_____
_____

» 7-9: How did your decisions and actions become your habits?

_____
_____
_____
_____
_____
_____
_____
_____

» 7-10: Would others define you by your habits?

_____
_____
_____
_____
_____
_____
_____

» 7-11: Did those habits become your values and put you where you are now?

_____
_____
_____
_____
_____
_____
_____
_____
_____
_____

Regardless of where authorities confine us, we can make decisions to influence a better future. We may start by defining our values, and to the extent that we align those values with the future we want to create, we live like a mastermind.

LESSON 8: SUPER SMART GOALS

What you get By achieving your goals is not as important as what you become by pursuing your goals.
—Henry David Thoreau

Take 10 Minutes

» 8-1: What did you do yesterday?

_____

_____

_____

_____

_____

» 8-2: How did your decisions move you closer to the person you intend to become?

_____

_____

_____

_____

_____

Asking such questions strengthened me while serving time in prisons of different security levels. It helped me to obliterate *misdirected* ideas that I would have to wait for prison administrators to offer programs. Although I could take advantage of every program available, circumstances often changed in prison. Sometimes administrators locked the institution down, or funding cuts or lockdowns could *suspend* classes.

Even in unusual times, a person could engineer a personal plan to prepare for success upon release.

All people who question what they're doing today to prepare for tomorrow can make better decisions. Those questions can lead to *incremental* steps that *restore* confidence and lead to better outcomes.

In August of 2013, when I transitioned from prison to Supervised Release, I had a higher level of liberty, and more opportunities. Had it not been for the lessons that masterminds taught, the Probation Officer overseeing me would have restricted my movements. Yet by showing a release plan that showed a pattern of defining success and setting clear goals at each stage of the journey, the Probation Officer allowed me to:

> » Work independently, as an ***entrepreneur***,
> » ***Interact*** with other people who were going through various stages of the criminal justice system,
> » Travel domestically at my ***discretion*** for the advancement of my career, and
> » Enjoy a higher level of liberty than others would have anticipated.

Those liberties after prison opened because of the preparations I made while going through the journey. To prepare for higher levels of liberty upon release, consider two concepts:

> » Our values define how we live, what we are, and what we consider success.
> » Our incremental goals advance us along our journey.

I'll reveal how those concepts influenced me through the 26 years that I served. Further, I'll show how adjustment strategies through decades in prison opened opportunities along the way.

I pledge that throughout this course, I'll never ask anyone to do anything I didn't do while in prison and that I'm not still doing today. In that manner, I hope to earn the trust of people who choose to continue participating in this program.

The previous lesson emphasized the importance of identifying the values by which we live. According to the masterminds who taught me how to prepare for success, we need to define our values. Once we understand what we're striving to achieve, we can set clear goals to close the gap between where we are today and the success we want to reach.

Working toward goals can help us advance.

As I wrote in earlier lessons of this course, Frederick Douglass, inspired me with how he used his life story to advance a cause. When he escaped from slavery, he invested his time and energy to become a force to ***emancipate*** all people in slavery. To succeed, he understood that he would have to communicate better. He set a goal of ***literacy*** and trained himself to read and write. Then, through three biographies that he published. Mr. Douglass used his life story to build strong ***coalitions***, convincing voters to ***abolish*** slavery laws.

When I began serving a lengthy prison term, I visualized how I wanted to return to society. Even from the confines of a solitary cell, I could see myself wearing a suit and tie and speaking in front of an audience. Like Mr. Douglas, I hoped to persuade people that we could improve outcomes of America's prison system if we changed the way we measured justice. Instead of waiting for calendar pages to turn, we should create incentives. Staff members could use those incentives to reward people for working to develop skills that would prepare them for success upon release.

To succeed, I would have to **emulate** Mr. Douglass. First, I would need to become more **literate**. If I could become a published author, others might take me more seriously. Rather than **dismissing** me as a convicted felon, the people would accept me as a contributing member of society. They might assess the ideas differently, judging me for the man I became—and not for the bad decisions that led to my imprisonment.

Since I could visualize success, which I'll describe in future modules, I could lay out a plan. As I wrote in the previous module, I laid out three value categories. To recap, I committed to spending every day working:

> » To learn and earn academic credentials,
> » To contribute to society, and
> » To build a support network.

Those value categories felt consistent with how I defined success. I anticipated that my avatars would recognize and respect those value categories. I wanted to walk into any group of law-abiding citizens and fit in. Whether I stood in a bank, a prospective employer's office, or a business, I wanted people to accept me. If I didn't **reveal** my past, no one would know I served a day in prison. If I succeeded, I would find support and opportunity. If I built credibility in those incremental ways, I might become more effective in advocating for prison and sentence reforms.

The strategy of earning academic credentials, contributing to society, and building a support network helped me frame decisions. Avatars would believe in my future if I lived by those values. Defining values would be the start toward building a better life—and I defined a better life as one that would free me from problems with the criminal justice system. Once I got past those problems, I would be more effective as an agent for change that would open opportunities to liberate others when I got out.

By living this values-based, goal-oriented strategy, I hoped to influence people that had discretion over my life. Those people may not have the power to release me from prison, but they could play a role in opening opportunities for me to make further progress. Before I could persuade others to change laws, I would need to persuade people that worked in prisons. They could include the incremental progress along the way. For example:

> » A case manager may recommend me for lower security.
> » A lieutenant may refrain from citing me with an infraction.
> » A warden may consider a special request.

Those leaders had discretion. Their decisions could ease my adjustment or **exacerbate** my problems. If I made good decisions, I could influence administrators and teachers in prison. They might view me more positively if I developed a values-based adjustment strategy while I served my sentence.

Likewise, by making values-based decisions, I believed that I could influence my future. A probation officer may consider my adjustment. An employer would want to know why I'm wor-

thy of a job. People that had the discretion to approve loan requests would like an explanation of my criminal background. I considered all those people as my avatars. My values would influence their perceptions and my prospects for success.

Before I could work to change laws, or advocate for incentives in prison, I first had to change my life. A jury had convicted me of crimes that led to a 45-year sentence. I had the onus of achieving a series of incremental goals. Otherwise, people would not take me seriously.

If I could make a favorable impression on my avatars, I could open better opportunities. Preparing for success required me to start my adjustment strategy deliberately, relying upon values to guide my decisions. The opinions of others wouldn't carry weight if those opinions did not align with how I defined success.

Many people in prison expressed different values. They focused on their time inside.

Take Ten:

» 8-3: How are values influencing your life today?

_____

_____

_____

_____

_____

_____

_____

» 8-4: How will people you meet in the future relate to your values?

_____

_____

_____

_____

_____

_____

_____

_____

_____

» 8-5: Describe the people who share the values that you use to define success.

_____

_____

_____

_____

_____

_____

_____

_____

As mentioned earlier, people in prison often give unsolicited advice. They have clear ideas on how to serve time. Some people mistakenly believe that they can't influence life beyond prison walls. They make decisions to **ease** their life in jail or prison. They think it's a waste of time to think about the outside and that such thoughts complicate time inside. While serving a sentence, they say it's best to forget about the world outside prison.

I didn't think like a leader before I went to prison. I didn't give much thought to my future. Since I wasn't thinking about my future, my decisions didn't matter. That type of thinking led me to problems. I didn't know how my decisions and actions influenced the lives of others. Instead of thinking about my role as a citizen (as I later learned from masterminds), I focused only on myself. That thinking led to bad decisions and actions leading to my prison term.

Making a Change:
I wanted a different life. During the many months of my pretrial detention, I saw and heard a lot. Hundreds of prisoners told me their stories. Many described serving time previously and spoke about the problems they faced after release.

Ironically, men spoke as if serving multiple terms gave them credibility. They were prison leaders **_dispensing_** advice. Indeed, they cultivated solid images as stand-up convicts. People in the jail "respected" them. Those cellblock leaders:

» Decided which television shows other people could watch,
» Influenced who could sit in which seats in common areas, and
» Perceived themselves as being stand-up convicts.

Such strategies and tactics may or may not lead to influence in prison communities. Yet in the broader community, people expect different adjustment patterns. For example, when going to a restaurant, no one knows or cares about people seated at a nearby table. When getting fuel, people typically don't concern themselves with the decisions of other customers.

» How does a stand-up convict differ from the path to preparing for success upon release?

» How would the avatars I chose respond to someone that built a reputation as a stand-up convict?

Those types of critical-thinking questions helped to guide the adjustment strategy I engineered.

When I understood that my conviction carried a mandatory-minimum term of 10 years, I knew that I would have to overcome many obstacles. Although ten years would be the minimum sentence, I could anticipate that my judge would ***inflict*** a much longer sentence. The ***statute*** gave the judge discretion to impose a life term.

Regardless of sentence length, my adjustment inside would influence my future. Even if the judge sentenced me to serve a life term, I could still work toward influencing a better outcome. I aspired to leave prison with my dignity intact at the earliest time.

My definition of success has always remained at the ***forefront*** of my mind. For that reason, these modules will repeat the three value categories that helped to frame every decision I made. I thought of how my choices would relate to:

» Educating myself,
» Contributing to society, and
» Building a support network.

The pursuit of those three value categories would define my adjustment strategy.

Anyone serving a lengthy term in prison (and I understand that a single day in prison might feel like a long term) could benefit from investing the time to describe their value categories. That exercise in personal development is essential for a person determined to grow. We all need clear goals.

Setting Goals:

We show our commitment to our value categories by setting clear goals. In my case, I understood that achieving goals would influence the perceptions of my avatars. Both the values and goals worked together. A values-based, goal-oriented adjustment strategy would prepare me for success, just as a values-based, goal-oriented adjustment could prepare anyone for success.

On the flip side, pursuing a reputation as a stand-up convict would be another option. That strategy would bring different consequences. The ***supplemental*** videos we offer with our courses profile people who talk about their prison journey. The people who spoke with me discussed how their early adjustment strategies in confinement (or lack of adjustment strategies)

led to problems. Without direction, individuals that did not set goals found new problems with administrators, or they had problems with other people serving time.

Let's think about how we want to emerge from challenging situations. We can set clear goals that may open new and better opportunities. Good goal-setting strategies may also lessen our *vulnerability* to further problems.

Defining a Stand-up Convict:

During the awkward months in pretrial detention, I heard many people offering unsolicited advice on how to serve time. They spoke about the importance of building a prison reputation. Rather than creating a "prison reputation," however, the decisions we make every day build our life reputation—not only while we're in prison, but always. Our choices put us on track for success or lead us into cycles of failure. People that identified as "shot callers" in jail sometimes revealed that they had complicated lives outside of confinement. In other words:

> » They didn't have good credit scores.
> » They didn't own a home.
> » Their most prized possession was a vehicle of some sort.
> » They didn't have financial resources.
> » They didn't have stable careers.
> » They couldn't buy items in the commissary.
> » They didn't have steady relationships.
> » They didn't have close or supportive families.
> » They described problems with substance abuse or other addictions.
> » They complained of ongoing problems while on supervised release.
> » Their family members had issues with the criminal justice system.

If that story applied to one person in prison, it would be easy to dismiss. Yet by the time I served a few months in custody, I heard similar stories from everyone who identified themselves as being leaders in prison. I saw a pattern. The way that a person adjusted in prison would influence the prospects for success after release.

People who valued a prison reputation minimized chances to live the way they envisioned after release.

As you work through this self-directed course, think about the life you want to lead upon release.

After a jury convicted me, I understood that prisons would confine me for at least a decade. I couldn't change that fact. Yet, I had the power to choose how I would adjust, and the adjustment strategies would influence my prospects for success once I got out. The value categories of focusing on education, contributing to society, and building a support network would influence the goals I set along the way.

» What clear goals would show a commitment to those values?

» Would they put me in a better position to succeed?

I wanted to succeed in prison and beyond.

Participants may want to engineer a new adjustment strategy to guide decisions going forward.

Take 20 Minutes

» 8-6: How can you use these lessons to start changing your life today?

_____
_____
_____
_____
_____
_____
_____
_____
_____

» 8-7: What relationship do you see between your circle of friends and your prospects for success—as you defined success with your values?

_____
_____
_____
_____
_____
_____
_____
_____
_____
_____

Transparency:

Establishing value categories influences our choices. Once I decided to transform my life, I wanted to go on record. I started writing to mark the day when I left criminal decisions behind. I wanted to show my commitment to living as a law-abiding citizen. By writing about that commitment, I drew a line and invited the world to hold me accountable. With that end in mind, I wrote a letter to a journalist in the local newspaper.

In the letter, I wrote how I regretted selling cocaine. Although I couldn't change the past, I pledged to the journalist to use my time in prison to make amends. The three-pronged strategy would include a commitment:

- » To earn academic credentials,
- » To contribute to society, and
- » To build a strong, positive support network.

I invited the journalist to visit me in jail with that simple explanation.

That letter represented a step in the right direction. It showed my quest to make things right. Writing the letter made it clear that I wanted to atone. I planted a seed for a new and bright future. The record would show the exact time I made a conscious, deliberate choice to change.

The journalist interviewed me in a small jail conference room. The week before sentencing, the newspaper published the article. That front-page story profiled how I said I would change. I put myself on record, pledging to spend every day working to reconcile with society.

With clear value categories to define success, I could start taking incremental steps to show my commitment to pursuing success. By going on the record, I started moving closer to liberty. As time passed, I would always be able to look back to those writings when I declared that I would never commit another crime.

The Sentencing Hearing:

I expected the prosecutor to oppose my request for mercy. Although I wanted leniency at sentencing, his job required that he pursue a harsh sentence. I anticipated that he would argue that I lacked **_remorse_** for the crimes that I had committed. Instead, he would contend that any sorrow I expressed resulted from getting caught.

Exposure to Socrates and philosophy changed how I looked at the world. When I read about Frederick Douglass, I understood that I would need to develop a life story. Instead of hiding from my past, I would need to respond and build a series of incremental progress that would influence a better future. If wanted to work toward changing laws, I would need change myself first.

Earlier, I lived by a philosophy that aligned with failure. I wanted to make things right. Writing to the journalist and participating in his interview, I believed, showed that I had changed my thinking.

On the day of my sentencing, jailers came to my cell before dawn. When I heard keys approaching, I got ready. They took me to another holding cell so I could change from my jail jumpsuit into my court clothes. Regardless of what term I received, I had my value categories. They would serve as a guide. They would help me build a path home.

Decades have passed since the day of my sentencing. But I will always remember the prosecutor's words. He told the judge:

> *"If Michael Santos spends every day of his life working to **reconcile** with society, and if he lives to be 300 years old, our community will still be at significant net loss because of the crimes he committed."*

After assessing the arguments, the judge **presiding** over my case sentenced me to 45 years. Strangely, I felt okay with the sentence. Under federal sentencing laws of 1987, I could earn "good time credits." By avoiding disciplinary problems, I could finish my sentence in 26 years. Still, 26 years felt like a long time, longer than I'd been alive at that point.

We can put that term in perspective. Imagine a young man going into prison today. Project 26 years into the future. Could a young man who began serving that sentence sustain a high level of energy and discipline through the journey?

Yes!

Still, we should learn and teach lessons that lead to lives of fulfillment and avoid **altercations** with the criminal justice system.

A values-based, goal-oriented adjustment strategy would bring energy and discipline to my life. Like anyone else, I could set clear goals once I defined success. Those goals would reflect a commitment to the values I set.

Experts who wrote about goals suggested that we adhere to the acronym "SMART."

S   — A goal should be *specific*.
M   — A goal should be *measurable*.
A   — A goal should be *action-oriented*.
R: — A goal should be *realistic*.
T: — A goal should be *time-based*

By setting SMART goals, I could work toward success. I defined success with my values. Those goals would help me break up the time. Those incremental goals would keep me go-

ing through the decades I expected to serve. Instead of dwelling on time, I focused on moving through the goals, completing one and moving on to the next.

Achieving goals felt like building a ladder. I could climb to liberty, to success.

Participants may want to set SMART goals that advance prospects for success, as they define it.

I again turned to my avatars to set SMART goals within each value category. Those avatars were like mentors to me—even if I had not met them yet. They included:

» The probation officer that would influence my life after release,
» The employer who could open an opportunity for me to earn a living,
» The creditors that might provide capital I could use to build businesses after I finished my prison term.
» The professionals who could help me work to change laws and open opportunities for more people to work toward earning higher levels of liberty through merit.

What steps could I take while in prison to influence those avatars?

That question led me to set the following clearly defined goals:

» To measure whether I lived by my commitment to educate myself, I needed to earn a university degree within my first ten years.
» I needed to become a published author within ten years to measure whether I lived by my commitment to contribute to society.
» To measure whether I lived by my commitment to building a support network, I needed to bring ten people into my support network within ten years.

I would achieve the three SMART goals during my first ten years in prison. I didn't know how. Yet, the goals became my guide. By completing the goals within ten years, I advanced my prospects for success. Then I could set new goals. The goals brought strength. I started on a path of recreating myself. I began the long process of transforming myself from a reckless youth into the man I aspired to become.

My term in prison began when I was 23, and it didn't conclude until 2013 when I was 49. Many years have passed since I got out. Experience has given me a different perspective from when I began serving my sentence.

» I've built businesses that generated millions of dollars in transactions with people in the private sector.
» I've negotiated business relationships with federal judges, US Attorneys, and directors of prison systems.

> » I've influenced judges, prison administrators, and people in academic to become a part of a coalition that would lead to prison and sentence reforms, such as the First Step Act.

None of those opportunities would have been possible if I hadn't been receptive to learning lessons from masterminds while serving my sentence.

As I look back, I can see the importance of defining success with values and using goals to guide adjustment strategies.

From masterminds, I learned that even though I made terrible decisions that put me in prison, I could start making better decisions. Those decisions could help me to grow stronger. The adjustment strategy may not have gotten me out of prison one day early, but it made a colossal difference in helping me to recalibrate and rebuild. I could seize opportunities that would accelerate prospects for success. By using values and goals to define an adjustment strategy, we may emulate masterminds who have conquered past struggles.

Take 10 Minutes:

> » 8-8: What SMART goals can you set to convert your adversaries into your advocates?

_____

_____

_____

_____

_____

_____

_____

_____

_____

_____

_____

_____

_____

_____

_____

_____

_____

_____

LESSON 9: DEVELOPING THE RIGHT ATTITUDE

Nothing can stop the man with the right mental attitude from achieving his goal; nothing on earth can help the man with the wrong mental attitude.
—*Thomas Jefferson*

Take 10 Minutes

» 9-1: What does it mean to have the right mental attitude?

_____

_____

_____

_____

_____

_____

_____

_____

_____

_____

_____

After a federal judge sentenced me to 45 years, I had to meditate on that question. Since I didn't know what it meant to have "the right mental attitude" to overcome challenging circumstances, I turned to masterminds for guidance. The right mental attitude differs, depending upon how the person defines success.

Course participants may want to consider the following questions to gauge whether they have an attitude that aligns with their commitment to success:

» In what ways does your attitude reflect a commitment to preparing for success?
» How would you articulate the ways that your activities over the past five days advance your potential for success?
» What further steps can you start taking today to prepare for the success you want to build in the future?

The earlier lesson on values prompted participants to think about how they would define success at every given stage in life. The lesson on goals encouraged participants to work toward success with a series of small, incremental steps. The small, specific goals we achieve prove our level of commitment to success, as we define it.

Remember that success comes in tiny steps, not all at once. Sometimes we're in difficult situations. Sometimes others attempt to pressure or influence us. They try to tell us what we can or cannot become.

We determine whether we want to listen.

Our values and goals should continually advance us along the pathway to success.

Fertilizer:

We can always take incremental steps to grow. First, we define success with our values. Then, we plant the seeds with our specific goals. If we plant seeds for success, we also must nurture those seeds with fertilizer. In time, as seasons pass, those seeds grow through the fertilizer. By nurturing the seeds appropriately, they will produce crops of ***abundance***. We can feed off those crops for a lifetime.

I see three critical points in the paragraph above.

> » We must plant the right seeds.
> » We must nurture seeds over time.
> » The seeds must grow through fertilizer.

What does that lesson tell us? It means we cannot ***merely*** "plant seeds" and expect to get everything we want. We've got to work the seeds, ***nourishing*** the soil with fertilizer to get the outcome we want. We know that one of the most effective types of fertilizer comes from animals—a polite way of saying a ***profane*** word that I pledged not to use in this course. We've got to grow through the fertilizer ("livestock manure") to build the future we want!

Start sowing your seeds for success regardless of where you may be today. Prepare yourself to nurture those seeds, growing through difficulties and struggles along the way.

Straight-A Guide:

In this lesson, we use our values and goals to move into the "Straight-A Guide." Before elaborating on the "Straight-A Guide," let me tell you how and why I created this tool.

I had about 20 or 22 years of prison behind me. I didn't know when authorities would let me out. There were some complications because federal sentencing laws had changed from when I committed my crimes. My release could come after I served 23 years, 24 years, 25 years, or 26 years.

Regardless of when I got out, I knew that I wanted to ***advocate*** for reforms. That would not be easy. I anticipated ***myriad*** complications. For example, from what others had told me, I understood that a probation officer would place restrictions on me. The officer would require me to have a job, or dependable income stream.

Further, when I finished my sentence, I'd be close to 50 years old—and I'd need to sow seeds for retirement. Although I ***aspired*** to teach others the strategies that masterminds taught me, I would have to ***anticipate*** complications and put myself in a position to overcome those complications.

Good strategies help all people who choose to live a values-based, goal-oriented life. They help people who want to succeed. We simply must apply values-based strategies to every area of our life. We can use the strategies to achieve success with fitness, relationships, finances, careers, and community involvement.

I knew that I hated every aspect of being in prison, and I hated that our country incarcerated more people per capita than any nation on earth. To overcome, I wanted to earn a living by creating products that would empower others. But that would require me to sow a lot of seeds. I would need to grow through a lot of "fertilizer."

Although I didn't quite know how I would start, I had many examples. Leaders such as Frederick Douglass, Nelson Mandela, Viktor Frankl, and Malcolm X used those personal stories to help others see the need for reform. If I could write in ways to document the pathway to change, I hoped to become more influential in being the change that I wanted to see.

During a visit with one of my mentors, I got inspired to begin writing this course.

My mentor asked how I intended to earn a living after I got out. In response, I told him about a book I had read by Suzie Welch, a management guru. She used to work as a journalist and editor for a business magazine. After she married Jack Welch, the legendary CEO and chairman of General Electric, she launched a new career with him. Together, they advised business leaders. Suzie Welch wrote a book called *Ten-Ten-*Ten, I told my mentor.

Using that simple concept, Suzy Welch advised leaders to think about how each of their decisions would influence life in the next ten minutes, the next ten months, and the next ten years. If a businessperson used that strategy, the person would make better, more deliberate decisions.

After my mentor listened to the story, he told me that I would need to develop a memorable teaching resource of my own. I wouldn't be able to build a career teaching someone else's story. He was right.

I told him I would use the story of my journey and other people's stories. By sharing those stories, I could show how all people that overcome struggles make small steps. When directed and deliberate, those small steps can take a person from struggle to success.

My mentor gave me some good advice. Besides stories, he said, I needed a simple tool that people could remember, like Ten-Ten-Ten.

After listening to his advice, I came up with the Straight-A Guide. The course's ***moniker*** would be easy to remember. As described earlier, we must identify our values and goals to start on the Straight-A Guide. Then, each subsequent lesson begins with the letter "A."

All masterminds start with the right attitude:

» Their attitudes align with how they define success.
» They follow a simple path to overcome challenges, clearly defining success.
» They set clear goals that align with how they define success.

With values and goals established, we move on to Attitude—the first "A" in our Straight-A Guide.

Masterminds like Nelson Mandela, Viktor Frankl, and Martin Luther King show the power that comes with the right attitude. Nelson Mandela's powerful and inspiring attitude carried him through 27 years of imprisonment.

» Viktor Frankl had the right attitude to make it through the challenges of a Nazi concentration camp.

» Martin Luther King had the right attitude to work toward restoring civil rights for all people.

Each of those masterminds defined the right attitude with a 100% commitment to success. With the right attitude, they overcome ***monumental*** struggles.

It isn't only world leaders that move through challenges with the right attitude. Business leaders like Steve Jobs, Bill Gates, and Jack Welch prove that we can create value from ideas with the right attitude. Steve Jobs built Apple, one of the most innovative companies in history. Bill Gates had the right attitude when he led his partners to start Microsoft and change the world with computer software. Jack Welch built General Electric with a commitment to grow companies that would lead their industries.

By sticking with the same lessons that drive masterminds, we all can succeed on a personal level. Those leaders start with the right attitude, and we should do the same. Masterminds teach that success depends upon what we profess to hold essential.

Take Ten

» 9-2: When it comes to the individuals I named above, how would you define their values?

_____

_____

_____

_____

_____

_____

_____

_____

_____

_____

_____

_____

_____

We can learn a great deal about preparing for success by studying people who've helped to shape history and our society:

Frederick Douglass:

Frederick Douglass was born into slavery. As an enslaved person, he didn't know the liberties that we take for granted. He lived in an environment of ***oppression*** until he escaped. After he escaped, he devoted his life to becoming an agent for change. He taught himself to read, to write, and to become an orator. Then he wrote three autobiographies. By writing his life story, he communicated at scale and became one of the most powerful voices that led to the abolition of slavery.

Nelson Mandela:

Authorities locked Nelson Mandela in prison, and he spent 27 years inside because he opposed the racist laws of South Africa. Those laws existed during the Apartheid era. Despite imprisonment for multiple decades, Mandela did not harbor any bitterness. He did not hate his oppressors after his release. Instead, Mandela worked to bring justice and peace. He became a leading world figure, personifying the best of human dignity.

Viktor Frankl

Nazis locked Dr. Frankl in a death camp, killing his family members as he watched. On any given day, Dr. Frankl knew the Nazis might murder him. He refused to show anger. He maintained his peace by devoting his life to helping others.

Martin Luther King

Authorities locked Dr. King in many jails. They did not like his efforts to expand civil rights for all people. Dr. King led the way in bringing awareness to injustice. Dr. King fought against inequality between races. He crusaded and united people of all races. People from around the world consider Martin Luther King a global leader. We celebrate his life as an American historical figure and role model.

Steve Jobs

Participants may not know Steve Jobs, but I'm sure that everyone know his company. He and his partner started Apple Computer. Later, business decisions forced him out of Apple. Rather than being bitter at losing the company he started, Steve went on to start new companies. Then he returned to lead Apple. With the right attitude, he grew Apple into the most valuable company in the world.

Bill Gates

Bill Gates and his partner started Microsoft. Their company began with an idea. Bill wanted to make computers more practical. He believed that every business and every home should have a computer. With Microsoft, Bill turned those ideas into a reality. In the process, he became one of the wealthiest people alive. And he pledged to use his wealth to improve the world for everyone.

Jack Welch

Jack Welch studied chemical engineering in college. He began building a career with General Electric after earning his doctorate. He rose quickly, eventually reaching the top position. Under Jack's leadership, the value of GE grew by more than 4,000 percent. Many people wrote books about his leadership philosophy and his commitment to success.

Learn from Leaders:

Leaders like those described above inspired me during my 26 years in prison. Each leader clearly defined what he wanted to achieve. Mandela, Frankl, and King valued equality for all humankind. Jobs, Gates, and Welch placed high importance on creating value. When I write about learning from "masterminds," I'm writing about people like them. They define success. Then they engineer the path that moves them closer to success. The journey never ends!

We should learn from masterminds. Their strategy can work for us. Notice how they identify values and make their values public. They invite others to judge them by their authenticity, integrity, and commitment to those values.

Take Ten Minutes

» 9-3: Describe a person you know who succeeded in one area, but failed in another.

_____

_____

_____

_____

_____

_____

Values and Goals in All Areas of Life:

The initial lessons on values and goals teach us how to excel in areas of our life that are important to us. But we can fail miserably when we don't use that approach in other areas of our life.

For example, we frequently hear or read about talented celebrities or superstars who set goals of becoming the best in the world at what they do. Take Whitney Houston, for example. She valued her talent as a singer, but her life ended tragically from a drug overdose. Whitney didn't place as much value on being free of substance abuse as she did on her professional singing career.

When I concluded my prison term, I heard the tragic story of Aaron Hernandez. He was a star athlete, and since childhood, he set goals to become the best at his craft. Yet when it came to other areas of his life, he failed. He lost his career in professional sports. He lost a criminal trial, and a judge sentenced him to life in prison. Then he committed suicide while locked inside his jail cell.

If being successful outside of football meant something to Aaron, he should have followed the same disciplined path he cultivated to become a best-in-class athlete.

Clear values and goals would have helped.

Values and goals advance our prospects for success. We should apply them to each area of life that can bring fulfillment. Some areas where we can use values and goals as a guide to success include:

- » Fitness
- » Relationships
- » Education
- » Spirituality
- » Career Development
- » Family
- » Hobbies
- » Substance abuse
- » Release preparation

To the extent that we use values and goals, we grow closer to success. We can learn from masterminds like Douglass, Mandela, Frankl, and King—we all can learn a great deal from those masterminds.

Values and Goals Guided Me Through Prison:

As I wrote previously, Socrates started me on the path to change my thinking patterns. After a jury convicted me, I thought about the decisions that led to my predicament. I needed to pinpoint where I started to go wrong.

What could I accomplish from inside a jail cell to make things right? I may not get out of prison early. But what could I do to make things better when I got out? That question led to my three-part plan. I would work:

» To educate myself,
» To contribute to society, and
» To build a support network.

I came up with that three-part plan by reading about people who succeeded. From them, I learned that I needed to define success. In my case, success would mean a return to society without complications. I wanted to live and interact with people that didn't have problems with crime or prison. Those people became my avatars.

My avatars want me to educate myself, contribute, and have a strong support network. As I wrote earlier, I didn't know those people. But someday I may meet them. If that happened, I would want them to accept me as a good person. If I didn't make efforts while I served the sentence, they would always wonder about my lengthy incarceration. I had to take steps to influence their perceptions of me.

Who is your Avatar?
An "avatar," for me, was specific. When I got out, I knew that certain people would advance my prospects for success. And certain people would threaten my access to opportunities. I needed to connect with people that would help me succeed.

I wanted to use all my time in prison to prepare in ways that would make it more likely for my avatars to support my efforts to succeed.

» I thought of my future probation officer.
» I thought of my prospective employer or business partners.
» I thought of my future creditors or investors.

When I got out, a probation officer would oversee the level of liberty that I would have. What would my probation officer expect of me?

Future employers would know about my criminal background and lengthy prison term. What would employers expect me to accomplish while I served my time?

I needed to make changes that would counter the negative background from my early 20s.

Prospective creditors or investors would also know about my criminal background. What could I do to make things right with them? I would need to find creditors and investors when I got out.

After 26 years inside, I would return to society without a vehicle, a place to live, or clothes. I knew that I would need help to get started.

Avatars could help. While in custody, I had to build a record that would make it easier for avatars to believe in me.

Who is in Your Future?

By thinking about avatars, I found my value categories. When my judge sentenced me to 45 years, I had to think differently. "Good time" credits would result in my release after 26 years if I didn't have disciplinary problems.

The release date felt far away. I hadn't been alive for 26 years, so I didn't have a frame of **reference** to **comprehend** that time. Instead of focusing on the time I had to serve, I kept my sights on the future I wanted to build.

>   » Who is in your future?
>   » Who influences your thoughts about what you can or cannot accomplish?
>   » What can you do while in prison to prepare for your future?

To sustain my energy and discipline level, I had to set clear goals that I could measure. Those goals would take my mind off what I could not control and help me focus on what I could achieve.

How to Become Successful?

A great management guru, Peter Drucker, is famous for advising companies on becoming more successful. He spoke about the importance of measuring incremental success. We could improve our performance by measuring each tiny step we took.

I took that message to heart. By reading from leaders like Peter Drucker, I learned to set clear metrics to define what it meant to commit. Like everyone else, I needed to measure progress if I wanted to work toward success.

>   » How could I measure a commitment "to educate myself?"
>   » How could I measure a commitment "to contribute to society?"
>   » How could I measure whether I worked "to build a support network?"

Finding Your "Why" with Questions:

To answer those questions, I thought about my avatars. What would they expect? Then, I set a time limit. Since prison would be a big part of my life, I set a time horizon focused on the first ten years. I could measure ten years. What could I accomplish during the first ten years? What would make a favorable impression on my avatars?

» In ten years, I committed to earning an undergraduate degree. My avatars would see me as an educated man if I had a degree.

» In ten years, I committed to publishing something. My avatars would consider a "published author" as someone who contributed to society.

» In ten years, I would persuade ten people to have a vested interest in my success. Those ten people would become my support network. If I built a support network, avatars would find it easier to believe in me.

Guides through the Maze of Confinement:

Values and goals became my guide through prison. By adhering to them, I could overcome struggles and achieve high levels of success.

» If you set values and live by those values, you're on the path.

» If you set goals that you can measure—with timelines—you advance prospects for success.

Use the Straight-A Guide to achieve new performance levels, starting with the right attitude.

An individual must have the right attitude to overcome. The right attitude leads to higher levels of success. Individuals may differ in how they define the right attitude. That's okay. We bring more clarity when we define the right attitude with a 100% commitment to success, as defined by our values and goals.

Is success the same for everybody? No. Success isn't the same for everyone because people set different values.

» Some people place the accumulation of wealth or financial security at the apex of their value system.

» Some people hold their commitment to family as their highest value.

» Some people value their faith in God as their highest value or contribution to society.

When we set our values, we take a step toward defining success. Our goals show our commitment to success.

Once we define success and show our commitment to goals, we can demonstrate that we have the right attitude. We can keep everything we say, do, and think in harmony with our values and goals. That's when we have the right attitude. That's when we follow the path of masterminds.

When you determine what you want, you have made the most critical decision of your life. You have to know what you want to attain it.
—Douglas Lurton

Determine what you want! Use values and goals. Then, advance your prospects for success with the right attitude. Make a 100% commitment by making decisions consistent with your values and goals. I learned the importance of this strategy from these true masterminds:

- » Frederick Douglass
- » Nelson Mandela
- » Viktor Frankl
- » Martin Luther King
- » Steve Jobs
- » Bill Gates
- » Jack Welch

I had the right attitude long before I left prison. While inside, I made a 100% commitment to my definition of success. Does that mean I was a model inmate? Not at all. It means that I made decisions that were consistent with my values and goals.

I made decisions that would influence my avatars. That 100% commitment defined my pursuit of excellence. My attitude guided my choices seven days a week. I explain when people ask what I mean by seven days a week.

I mean seven days a week!

When people ask whether I obsessed over those goals on weekends or holidays, I tell them I had the right attitude seven days a week. If weekends and holidays fell within a seven-day week, I adhered to the strategy.

I am not in prison anymore. But I still follow the strategy of having the right attitude. I make a 100% commitment to success because I know what I want to achieve. That strategy powered me through prison. I am convinced that it opens opportunities for me in society.

A conscientious, values-based, goal-oriented adjustment through prison allowed me to seize control of my adjustment. My attitude may not have influenced an earlier release date, but it certainly influenced how I passed each day. By making a 100% commitment to my values and goals, I put myself on a path to receive support from "avatars." The strategy made all the difference during my journey through prison. More importantly, the process empowered me to return to society precisely as I anticipated—with my dignity intact and opportunities for a life of fulfillment.

By adhering to the principles of this Preparing for Success After Prison Course, participants advance prospects for a better outcome. But it all begins with attitude.

Take 20

- » 9-4: How would you measure a 100% commitment to success?

LESSON 10: ASPIRING TO MORE

A noble man compares and estimates himself by an idea which is higher than himself. Such pursuits produce aspirations.
—Marcus Aurelius

We open this section with a quote from Marcus Aurelius. His book, *Meditations*, inspired me while I served my sentence. I always found it helpful to read about people who began their lives in a challenging environment. If they triumphed over the disadvantageous and difficulties they faced, I believed I could learn lessons from them.

Success always leaves clues that we can follow.

From Marcus Aurelius, I learned the importance of aspiring. If we can train ourselves to learn from others, we gain the power to suppress worthless emotions such as envy. Rather than **begrudge** the success that others have, we should open our minds to learn the steps they took to reach the position they aspired to achieve.

Marcus Aurelius began his life in an orphanage during the Roman era. As a child, he knew he did not want to live in disadvantaged or **marginalized** circumstances. Since he was poor, he chose to open his eyes and observe the patterns of behavior that he saw in leaders.

To record what he learned, he kept a journal. That journal guided him on what he should do and should not do. Later, publishers brought his journal to market with the book **Meditations**.

As I recall, Marcus Aurelius wrote that book to guide his future decisions and to teach lessons to his son and others. Although he lived more than 1,000 years ago, *Meditations* by Marcus Aurelius remains one of those influential books in the self-help genre.

From Marcus Aurelius, I learned the importance of journaling. Through journaling, we can **memorialize** the methodical steps we take to prepare for success after prison. Participants who document their journey inside may have more power in reaching their aspirations.

First, a person must aspire to something more than what they're currently experiencing. While living with the pressures of confinement, we need to **muster** the strength to fight off the stress. Those walls and bars can feel like they're closing in, and our aspirations can free us from the pressure.

Like many others in prison, I felt the pressure. Yet leaders teach us that if we remember how every decision influences our prospects for success, we empower ourselves.

Never forget the reality that at any time, we can choose to work toward empowering ourselves.

Had I learned that concept in school—before I broke the law—I may have made better decisions as a young man. By reflecting, I could see that my choices before I turned 20 had as much to do with my imprisonment as my crimes. Instead of learning from leaders, I learned from people of questionable character. That failed strategy put me on a destructive path.

Fortunately, it's never too early and never too late to begin working toward self-improvement. The strategy I learned from leaders like Marcus Aurelius is twofold.

We must reflect on our past decisions and connect the dots, so we know how those decisions led to our current situation, and

We must aspire to what we want to become and then figure out the changes we must make to reach our full potential.

As a **reckless** adolescent, I chose to ignore my teachers, guidance counselors, and advice from my parents. The friends with whom I surrounded myself used similar judgment. All those choices led me into a life of crime by the time I turned 20. At 23, I started serving a 45-year prison term.

I should have made better choices while in school. Fortunately, I started to make better decisions when I began my prison term. By aspiring to something better, I could carve out a strategy to help me succeed when I would walk out of federal prison—26 years after my arrest.

How to Aspire:

After my arrest, I learned what living in a total institution meant. I felt like a **cog** in a machine. Regardless of how much I would have liked to change the machine, I couldn't. Administrators would determine the clothes I wore, the food I ate, the books I read, and my ability to interact with others.

I'd lost my liberty. I didn't know how to **liberate** myself, but I knew I **loathed** living in prison. Despite the challenge, like every person striving toward a better life, I had to build a positive mindset and prepare. Without preparation, I wouldn't be able to seize opportunities around me or create new opportunities.

When we look beyond our current struggles, we may find light, something worth working toward. Forcing ourselves to ignore the concrete walls and barbed-wire-topped fences requires discipline. As Socrates taught me, we can always ask good questions to develop our critical thinking.

Take 15 Minutes

10-1: Develop your critical thinking by responding to any of the following questions:

» What does the best possible outcome look like for me?

_____

_____

_____

_____

_____

_____

» Who would be the people that could influence my prospects of getting that outcome?

_____

_____

_____

_____

_____

_____

» How can I influence people to invest in the future I'm building?

_____

_____

_____

_____

_____

_____

» In what ways will the decisions I've made over the past month open new opportunities?

_____

_____

_____

_____

_____

» What are the characteristics of people who have overcome the challenges I face?

_____

_____

_____

_____

_____

_____

» What lessons can I learn from reading about those people?

_____

_____

_____

_____

_____

_____

Let me recap what we learned from earlier lessons:

» We define success by stating our values.
» We commit to values by setting clear goals.
» We succeed by living with the right attitude.
» We show our commitment to having "the right attitude" with our 100% commitment to the values and goals we set.

When I write about "aspiring," I want to convey the importance of seeing the best possible outcome. Instead of **_dwelling_** on the pain we're living with today, we can focus on what we're going to become by **_adhering_** to our disciplined, deliberate adjustment plan. We need a program that will help us reach our highest potential. That plan will require us to put priorities in place.

One priority may be to visualize success. We can project the future we want to live as Marcus Aurelius did. Instead of seeing himself as a disadvantaged child in an orphanage, he saw himself as a community leader. He trained himself to become a person of influence by learning from others. In time, those aspirations led to actions that lifted him to become one of the most influential emperors of the Roman empire. He wrote a biography to help him stay on track, and to show others how to grow from struggle to self-empowerment.

To develop better critical thinking, Consider the following exercises to begin developing your release plan:

Take 15 Minutes

10-2: Respond to the following questions:

» Describe the future you see for yourself.

_____

_____

_____

_____

_____

_____

» Write at least three persuasive paragraphs that explain the steps you've taken over the past month to move you closer to the success you aspire to become.

_____

_____

_____

_____

_____

_____

_____

» Write how your actions over the past three months have put you in a position to seize opportunities over the next three months.

_____

_____

_____

_____

_____

_____

_____

_____

_____

» How would people that you want to influence respond to the adjustment strategy you engineered?

_____

_____

_____

_____

_____

_____

» How would the people you admire most respond to what you're striving to achieve?

_____

_____

_____

_____

_____

_____

Our aspirations strengthen us and help us conquer challenges. They weaken the pull of anything that could potentially hold us back. When we aspire to create a better future that we can see, we empower ourselves to engineer a path that will lead us to where we want to go.

Leaders like Marcus Aurelius taught me that success is a journey, not a destination. The day we stop pursuing success, we **wither**. Over time, our values and goals will evolve, depending upon what we achieve. For example, immediately after my arrest, I only wanted the system to release me.

After reading and learning from leaders, I started to **perceive** life differently. I wanted to build a record that would restore confidence and allow me to live a life of meaning, relevance, and dignity.

Wishing to **emulate** Socrates or Mandela, I wanted to develop inner strength. I didn't want to complain about my predicament. I made terrible decisions that put me in prison. I wanted to create a path that would lead to something better, pursuing aspirations that I believed would bring more meaning to my life. I wanted to make an impact on building a better society.

As I strive to show through the various **modules** of this course, my values and goals evolved during my adjustment. They always aligned with my aspiration of how I wanted to walk out of prison—and the life I wanted to lead once I got out. Our values and goals should **harmonize** with our aspirations.

Take 15 Minutes

10-3: Respond to the following questions:

» How will your values and goals evolve?

_____

_____

_____

_____

_____

_____

» What will change with your values and goals as you advance through the stages of your confinement?

_____

_____

_____

_____

_____

_____

» In what ways are you working to reach your highest potential?

_____

_____

_____

_____

_____

_____

The Labyrinth

When I was locked up, my aspiration served as a light. I had a long way to go, but I could always see the light at the end. The light guided my decisions. I didn't see that light as a student in school, and during those first days after my arrest, I didn't know how to find a light that could guide my future decisions.

Leaders helped me to see the world differently. They helped me learn how to project the future I wanted to build, and they helped me understand why I would have to make decisions differently from how I spent my teens.

Although I didn't start selling cocaine until I was 20, I started making bad decisions during my troubled adolescence. Those decisions led me into a dark pit or a *labyrinth*. Aspirations could provide the light I could follow to lead me out.

I learned about labyrinths (pronounced lab-i-rinth) when I began reading the work of masterminds. While locked in my cell at the Pierce County Jail (before my sentencing date), I escaped the *monotony* by reading. One book I read included a story about a labyrinth.

Some readers may not grasp the definition of a labyrinth. I didn't. But the concept of finding my way out of the labyrinth inspired me. This concept could empower anyone who is in prison. We need stories of self-mastery and discipline to help us make better decisions.

Just as Socrates influenced me to change the way I thought, other authors from ancient Greece gave me a lot to consider. I especially liked to read from the *stoic* philosophers—who taught a great deal about being self-reliant and self-directed. Those virtues could help anyone commit to making better decisions.

Greek Mythology

From the many stories of Greek mythology, I learned lessons. One story described Theseus, a *mythological* king who offered hope and an example of self-mastery. That story introduced me to the concept of a "labyrinth," an *intricate* maze buried deep underground.

Theseus had to save his community from a beast known as a minotaur. The minotaur resided in the labyrinth buried deep in the ground. It had a pattern of killing the youth in the Greek community. To resolve the problem, someone needed to kill the beast—but no one that *descended* into the minotaur's labyrinth ever made it out alive. Either the beast *devoured* those that entered, or the individual got lost within the maze and died.

Theseus valued his community and aspired to save its youth. To kill the beast, Theseus made a plan. Before entering the labyrinth, armed with a sword, he tied one end of a string around his ankle and the other around a tree at the maze's entrance. After killing the beast, Theseus used the line to find his way through the labyrinth and back out to safety.

Identifying with the Labyrinth

That *analogy* gave me hope. Although I could reflect on my youth's influences and bad decisions, I could also project a better life. Like Theseus had to kill the beast to build the future he wanted for his community, I would have to develop the discipline to reject or resist triggers that could lead me to further problems. I would need a plan that would lead me out of the labyrinth of confinement and into the future I aspired to build.

In my youth, I hated getting up in the morning for school and couldn't relate to how learning would lead to a better life. Since I didn't have any aspirations, I didn't have a reason to learn. Going to school didn't inspire me because I didn't connect reading and studying with success. Without an aspiration for something better, I made decisions that led me into prison—a labyrinth that keeps many people locked in struggle.

Statistics show that most people struggle when they leave prison. For this reason, a person must live like the stoics—becoming self-reliant and self-directed.

I wanted a fulfilling life in prison and beyond. To succeed, I would need a release plan.

Take 15 Minutes

10-4: Develop your critical thinking with your responses to the following questions:

» What do you want?

_____

_____

_____

_____

_____

_____

» When will you start pursuing what you want?

_____

_____

_____

_____

_____

_____

» How much effort are you willing to invest in getting what you want?

_____

_____

_____

_____

_____

_____

» What preparations are you making to build a better life?

_____

_____

_____

_____

_____

_____

» In what ways are your decisions influencing your community?

_____

_____

_____

_____

_____

_____

» Who bears responsibility for the success that you want to achieve?

_____

_____

_____

_____

_____

_____

_____

Those questions helped me accept that if I wanted a better future, I would have to prepare. To start preparing, I needed a plan.

Without an effective release plan, the avatars I tried to bring into my life would dismiss me as a person prone to "happy talk," offering words without backing things up. Or a person with "happy ears," prone to believing others who would define my future. To move closer to my aspirations of a fulfilling life, I had to make the right choices.

Every person bears responsibility for the choices we make.

I rejected education as a youth. That choice brought consequences that I didn't intend. Once I started to serve my sentence in prison, I had to make adjustment choices about how I would live in the culture of confinement. Other people in prison offered advice of dubious value. They advised me on the best way to serve time, admonishing me to "Forget about the outside world and focus on life inside."

If I made that choice, I had to think about what would follow.

Take 5 Minutes

» 10-5: What do you think will follow if you adjust to the prison culture and dismiss a personal responsibility to prepare for success upon release?

_____

_____

_____

_____

_____

_____

_____

I can give you an example. Think of a shot caller in prison. The choice to live as a shot caller brings consequences. The shot caller may control the television. He may direct where people sit in common areas.

What would you say follows for someone that pursues such an adjustment?

» From my recollection of living in prison, a shot caller can expect the following:
» They face problems with staff.
» They spend time in SHU.
» SHU time can also mean a more extended stay in prison.
» SHU time means less access to opportunities to prepare for success.
» Lower preparations for success can mean fewer opportunities for employment after release.
» Fewer opportunities for jobs may translate into a more difficult time generating resources.

» Without resources, it's harder to gain traction in society.
» Without traction, it's harder to resume stability.
» Without stability, more problems with the law follow.
» Problems can lead to more time in prison.
» The cycle of failure would continue.

Without a doubt, I wanted a different outcome. I set values and goals to define success. My attitude showed a 100 percent commitment to staying out of prison. My aspiration kept me on course.

Aspirations:

Masterminds teach that we always aspire to success. When we see success, we begin to build. Pursue the deliberate path, even if you're locked in a cell.

Leaders like Frederick Douglass, Nelson Mandela, Mahatma Gandhi, Viktor Frankl, and Martin Luther King aspired to end social injustice. They took clear steps to succeed. Even while living in a struggle, they knew what steps to take. Leaders like Bill Gates, Steve Jobs, and Jack Welch aspired to build businesses that would ease life for millions of people. They knew what they wanted. They set a path to success, and they inspired others to follow their path.

Participants in our course can choose to prepare for the careers they want to lead, or they can make choices without a disciplined plan. Either way, they make a choice. And the choices we make have consequences, as recidivism rates show. We may develop the power to make better decisions when considering likely outcomes.

Aspirations Mean Looking Ahead

At the start of my sentence, I thought about the best possible outcome. I had to look far ahead, decades ahead. Unless I made changes, my return to society would bring many struggles:

» I would not have a work history.
» I would not have financial resources.
» I would not know anyone other than those serving time with me in prison.
» I would not have any credit.
» I would not have any clothes.
» I would not have a place to live.
» I would not have resources saved for retirement.
» I would not have a car.

Those thoughts could weigh me down. Fortunately, I found courage and hope in stories like Theseus in the labyrinth. All I needed was a string. A string could guide me from the depths of my labyrinth to the brightness of a better world.

I wish I had found that string at a younger age—but I didn't. Nevertheless, stoics like Marcus Aurelius taught me that it's never too early and never too late to start making better decisions.

My values, goals, and attitude would become my string. By following that string, I could reach the aspirations I wanted for the new life I would lead.

Ten-Year Aspirations:

Another Greek myth, the story of Homer's Odyssey, inspired me. The tale describes Odysseus, a man separated from his family and home after fighting a war. Despite his separation, he never lost sight of home or his aspiration to return. Odysseus spent ten years fighting battle after battle. His aspiration *sustained* him, and he made a 100% commitment to succeed. Knowing what he wanted, Odysseus had the right attitude! That attitude brought him closer to his aspiration. After ten years, he reached his aspiration, returning home in victory.

Homer's Odyssey inspired me to set a ten-year plan. I didn't expect to return home in ten years, but if I stayed true to my values and goals, I would be farther ahead. New opportunities would open. I knew that every decision I made during the first ten years in prison would influence my life.

I learned about aspirations during the *nascent* stages of my journey. Back then, I couldn't think of 26 years in prison. I hadn't even lived that long. To put the term in perspective, project into the future by 26 years. A person needs an aspiration to maintain a high level of discipline and energy throughout the decades. My strategy followed the path of Theseus and Odysseus—using aspirations to help me see the reasons for the decisions I would make. I set my initial aspiration for ten years.

During that first decade, I knew what I would need to achieve. I could see success.

» And what would success look like for me?
  ◊ Within ten years, I would have at least one university degree.
  ◊ I would find someplace to publish an article, chapter, or book I wrote within ten years.
  ◊ Within ten years, I would start my support network by bringing ten new people into my life.

Those aspirations strengthened me, helping me to see success and empowering me to measure progress on the journey. I didn't perseverate over matters beyond my control, like my sentence length. Instead, I aspired to a better life and worked to prepare. Advancing along the path led me to restore the strength and confidence that the prison system and my sentence had once obliterated.

Restoring Strength and Dignity:

Masterminds teach us that we shouldn't live like a prisoner. We shouldn't allow calendar pages to anchor us in a pool of hopeless thoughts. We shouldn't dwell on the past or parts of life we can't control.

We should focus on what we have the power to change. Like the stoics, we can choose to live in the world as it exists, not as we want it to be. Each day brings an opportunity to work toward something better. We can make decisions that show we want to climb out of the labyrinth of confinement.

Throughout each of my 9,500 days in prison, I considered my values and goals. Adhering to this disciplined strategy positioned me for the best possible outcome. If I ignored those values and goals, I became vulnerable. The wrong decisions could quickly ***derail*** my progress. After all, I lived in prison, where I would remain for decades. People around me could be volatile. Fights would erupt over trivial issues. Television programming, noise, personal space, or perceived respect could bring problems. I couldn't ignore those realities. Instead, I needed a strategy to succeed despite threats that could block progress.

Good decisions could lead me closer to my aspiration. Wrong choices could threaten progress. This insight helped me assess flawed ideas that I heard from others. Bad ideas can derail people in prison. For example, consider how some people in prison think about "respect" and what the term means.

Respect or Fear?

As a young person, I heard many experienced prisoners talking about respect. For example, Stump said anyone in prison could get respect by being willing to pay the price, and he said the cost would be to respond immediately with ***treacherous*** or lethal violence at any sign of "disrespect." Others would "respect" a man, he said, if they knew that he would retaliate to any disrespect with a knife.

Stump's perspective matched the prison culture. Yet, that perspective differed from my avatar's concept of respect.

I never aspired to become "the man" in prison. Instead, I wanted to succeed when I returned to society, which would require preparation.

With success in mind, I had a reason to avoid problems. I wanted to sidestep the cycles of failure that others faced when they finished their terms. My avatars defined respect differently from Stump and the general mentality of the prison environment.

I wanted respect from my avatars, and I made decisions that were consistent with my aspiration.

Who Will Facilitate Your Success?

My avatars would not respect me if I pursued a path involving violence. They would "fear" people that responded to problems with violence. They would want that person to stay in prison.

My 100% commitment to living a values-based, goal-oriented life influenced my decisions, adjustment, and the release plan that would lead to the life I aspired to build. My aspiration influenced every step I took and every decision I made. I made decisions that would minimize exposure to problems.

What did avoiding problems and pursuing success mean for me?

>> I avoided hustles.
>> I avoided television rooms.
>> I didn't participate in team sports or table games.
>> I selected jobs that would allow me to work toward my goals.
>> I was deliberate about my conversations, the words I used, and the activities I pursued.

Every step felt like crossing a high wire, with each deliberate action leading closer to my aspiration. One false step could lead to my fall. The clear aspiration gave me reasons to continue the journey to success as I defined it.

My wife picked me up from USP Atwater to drive me to a halfway house on August 13, 2012. I'd serve six months in the San Francisco halfway house and the last six months of my sentence in home confinement. While driving to San Francisco, I told Carole I intended to follow the same disciplined, deliberate strategy that got me through prison to adjust to society.

I had values and goals in place. But they evolved from the values and ideals I set when I started my term. My decisions in prison lifted me to a higher status, opening more opportunities. I had bachelor's and master's degrees. I contributed to society, as evidenced by the many books I published. I had thousands of people in my support network.

When my wife drove me from the prison in Atwater to San Francisco, I told her of my new aspiration:

>> I'll control assets worth more than $1 million within five years of finishing my sentence.

I aspired to make an impact on the lives of other people in prison. If I achieved that goal, I believed that I could inspire more people to adhere to the values-based, goal-oriented principles I would teach through the Straight-A Guide. As we try to teach through our Preparing for Success after Prison series, a person must:

>> Define success with values,

» Set SMART goals that align with how the person defines success.
» Go forward with the right attitude, showing a 100 percent commitment.
» Act in ways that align with a person's responsibility to prepare for success.
» Use an aspiration to stay motivated through the challenges ahead.

Success follows for anyone that adheres to that principled path. Future modules will show you what comes next in our Straight-A Guide. For me, that path led to a portfolio of assets worth far more than $1 million. Decisions in prison influenced my ongoing commitment to preparing for success.

Take 15 Minutes

» 10-6: Where will you be in 10 years?

_____

_____

_____

_____

_____

_____

_____

» 10-7: How will your decisions today lead you closer to your aspiration?

_____

_____

_____

_____

_____

_____

» 10-8: Will you be closer to the aspirations you set?

_____

_____

_____

_____

_____

_____

_____

LESSON 11: ACTION AND PURPOSE

Successful people maintain a positive focus in life no matter what is going on around them. They stay focused on their past successes rather than their past failures. They also look to next action steps they need to take to get them closer to the fulfillment of their goals. They refuse to be distracted by obstacles that life presents.
—Jack Canfield

I updated this module while on airplane bound for New York City from California. I could choose to:

» Sleep,
» Watch a movie,
» Read a book,
» Listen to music, or
» Work toward projects that align with my goals.

Since neither emails nor phone calls will disturb me while flying, I'll use this time to read and edit the remaining modules of this course. It's an example of acting and purpose—the very subject of this module.

We should always work to accomplish the goals that we say are important to us.

As a younger man, I didn't understand the importance of action. If we want to reach our highest potential, we've got to begin by taking small steps. With incremental progress, we put ourselves in a position for new opportunities. When we understand this lesson, we can more easily appreciate the urgency of making good decisions. A relationship exists between our choices today and our prospect for success in the weeks, months, and decades ahead.

This reality is as true after a person's release from prison as it is valid during the time a person serves.

When I transferred from the county jail to a high-security penitentiary, I didn't understand how the system operated. Since I defined success as emerging from prison strong, with my dignity intact, and with opportunities to build a fulfilling life, I had to prepare. When I transitioned to the community after finishing my sentence, I wanted to work on projects that would have an impact on making a better community. But I also would need to earn a living.

With that vision, I could take the next step toward preparing, acting in ways that aligned with the SMART goals I set. For example:

» I would earn a university degree within my first ten years of confinement.

» I would become a published author within my first ten years of imprisonment.
» Within my first decade, I would persuade ten mentors to help me prepare for success.

I could measure progress toward achieving each of those specific goals if I pursued them with a 100% commitment. That commitment would lead to my ***aspiration*** of getting out of prison successfully—as I defined success. On the flip side, if I didn't act in deliberate, ***decisive*** ways, I would have a plan that lacked follow through. Without action, I could not ***convert*** my aspirations into reality.

I would have to act, taking ***incremental*** steps every day.

People in prison face obstacles, just like everyone else. While incarcerated, people may spend weeks or months on lockdown or in the Special Housing Unit. From the time I served in solitary confinement, I know the limitations of living in isolation. I also know that regardless of where administrators confine us, we can always choose how we will act. We can advance our progress toward goals, or we can complain.

We take incremental action steps while locked in a cell, just like we can take incremental action steps if we're sitting on a cross-country flight in an airplane seat.

When we're locked in a cell, we may not be able to attend programs. We cannot connect with family as easily. I spent months in the SHU during the decades that I served in prison. While alone, I took small steps that aligned with my values and goals to keep productive. With small action steps, I could move closer to success.

When people act in ways that align with how they define success, they develop strength and confidence, knowing that they're taking another step toward reaching their aspirations.

People in prison must become comfortable with being uncomfortable. They should expect to pass through tough times now and in the future. Those tough times represent a part of the success journey, and we must accept reality: There is always more struggle to come.

Take 5 Minutes

» 11-1: What does "being comfortable with being uncomfortable" mean to you?

_____

_____

_____

_____

_____

_____

The Mindset of Success:

To build strength in times of difficulty, I rely upon the Straight-A Guide as a sailor depends upon a compass. A compass can help a sailor navigate *treacherous* seas, and we can use the compass to stay on our course toward reaching the goals we've set for our life.

We sometimes need self-motivation to act when times are tough. Those action steps require the mindset of success. Without self-discipline, we leave ourselves vulnerable to influences from others.

I remember Wayne, a person I met in prison. Wayne told me about growing up in a community rife with crime, substance abuse, and gang prevalence. In that community, he said, people adjusted as if they were crabs in a bucket.

I asked Wayne to help me understand the crabs-in-a-bucket analogy. He said if you put a batch of crabs in a bucket, one would try to scale the wall and climb out. Before the escaping crab progresses, the other crabs would gather and try to pull the aspiring crab back inside.

People that lived in his community, Wayne told me, were the same way. They didn't want to act in ways that would help them succeed—but neither did they want others from their neighborhood to prepare for success. If every person in the community failed, people wouldn't feel so bad about their inability to get their life together. On the other hand, if a person from the same community succeeded in making it out to a better life, he said, everyone else would realize the *colossal* disappointment of life—and failure stings.

People that want to conquer their environment must start by defining success. Then they should set clear goals and pursue them with a 100 percent commitment. It's one way to show they have the right attitude. We can always take small action steps to advance toward the aspirations we want to pursue.

This disciplined, deliberate strategy fundamentally differs from Wayne's crabs-in-the-bucket theory. Instead, it aligns with someone who commits to building a strong mindset.

In 2017, when I wrote the original version of this module, I was launching a health-care business with my wife. From my perspective, the health-care industry offered promising prospects to accomplish many goals. With an aging population, I *surmised* demand for homes with 24-hour caregivers would grow.

My wife's credentials as a registered nurse gave us a strategic advantage to succeed in this business; she could oversee staff while I would oversee operations. The business would generate revenues we could use to service debt on the real estate we would acquire. The end goal would become possible with a series of incremental action steps.

Consider the infinite number of incremental action steps that would have been necessary to reach the goal:

> » Write a plan to get a good understanding of how much capital the business would require.
> » Identify potential partners that could provide financial resources to build the business.
> » Make enough presentations to advance prospects for funding.
> » Locate the property and make the acquisition.
> » Complete modifications to the property.
> » Obtain licenses from regulatory agencies.
> » Create marketing campaigns to generate revenues.
> » Hire and train staff.
> » Operate the business.

Regardless of how much we plan, as captains of our ship, we must be flexible. When plans don't work out, rather than make excuses, we adjust.

Although I set out to build a health-care business with Carole, anticipating the ***venture*** would grow, I had to modify the plan. My felony conviction from 1987 proved more burdensome than I expected, complicating my ability to get the license I needed to operate the health-care business.

Fortunately, prison conditioned me to face resistance with ***equanimity***. To overcome this hurdle, I could reflect on the action steps I had to take when I served my sentence. Those action steps did not seem relevant to other people around me in prison, but they put me on a pathway to develop business opportunities upon release.

When we connect the dots from yesterday's decisions, we can see how incremental action steps opened opportunities. That strategy leads to the mental ***fortitude*** necessary to overcome new challenges. Those challenges arise continually while serving a prison term or on the other side of the sentence.

We advance prospects to succeed over challenges when we take small, incremental action steps. We must prepare to climb hills to get where we want to go. We can develop tools, tactics, and resources to help us jump over gaps. We can wake early and work late into the night.

Since getting out of prison, I rely upon the same strategies that strengthened my mindset while serving portions of my sentence in special housing units.

When I reflect, I see the power and influence of my early decisions. I read about Socrates for the first time while inside a jail cell during that awkward transition between the day a jury convicted me and the day a judge sentenced me. That story changed the way I thought.

I began thinking of avatars. The avatars helped me think about values and goals. That process gave me the right attitude, and it gave me an aspiration. Action steps led me to the right programs. By finishing programs, I built my skillset. Each action step helped me get through prison. As a result, I ended my prison term with many opportunities to succeed.

The action steps we take today make a difference in our life. Regardless of what stage in the journey we're in or what eternal circumstances we endure, we can take small, incremental action steps that will lead to better outcomes.

For that reason, I encourage people to begin action steps that will advance prospects for success as they pursue their aspirations. This strategy helps to build a stronger mindset.

We can become more than past bad choices and more than tough times of the moment. By reading about leaders, I saw traits that they shared. Consider what you know about:

- » Socrates
- » Frederick Douglass
- » Nelson Mandela
- » Viktor Frankl
- » Mahatma Gandhi
- » Martin Luther King
- » Malcolm X
- » Steve Jobs
- » Bill Gates
- » Michael Jordan

They all spent time reflecting on past decisions and using those reflections to make projections on how they could improve. Those masterminds saw how small steps could lead them to their fullest potential. They never stopped acting in ways that aligned with their plan.

By thinking about our past decisions, we strengthen ourselves to climb our way through tough times. Introspection will help us make better decisions, giving us the energy to persist with the next step.

Leaders leave clues that teach us how to make progress, and we can learn from the clues they leave us:

- » Leaders know how to state their values.
- » Leaders set goals.
- » Leaders live with the right attitude.
- » Leaders have high aspirations.
- » Leaders act in ways that harmonize with what they aspire to become.

Leaders change the world by acting. They know how to prepare in ways that will lead to new heights of success. They make life better with every decision, with every thought, and with every action step they take.

Take 15 Minutes

» 11-2: What can you learn from those leaders?

_____

_____

_____

_____

_____

_____

» 11-3: What's your release plan?

_____

_____

_____

_____

_____

_____

Make Good Choices:

Suppose we don't take action toward the goals we set. In that case, we risk deluding ourselves. Anyone can talk about what he wants to achieve. Those who genuinely aspire to build a life of meaning, relevance, and fulfillment after prison take daily action steps, regardless of what external influences may complicate their lives.

While in prison, I interacted with many people that waited for calendar pages to turn, saying they would make changes once they got out. They didn't act. They didn't pursue the small, necessary steps to succeed. They could have been:

» advancing their reading skills,
» developing their vocabulary, and
» improving their ability to comprehend mathematical equations.

Every day, we should act in ways that align with our values and goals; those actions should advance our prospects for success.

» Describe the effort you put into personal development.
» How could reading books in the prison's library influence your prospects for success?
» What steps could you take to master arithmetic?
» In what ways would learning algebra, geometry, and calculus open opportunities for you to earn an income upon release?

> » How would your income capacity change if you habitually write at least 1,000 words every day?

Incremental Action Steps

From Marshall Goldsmith, a mastermind teacher, I learned a great deal. He distinguished himself as one of the top business coaches in America. I read his influential business book, *What Got You Here Won't Get You There*. Besides writing books and articles for business, Dr. Goldsmith built a second career as a coach. People on the path to becoming CEOs hire him to learn the best action steps they can take to reach their potential.

People who had already achieved a high level of success hired Dr. Goldsmith to learn action steps. In his book, *What Got You Here Won't Get You There*, I considered how I could take those same action steps while serving my sentence. He didn't write the book for people in prison, but the message certainly applied to anyone that wanted to change.

If you want to influence people who can hire you, start acting today. If you contemplate what people might expect from you, take action with purpose. That process led me to think about avatars.

Who were my avatars?

They were people who could help me build a life after 26 years in prison. My avatars included:

> » My unit team and staff members in prison that could influence my future,
> » My future probation officer,
> » My prospective employer or business partners
> » My future creditors who could provide the resources I would need to start a new life.

Who can serve as your "avatars."

Take action to prove worthy of their trust. That strategy worked well for me. If you take action, you will develop the strength to persevere through tough times and position yourself for success.

The action steps will change as time passes. First, you master a lesson at one level. Then you can advance to the next level. Growth comes from taking small steps. If you don't act today, you miss an opportunity to take a new action step tomorrow.

What action step can you take today?

> » Can you read?
> » Can you learn?
> » Can you write?
> » Can you do pushups?

» Can you do leg lifts?
» Can you do crunches?
» Can you pray?
» Can you ask for help?
» Can you help others?

Align actions with values and goals.

Take 10 Minutes

» 11-4: Who are the people you want to impress in a positive way?

_____
_____
_____
_____
_____
_____

» 11-5: Who should believe in you?

_____
_____
_____
_____
_____

» 11-6: What steps will lead you through prison?

_____
_____
_____
_____
_____
_____

» 11-7: What steps will open options for you when the gates let you out?

_____

_____

_____

_____

_____

_____

_____

I started acting with purpose toward change after a jury found me guilty. As I rested on the concrete slab of my cell, I stared at the ceiling and the walls and thought about the life I'd been living before prison, and how poor decisions led me into my predicament. I had to block out the noise and think about what I could do to change.

» Asking that question was an action step.
  ◊ The question led me to look for an answer.

» I read about Socrates.
  ◊ Reading was an action step.

» By reading about a leader, I could start to think in different ways.
  ◊ I thought about avatars, another action step.

» By thinking about avatars, I could see the following action steps to take:
  ◊ Avatars would want me to educate myself.
  ◊ Avatars would like me to contribute to society.
  ◊ Avatars would want me to build a support network.

By thinking about avatars, I devised a strategy to guide my journey. It led to my values: Education, contribution, and support. I set clear goals. I said I would achieve those goals during my first ten years.

» I would earn a university degree.
» I would find a way to publish
» I would persuade 10 people to help me succeed.

To achieve my goals, I would need to take small action steps. First, I had to find a school that would allow me to earn a degree. I neither had the money for tuition nor an exemplary academic record that would qualify me for a scholarship. Still, I had to start somewhere.

As I wrote in a previous lesson, I took the following action steps:

» I found a dictionary.

> » The book included the names of universities, and I wrote out the names.
> » The book also gave the cities and zip codes for the schools.
> » I wrote an ***unsolicited*** letter to each school.

Persistence:

We need patience, persistence, and perseverance. Since my struggles were in prison, I had to figure out ways to transcend the walls that separated me from the community. I wrote more than 100 letters, exercising patience. I might have to wait months for a response. Sending a letter would be one step, but sending 100 letters would be 100 steps. I might not have found the right person if I had only sent one letter. By sending more than 100 letters, I had a better chance. I had to keep acting intentionally, with purpose.

We all must be persistent with the action steps we take to prepare for success.

Small action steps each day would lead to my goal. I could not control whether a school would respond.

But I could control how many letters I wrote to different schools.

By hand, I wrote letter after letter. I bought stamps, and I wrote to as many schools as I could find. I wrote about four letters per hour. In eight hours, I wrote about 30 letters. In two days, I sent 60 letters. Then, I could wait, or I could write more.

Those small action steps brought me closer to my goal. Ohio University accepted me. Once I started school, I felt a change. At that moment, I felt as if I were transitioning from prisoner to a student on my way to earning a university degree.

I wanted more than a credential. A degree was a piece of paper. More than the degree, I wanted to learn. By learning, I could persuade avatars to invest in me. They would see me as something more than my bad choices when I was 20. Acting with purpose would influence avatars I would meet in the future.

Action Plans Lead to Success:

Marshal Goldsmith taught the leaders that hired him how to keep growing. We must keep growing, too. If we act with intentional purpose today, we will advance our preparations to succeed. Our growth will put us in a position for new action steps. We cannot reach higher levels of growth tomorrow unless we take our first action steps today.

I am always looking back. When I reflect, I can see the pivotal points in my journey. I finished my prison term in August 2013. When I transferred to a halfway house in San Francisco, I started to grow my business with incremental action steps.

> » When did I begin sowing seeds that would lead investors to partner with me?

» How did I start?

I started with small, incremental steps, such as reading a book in a jail cell. The book led me to think differently and helped me to develop a mindset of success. I started to think about avatars. I took small steps that would show I wanted to earn their trust. I wrote to schools, which led to my studies and earning degrees. I wrote articles, chapters, and books, opening more opportunities to grow my support network.

My commitment to preparing for success after prison gave me a reason to avoid problems with staff or other people serving sentences alongside me.

Each step led me closer. Now, when I face tough times, I look back. I see how small action steps got me through tough times before; there will always be struggles. The tough times are part of the journey. By focusing on success, I know I can take another action step. As in the past, the action steps I take today will lead to new growth. Countless action steps allowed me to pivot from struggle to prosperity:

» I earned a bachelor's degree in my fourth year of imprisonment.
» I published my first article in my sixth year.
» I earned a master's degree in my seventh year of the term.
» I published my first book in my 10th year.
» By publishing, I built a massive support network.
» The support network led to marrying the love of my life in prison.
» Marriage allowed me to publish more, and the writing brought income.
» Income from my writing supported my wife, who went to nursing school.
» With my wife's degrees in nursing, I could learn about health care.
» My track record led to job offers and income opportunities before I got out.
» I became a professor at a university within three weeks of finishing my sentence.
» As a professor, I could more effectively work toward prison and sentence reform.
» I worked with law schools to build more influence with judges, prosecutors, and prison officials.
» I leveraged those relationships to begin bringing products I created into jails and prisons across America.
» I persuaded investors to partner with me.
» Those relationships led to my building many different businesses.

Take 10 Minutes

» 11-6: What incremental action steps can you start taking today?

_____

_____

LESSON 12: PERSONAL ACCOUNTABILITY

Great companies operate with high cultures of accountability. Those accountability metrics help us determine whether we are succeeding. Accountability systems let us know when we must correct course and pursue new strategies.
—Steve Ballmer

Sometimes we feel like we're trying to accomplish a task that we deem essential to our preparation for success. The system may not allow us to progress, bogging us down with all types of red tape or bureaucratic procedures. From our perspective, the reasons don't make sense.

People can get in our way, obstructing or discouraging us. Authority figures may vehemently argue that we won't ever be able to succeed in the ways we want due to our past decisions.

When preparing for success after prison, we must stay on the path, holding ourselves accountable daily, even though we encounter obstacles. Going through the challenges or responding responsibly to them is another step in our preparation.

If we're determined to succeed, we can learn a great day from the mindset of the Stoics. They teach us the importance of personal accountability.

Either we blame ourselves for not achieving our goals, or we don't blame anyone at all. If we look for excuses, we're not going to lead a very productive life. Although we may face challenging circumstances that limit our progress, we always have the power to choose how we respond.

Rather than allowing other people's decisions to anger us, we can focus on our ***deficiencies*** and push ourselves to do better. If other people refuse permission that we may need, ideally, we've invested enough time and energy to develop the art and skills of persuasion. If rules are stopping us, consider the ways that those rules could potentially work in our favor. We must be ***tolerant*** of other people's mistakes or bad decisions.

Remember that each of us has made plenty of mistakes and bad decisions in the past.

We may live in an environment that makes us feel like everyone is conspiring or plotting our demise. Yet, we grow stronger when we hold ourselves accountable, accepting that we have the power to focus on what matters.

Leaders, or masterminds, taught me this lesson on personal accountability:

Our attitude, decisions, and actions determine whether we succeed—not the decisions of others.

Accountability metrics aren't new. Whether we're fathers, mothers, sons, or daughters, we've relied upon accountability tools to track progress. For example, parents expect school-age children to bring home report cards. What purpose do report cards serve? They help us assess progress, showing what students are doing well and where they can improve. The report cards hold students accountable.

Sports enthusiasts, either coaches or fans, use accountability logs to assess how well players or teams are doing. They help us measure performance. We count wins, losses, batting averages, passing, or rushing yards. Depending on the sport, we count runs or points. Each metric gives us an idea of future performance.

Investors rely upon accountability logs to assess how stocks perform in different time frames. They measure whether the pace of sales will meet growth targets. Financial reports let us know whether a company is poised to lead the market.

An investor or business leader may rely upon accountability metrics to ask Socratic questions.

For example, in what ways would merging with a supplier or a competitor increase efficiencies?

Those types of questions give investors an idea of the company's health. Investors hold themselves accountable by **assessing** all sorts of metrics. Similarly, accountability metrics can help us determine whether we're on the right track, personally. By creating accountability metrics, we can examine our choices and performance.

Aristotle, another teacher from ancient Greece, wrote that we should always examine performance. Many scholars of the **Hellenic** period credit Aristotle with saying:

"The unexamined life is not worth living."

If people of wisdom use accountability metrics to examine their past decisions and project future performance, shouldn't we do the same?

Take 10 Minutes

> » 12-1: What takeaways on personal accountability do you get from the leaders around you?

_____

_____

_____

_____

PREPARING FOR SUCCESS AFTER PRISON
BE THE CEO OF YOUR LIFE

_____

_____

_____

» 12-2: In what ways have you examined your choices?

_____

_____

_____

_____

_____

_____

» 12-3: How have the choices you've made in the past influenced who you are today?

_____

_____

_____

_____

_____

_____

» 12-4: What choices can you make today to influence the success you want to achieve tomorrow?

_____

_____

_____

_____

_____

_____

I examine past choices a lot. When I think about past decisions, I also think of costs. How would you respond to the following questions:

» What did I gain or lose from my past decisions?
» If I made a different choice, would I be better off today?

Interns@PrisonProfessorsTalent.com / Page 155

»   What options can I choose today?

»   Which choice will put me on track for the best future?

These types of reflections cause us to examine our life. They help us make better choices. From inside jail cells, I started assessing how my past decisions led to my confinement. Then I began thinking about tools I could create to measure progress. Those thoughts helped me to develop a release plan that I could use to leverage my way into new opportunities.

I needed to create accountability logs to keep me on the path to success. I used that strategy throughout the entire 26 years that I served. I still use that strategy today, even though I completed my obligation to the Bureau of Prisons on August 12, 2013.

Starting Over:
Being in prison gave me a chance to start over; ironically, since writing the first version of this Preparing for Success After Prison course in 2017, I've found that I routinely use the lessons in this course. I use them in my business, and I use them in my life. They always help me to recalibrate and get back on track.

While stuck in a jail cell, I knew that I wanted to change. In some ways, being in jail opened opportunities to recalibrate. I had a place to sleep, and the system would provide for all my necessities, including food and water. Institutions would provide clothes. Access to financial resources would ease the pain of confinement, but I did not need money. Had I not been incarcerated, I would need an income to provide for myself.

I needed tools to measure my progress. Progress would help me build a powerful case, showing my commitment to personal development. By making accomplishments from prison—despite the obstacles—more support could follow. That support might prove essential to my preparations for success.

I could count the number of months that passed. Each month would lead me closer to my release date. But a release date wouldn't set me free. Sadly, when many people conclude their prison term, they find enormous struggle on the other side. While going through my journey inside, I listened to many people who told me about the challenges they faced when they got out from previous terms:

People that served time and then returned to prison told me they could not overcome:

»   employment hurdles,

»   challenges finding housing,

»   feelings of being unwelcome in society,

»   the need for resources to make a clean start,

»   the pull from a criminal lifestyle.

Some people told me that they preferred to live in prison than live with all the challenges in society.

Those people could change their life if they wanted, but they adjusted in ways that conditioned them to live in prison. They believed in prison maxims:

"The best way to serve time is to forget about the world outside."

Later, they learned the disappointing reality that their choices in prison made them less able to fit in with society. They developed a tone, mannerisms, and attitude while living in the prison adjustment. In the broader community, the prison vibe didn't bode well for people who said they wanted to get on the pathway to success.

By the time I returned to society, the lessons I had learned from masterminds had left an indelible impression on me. Books I read about leaders and masterminds or the lessons I learned from listening to those people taught me the importance of personal accountability.

When I finished serving my sentence, I wanted to pay it forward by showing others how they could grow by learning the same lessons that leaders taught me. Any person could choose how to adjust in prison. If they understood the power of creating personal accountability tools, they might develop new resources to restore confidence. The accountability tool would show the relationship between decisions, actions, and prospects for higher levels of success.

To become more persuasive in helping people see the potency of accountability metrics, I needed to develop the credibility that would come from a successful reentry. To paraphrase a well-known cliche, when we give a person a fish, the person eats for a day, but when we teach a person to fish, the person eats for a lifetime. Assisting others would be one way to be the change I wanted to see in the world.

I truly believed that other people could build better lives if they learned the same lessons masterminds taught me. All of us could work to:

> » define values,
> » set clear goals,
> » improve our attitude,
> » visualize aspirations,
> » take small action steps, and
> » hold ourselves accountable.

As I studied, I read the work of John Locke, a philosopher. John Locke lived during the late 1600s. In his epoch, the world was coming out of the Dark Ages and into an era of hope. People referred to the new era as The Enlightenment. People were learning more.

Locke wrote that all humans came into the world with "a blank slate." He said that human beings were neither good nor bad. We saw things and heard noises. Those things we saw and noises we heard made an impression on our minds. Some people had positive role models all around them, and they learned to make good decisions. Others lived in environments that taught them destructive habits. We became the product of what we learned.

Many of us can appreciate the wisdom in the saying: "But for the grace of God, there go I." That mindset may make us more critical of our decisions and more tolerant of the choices that others make.

John Locke said that even if we made bad decisions in the past, we could learn new concepts. We could start at any time to make good decisions. Leaders know we must hold ourselves accountable to make changes and better decisions.

From the writings of John Lock, I learned a great deal. Early "learning" led me into a criminal lifestyle. Reading John Locke's work taught me that what I "learned" could also be "unlearned." I could build a better life by following clues from successful people.

With certainty, people who achieve high levels of success hold themselves accountable. They don't wait for others to tell them whether they're on the right path. They know where they're going. They engineer success, and they don't make excuses. Accountability metrics inform them about making acceptable progress to succeed or whether they need to adjust.

Successful people taught me how to create my tools and measure progress. To build an accountability metric, I had to:

» define success,
» set a timeline, and
» measure progress on the timeline I set.

It's the same as what we see in others:

» Like a parent who uses a report card to hold his child accountable, I could hold myself accountable.
» Like a coach who uses statistics to measure athletic performance, I could create an accountability metric to grow from one goal to the next.
» Like an investor assesses the pace of a stock's growth, I could measure if I were on track to succeed.

◊ In what ways can accountability tools help you emulate the habits and performance of successful people?

Why Use Accountability Metrics?

My avatars spoke the language of accountability. They understood that "we get what we measure."

My actions would influence whether avatars would believe in me or move on. By holding myself accountable, I anticipated that I could earn their trust, despite the bad decisions of my youth.

At the start of my sentence, I thought of how I could use my time in ways to persuade people to believe in me, even though my past included the following record:

- » I sold cocaine.
- » A jury convicted me.
- » A judge sentenced me to 45 years.
- » I would complete my sentence in 26 years if I didn't lose credits for statutory good time.

Accountability metrics could help me overcome challenges. I simply had to begin with a clear understanding of what I wanted, and then create a plan. Setting clear values and goals was essential to my personal growth and development plan that would guide me to release. I needed to be clear about how my decisions would influence the opportunities I could open in prison and when I came to the end of my sentence.

I thought about my avatars to set my strategy and the growth I would make.

Take 15 Minutes: Develop critical thinking with your responses

- » 12-5: In what ways does your past record or decisions influence the way that others perceive you?

_____

_____

_____

_____

_____

_____

_____

_____

_____

_____

» 12-6: How will your life change when you finish serving your sentence?

_____

_____

_____

_____

_____

_____

_____

_____

» 12-7: What could I do in prison to ease my path to success after I got out?

_____

_____

_____

_____

_____

_____

_____

_____

All people serving time should ask similar questions. Then they should build accountability metrics that will help them stay on track. In my case, I considered how my avatars:

» would consider me worthy of their trust if I earned a degree from prison,
» would find it easier to employ me or extend me credit if I could show that I gave back to society while I was in prison,
» may be willing to invest in me if they saw that others believed in me.

With accountability logs, I could measure daily progress and work toward the goals I set daily.

Since I went to jail at age 23, I didn't know how to grasp 26 years inside. Instead, I thought about what I could accomplish in the first ten years. When I hit the ten-year mark, I wanted a record of accomplishments that would speak louder than words:

» I wanted a university degree.
» I wanted to publish something.
» I wanted a support network of at least ten people.

I had to hold myself accountable to achieve those goals and not blame anything on my environment. I could succeed or fail based on the chart I set out for myself, and everything would matter. From leaders, I learned that I should:

» Visualize success,
» Create a plan,
» Prioritize goals,
» Develop tools, tactics, and resources, and
» Execute the plan.

The accountability logs I created could show whether I was making sufficient progress or whether I had to adjust.

If I could define success at ten years, I could reverse engineer and figure out how far along I should be in five years. If I knew where my progress should be at five years, I could reverse engineer my progress at two and three years. An accountability log would show where I should be when I hit my first year. With that insight, I could figure out where I had to be in six months. I could extend that process back to the next month, the next week, and the next day.

How To Create Accountability Logs (from anywhere):

I had to accept that I could control some things in prison, and I could not control other things. Staff members would determine where I served time. They would order where I slept. Rules would dictate how many contacts I had with society. Other people would determine what, when, and how much I ate.

Despite the external controls of every prison where I served time, I could control my adjustment. I could set values and goals, take incremental actions that would lead me closer to my aspirations. And I could create accountability logs to measure progress. I believed that using those accountability logs wisely would lead me out of the prison labyrinth.

In a previous lesson, I described how I wrote more than 100 letters to schools, hoping to persuade a university to admit me. I wanted a university degree. I had to convince those universities to overlook my crimes and allow me to enroll, even though I didn't have any financial resources. Although I did not control how a school would respond, I could control how hard I worked to persuade administrators that I was a worthy candidate. With my accountability logs, I could measure progress.

My accountability log would resemble something like the following:

» Value category: Education
» Goal: Earn a university degree
» Purpose: A university degree would persuade my avatars to respect and invest in me.
» Action Plan: Write five letters daily until I sent 100 letters to 100 schools.

»   Accountability Metric: Write letters to five different schools each day.
»   Timeline: Connect with 100 universities over 20 days.
»   Intended Outcome: Persuade at least one university to admit me.

The accountability metric gave me a clear plan. I had to set priorities and execute the plan. The project gave me a deliberate path. I didn't know whether a school would admit me. But I could measure whether I followed the plan. If I executed the plan, I would increase my chances of getting into school.

The plan worked. Ohio University accepted me. I then began to track my progress through school, measuring the number of lessons I completed and the credits I earned. By May 1992, I met the requirements for my undergraduate degree. Then I followed the same plan to get into graduate school. And in 1995, Hofstra University awarded my graduate degree.

As described in a previous lesson, *The Autobiography of Malcolm X* influenced me. Reading that story gave me hope. I could increase my value by learning how to communicate better. By building my vocabulary, I could become a better writer and speaker.

I needed a plan and an accountability log. I thought about my avatars. I could learn to communicate like the people I wanted to meet in the future. I could refrain from using language, *syntax*, or *inflections* that left others with the impression that I had served decades in prison.

With a more advanced vocabulary as my goal, I chose my words carefully. I would avoid words like "homie" when referring to friends. I would not refer to a woman in my life as my "old lady." I set a clear path to build my vocabulary:

Value Category: Education
»   Goal: Add 500 words to my vocabulary within 100 days.
»   Purpose: Communicate in the language of my avatars.

Action plan:
»   Keep a sheet of paper beside me while I read each book.
»   Write down each word that I didn't understand.
»   Learn to define each word on my sheet.
»   Write and define each word and part of speech (adjective, noun, or verb).
»   Create flashcards.
»   Write the word on one side of the flashcard; define the word and name part of speech on the other side of the flashcard.
»   Carry a stack of flashcards with me at all times.
»   While waiting in lines, I would test my knowledge by flipping through flashcards. Make each word a part of my vocabulary.
»   Accountability metric: Incorporate an average of at least five new words into my vocabulary each day.
»   Timeline: 100 days.
»   Intended outcome: Build my vocabulary by more than 500 words within 100 days.

I could measure progress with accountability metrics, and the tools kept me on track. Other people in prison advised me to slow down, saying it didn't make sense to **obsess** over making such rapid progress when I served such a long sentence. They **ventured unsolicited** advice, telling me that progress toward goals would not result in my getting out earlier.

Success requires people to know when to accept advice and when to dismiss what others tell us about what we should or should not do. Instead, we should rely upon our values and goals.

I thought carefully about where I would turn for advice. We get a sad story if we use recidivism rates to define success or failure after release. Statistics tell us that more than half of the people that go into prison fail after release. We cannot ignore that accountability metric.

We should ask whether our adjustment patterns mirror successful people. If they mirror the habits of people who fail, we should change. Choose a deliberate path. Use accountability metrics to make progress toward goals. Leaders teach us the strategy to follow if we want to embrace the mindset of success.

By using accountability logs, I beat timelines that I set at the start:

» Instead of earning one college degree within ten years, I earned two university degrees within eight years.
» Instead of becoming a published author within my first ten years of imprisonment, I published more than 20 articles or book chapters within my first ten years.
» I set a goal of finding ten people to believe in me during my first decade of imprisonment. Yet, the published writings allowed me to bring many mentors into my life during those first ten years. Those people were community leaders who visited me in prison and opened more and more opportunities.

In the next lesson, I'll reveal how accountability logs led to my building a vast support network before I got out of prison. Then, I'll show how that support network influenced my liberty and income opportunities from when I transferred to a halfway house in 2012 to the present day.

The takeaway: every decision we make in prison influences prospects for success upon release.

Take 10 Minutes

» 12-8: How does waiting for calendar pages to turn influence prospects for a triumphant return to society?

_____

_____

_____

_____

» 12-9: How would creating accountability logs and measuring progress influence confidence and self-esteem?

LESSON 13: STAYING AWARE

The ultimate value of life depends upon awareness and the power of contemplation rather than upon mere survival.
—Aristotle

In the previous module, I pledged to reveal how accountability logs led to my building an **extensive** support network before I got out of prison. At this stage, participants have worked through seven modules. Every lesson encourages participants to work toward developing better verbal, writing, and reading skills. If people also work toward mastering critical thinking, they'll also become more intrinsically motivated with a self-directed work ethic, realizing how:

The decisions a person makes today influence prospects for success in the months, years, and decades ahead.

With each revision I make to this module, I reflect on those earliest days of my journey when authorities first locked me in prison. On August 11, 1987, the system replaced my name with registration number 16377-004. For the first several months, I fantasized about getting out instead of reflecting on the bad decisions that led to my criminal charge.

Following the criminal trial, members of the jury convicted me. That's when my eyes, my mind, and my heart opened. I became aware of my responsibility to understand more about my role as a citizen. Reading stories about Frederick Douglass and Socrates' life changed my perspective, helping me to ask better questions.

Dreams of the system releasing me **vanished**. Instead, I became more aware of how others perceived me. Then I began introspecting on all the decisions that led to my **demise**, asking different questions, such as:

» What, if anything, could I do from prison to reconcile with society?
» What actions could I take to make amends?
» How does preparing to live in prison differ from preparing for success after release?
» How could I make others aware of my commitment to change?
» How could I develop a network of supportive people that would have a vested interest in helping me to succeed after release?

Lessons on the value of staying aware of my surroundings proved especially valuable, and I'm confident it will also help all participants.

We can start with a question:

» What does awareness mean to you?

When I think of awareness, I think of coaches. Coaches frequently tell athletes to keep their heads in the game. When they give such guidance, the coaches encourage the players to stay aware of every opportunity. When we keep our head in the game, we see opportunities, and we seize those opportunities. The concept of awareness is central to our series on Preparing for Success After Prison; we're always looking for options that can accelerate progress on our goals and our end game.

In prison, we must be ***indefatigable*** in our commitment to overcome the challenges and complications that keep many formerly incarcerated people in the cycle of struggle. Regardless of what goes on around us, we must keep our heads in the game.

As a young man, I lacked awareness. I didn't consider how early decisions could influence my future. My parents tried to put me on the right track, though I ignored them. Both teachers and guidance counselors warned me about the problems likely to follow my decisions. I dismissed those ***admonitions***, thinking I could avoid problems.

I didn't keep "my head in the game," and ignored the possible consequences of my actions, telling myself I didn't care.

I may not have been aware of the ***sanctions*** associated with my criminal behavior. Still, my lack of awareness didn't ***absolve*** me of the consequences that would follow the government's charges against me.

In contrast, the DEA agents kept their heads in the game. Once they became aware of my crimes, they were relentless in their pursuit. They worked behind the scenes to arrest me. With the evidence gathered, prosecutors worked to convict me.

Awareness: You and Others

With awareness, we should consider two perspectives. We can choose to become aware of opportunities around us or choose to remain ignorant of those opportunities. Either way, every day, we're making decisions that advance us closer to a triumphant return to society or a lifetime of continuing struggles. Many people leave prison to face further problems with the law, unemployment, or homelessness.

Regardless of our choices, other people become aware of us and make judgments about who we are. To use a metaphor, "we live in a fishbowl," with others watching and assessing our judgment or how we spend our time. Our choices will influence how others perceive us and what opportunities open in our future.

Regardless of where you are right now, start preparing for success.

Take 30 Minutes

» 13-1: What level of awareness do you have about opportunities around you?

_____
_____
_____
_____
_____
_____
_____
_____
_____

» 13-2: How do your actions show that you're keeping your head in the game?

_____
_____
_____
_____
_____
_____
_____
_____

» 13:3: How will your decisions influence your future?

_____
_____
_____
_____
_____
_____
_____
_____
_____
_____

Your responses to those questions influence how others perceive you. Based on what other people see, they become more "aware" of who you are and whether you're a worthy candidate for their time and attention. Your daily choices and behavior determine whether other people will want to invest time, energy, or resources to help you develop.

Consider the wisdom of Zig Zigler, a mastermind who developed training materials for sales professionals. Zig Zigler said:

» "If you can help other people get what they want, you can get everything you want."

A person who is less committed to preparing for success may show signs of being intellectually lazy. In prison, I frequently heard others say, "There aren't enough programs here," or, "no one cares about rehabilitation."

Take 15 Minutes

» 13-4: How do your daily activities relate to your values and goals?

_____

_____

_____

_____

_____

_____

_____

» 13-5: In what ways do my actions show that I want to succeed upon release?

_____

_____

_____

_____

_____

_____

_____

_____

» 13-6: How would a well-developed release plan show my commitment to succeed?

_____

_____

_____

_____

_____

_____

_____

_____

_____

_____

» 13-7: What accountability metrics can I show that I adhered to my release plan?

_____

_____

_____

_____

_____

_____

_____

_____

_____

_____

_____

Since my release from prison, I have spoken to many audiences. When giving presentations in universities or professional conferences, I strive to help influential people understand why we need to collaborate in ways that will improve outcomes for justice-impacted people.

Frequently, I refute arguments from people who tell me that others cannot do what I did. My response is always the same. Anyone who served time with me could have opened the same opportunities that I opened. The only difference is that Socrates, Frederick Douglass, Nelson Mandela, Viktor Frankl, Mahatma Gandhi, and Malcolm X inspired me. They helped me grasp the importance of keeping my head in the game. Leaders like Bill Gates and Steve Jobs helped me understand the power of being aware of opportunities and making others aware of me.

I offer examples to show how being aware changed my life, hoping others will see the value of introspection and projection.

Sowing Seeds with Awareness:

As described in earlier lessons, I started selling cocaine after high school. A jury convicted me, and a judge sentenced me to serve 45 years. I kept my head in the game from the start of my sentence. I didn't want to repeat the same types of bad decisions that I had made when I was in school.

The custody and classification system that the Bureau of Prisons developed had a scoring system. Among other factors, the scoring system considered sentence length and offense type. Based on my sentence length and high-severity offense, administrators designated me to serve my sentence in a high-security US penitentiary.

During my first meeting with the unit team, I asked whether I could ever transfer to a lower-security prison. Based on my sentence length and offense, the unit manager told me that I would remain in high-security prisons until my release.

He judged me based on the papers before him. But he did not know the depths of my commitment to preparing for success. Decisions while in prison led to my gradual transition to medium-security, low-security, and minimum-security camps.

When we keep our heads in the game, we become aware of opportunities we can seize or create. As described in *Earning Freedom: Conquering a 45-Year Prison Term*, we can convert our ***adversaries*** into ***advocates*** when we make others aware of our commitment to change.

Besides avoiding problems while in prison, I also prepared for a better future. By training, I opened opportunities to grow and orchestrate a pathway that I anticipated would lead to success. I was always aware of opportunities I could seize. My term with the Bureau of Prisons ended on August 12, 2013, after 26 calendar years. But I wasn't finished with the criminal justice system.

Once I finished the prison portion of my sentence, I had to serve time on probation. First, there would be seven years of Supervised Release. Then I would start parole. My sanction required 26 years inside and 19 years on parole—but I couldn't begin the parole portion of my sentence until after I finished Supervised Release. When I finished Supervised Release and parole, three years of special parole would follow. Federal probation officers would oversee me through the entire post-release term.

My term required 29 years of supervision from federal probation. Day-to-day life would be the same on Supervised Release, Parole, or Special Parole.

I put a plan in place to ***terminate*** that supervision early. The same strategy that got me through prison would help. I had to stay aware of how every decision would matter. I had to keep my head in the game. I stayed mindful of what I could do to make myself a good candidate for relief. I also stayed aware of the efforts I could make to earn support from others.

I couldn't control what others would do. Yet by being aware, I could always keep my head in the game. I could create ways to make my case stand out in a more favorable light.

Double Concept:

Each previous lesson only had one concept to grasp. With awareness, we need to consider two perspectives. We can make different choices, yet each option comes with a cost. If we ***assess*** the cost, we can make the best choice. We should remain aware of how each choice relates to our prospects for success or the threat of failure.

Our choices make others aware of us. They see how true we are to our values and goals. As a result of our work, they begin to believe in us. Then they offer to help us on our path.

> » Awareness perspective 1: We become aware of opportunities,
> » Awareness perspective 2: Others become aware of our commitment to success.

Preparing for Supervised Release:

Early in the journey, I identified the values and goals that would characterize my adjustment through prison. I wanted freedom as soon as possible. I wanted to build a career and stability upon release. I would need support from the probation officers supervising my release to succeed.

Many years before I finished my term, I began preparing to build a record that would result in the best experience on Supervised Release. In prison, I stayed out of trouble. A clean disciplinary record would have a positive influence on my probation officer. To validate my preparations for success, I earned two university degrees, many certificates, published books, and built a strong support network. In its totality, I hoped my prison record would make a favorable impression on the probation officer assigned to my case.

By 2011, I had more than 23 years of prison behind me, and I had advanced to within a few years of my release date. I set a goal of writing a monthly letter to the federal probation office, hoping to influence the probation officer that would supervise me. I didn't know the probation officer, but if I wrote the letter, I hoped to reach someone of influence.

In the initial letter, I introduced myself. I told the probation officer how hard I worked to prepare for a law-abiding, contributing life from the start of my sentence. I also explained the career that I wanted to build. The subsequent 24 monthly letters provided an update. As an example, the followed a pattern:

Dear Probation Officer:

If you've read my previous letters, you know about my commitment to prepare for success upon release. While I work through these final months of my lengthy sentence, I consider it important to connect with the leaders that will supervise my release. For that reason, I'm continuing to send these updates.

If you haven't done so already, I encourage you to review my release plan. I published my release plan on my website, at PrisonProfessors.com. It shows the way that I began to architect a plan for release at the start of my journey. It led to my following a principled path, including:

» *Earn academic credentials,*
» *Contribute to society,*
» *Build a positive support network of mentors.*

Those strategies influenced a release plan that I'm still building upon today. It influenced the books I read, the courses I completed, the friends I chose. Because of that plan, I opened a broad support network that will support me upon release. It even led to my getting married inside a prison's visiting room.

Since writing you last, I've opened new opportunities with universities. Relationships with people in academia are part of my strategy to work toward prison and sentence reform upon release.

Although I know that rules prohibit people who leave prison to interact with other justice-impacted people, I am hoping to earn your support. I will seek permission to build a career around my journey. That career will require me to travel and interact with others who have criminal backgrounds.

My release plan clearly shows how hard I've worked to prove worthy of your trust. I a hopeful you'll support those efforts.

I look forward to discussing my release plan with you further when I'm released.

Respectfully,
Michael Santos
Number 16377-004

Probation officers didn't write back. I didn't have any way of knowing whether anyone read those letters I sent. But in August of 2013, I concluded my term with the BOP. When I went to meet with my probation officer, she was aware of how hard I worked. Those efforts I made to influence her yielded a great return on investment of time and energy. The probation officer gave me a much higher level of liberty. She allowed me to travel, and she approved my request for permission to build a company that would necessitate my interaction with other people that had criminal charges or convictions.

That is an example of how the Straight-A Guide got me through prison and led to my success upon release. As I became aware of opportunities, others became aware of my efforts to succeed.

From a prison cell, I could choose what I wanted to learn. Like anyone else, I could learn from people I would never meet. Leaders offered valuable lessons.

I chose lessons that would put me on a path to success. I wanted to learn the patterns of people with a record of succeeding in their chosen fields. They knew what they wanted and made deliberate choices. Aware of opportunities, they marketed themselves in ways to make investors aware of their work. The more aware investors became of leaders, the more resources investors provided.

Take 15 Minutes

» 13-8: What would you like your future probation officer to know about you?

_____

_____

_____

_____

_____

_____

_____

_____

_____

» 13-9: In what ways could you develop a release plan that would help you influence your probation officer?

_____

_____

_____

_____

_____

_____

_____

_____

_____

_____

_____

» 13-10 How will your accountability logs reflect your commitment to your release plan?

_____

_____

_____

_____

_____

_____

_____

_____

_____

Examples of Leadership and Awareness:

Bill Gates started Microsoft with his partner, Paul Allen. Bill Gates and Paul Allen were great examples of masterminds. Together, they built and led one of the most influential companies in the world.

Unlike me, Bill Gates and Paul Allen made good decisions when they were young:

» They studied on their own to learn and master computers,
» They knew their values,
» They set clear goals,
» They worked on writing software code in a short time.

They wrote the computer code that would launch Microsoft in less than a week. As they succeeded, investors from all over the world invested resources to help Microsoft grow.

Bill and Paul's early preparations put them on a path to success. When an opportunity of a lifetime opened, they were ready. We all can make choices today that will allow us to take advantage of opportunities later. We need to sow our seeds.

We see many examples showing us how people succeed. The only question becomes whether we want to learn from them. By studying their patterns, I learned a great deal. I wrote the Straight-A Guide's principles to convey what I learned to others.

As a case study, let's consider more about the story behind the founders of Microsoft.

Attitude:

They committed to success with 100% effort. Bill Gates studied independently, learning as much as he could. When he saw an opportunity to start his company, he went all in. He quit

Harvard and moved to New Mexico to work with his first client. Gates did not allow anything to get in the way of his success.

Aspiration:

They had a vision, wanting every office and every home to use personal computers. They wrote the codes that would drive computers and taught others how to use the code to write programs. It was all part of a grand vision to build Microsoft.

Action:

They took incremental action steps, first writing the code. Then they got the client, generating resources to hire staff to help them find more clients. Then they repeated the process. Then they found investors that would provide resources to accelerate success.

Accountability:

They set clear goals. Each goal had a timeframe to complete. A timeline let them know how much progress they needed to make each day. By meeting timelines, they earned the trust of their partners.

We see these kinds of examples all around us. We should follow the clues. The Straight-A Guide shows us how to follow a pattern of success. Define success and commit to it, then make decisions to deliver success. Those who follow this pattern know that their choices rather than chance led to success.

Hence, we see the first prong of Awareness.

But there's a second prong. Others become aware of people that put themselves on pathways to success. Everyone wants to be a part of success.

Being Aware in Prison and Life:

I didn't get this concept of awareness as an adolescent. My lack of awareness had a bad outcome. I chose friends poorly, and I made terrible decisions that locked me in conflict with authorities. Then I went to prison for multiple decades. While inside, from the masterminds I studied, I learned that I could step onto a path to success regardless of where I was. Or I could stay unaware and follow the path that derails success and leads to further demise. I had to choose and pursue success regardless of my environment.

» What are you choosing?

To follow patterns of success, we may need to change how we think. We need a new mindset. To change how we think, we should start by thinking of our teachers. Learn to think like people who succeed. They leave clues that show how they became successful. Reject patterns of failure that we see so frequently in jails and prisons.

The example of Bill Gates and Paul Allen shows how we can reap big rewards if we prepare early. They studied science and math. When they began, neither Bill Gates nor Paul Allen knew they would start a valuable company. They applied themselves, and they learned. As a result, they were ready to seize the day when others could not. They were "aware" of opportunities. Later, others became aware of their success and joined them.

People in prison could follow the same steps. In the Straight-A Guide, we list those steps as follows:

- » Values: Identify values to define success.
- » Goals: Set clear goals showing how you commit to your values.
- » Attitude: Show that you have the right attitude with 100% effort.
- » Aspiration: See the success that you're going to become.
- » Action: Take small action steps each day.
- » Accountability. Use clear timelines to measure your progress.
- » Awareness. Stay aware of opportunities to seize, and more people will become aware of you.

People who follow the principled steps of the Straight-A Guide are more aware. They know a lot of negative energy exists in prison, but their mindfulness helps them triumph over that energy. They choose friends carefully, knowing they can control their behavior but cannot control others' behavior. Accordingly, they make choices that will lessen their exposure to problems. They are aware of the power of each choice they make. The choices they make today put them on a path to success tomorrow. Every choice matters.

It's never too early—and never too late—to start preparing for success. The earlier we prepare, the more we can accelerate prospects for success, as we define success.

Leaders know how decisions matter. They understand how actions matter. They are aware of how their choices, their decisions, and their efforts will influence others. Make choices today to prepare for a better life tomorrow. Every decision can affect success.

- » If problems erupt from table games, be aware. Avoid table games. Read instead of playing games.
- » If sports teams lead to tempers flaring, be aware. Avoid playing on sports teams. Exercise alone or with people who share the mindset of success.
- » If people value seating rules in common areas, be aware. Avoid common areas. Spend time introspecting, thinking about the future you will build.

If you follow principled steps, you will become aware of opportunities. Because of your awareness, you can seize those opportunities to achieve increasingly higher performance levels. Simultaneously, others will become aware of your commitment. They, too, will want to invest in your success. They will help you, assist you, and encourage you.

That principled strategy works everywhere. It works in prison and beyond. It worked for all the leaders who inspired me and kept me climbing toward the goals I wanted to achieve through the 9,500 days I lived as a prisoner. The strategy allowed me to return to society successfully. Because I followed the patterns of successful people, income opportunities opened. For example, before I finished serving my time, San Francisco State University hired me to teach as a professor.

People provided me with resources to begin investing in real estate when I was still in a halfway house. By being resourceful while I served my sentence, I influenced the value they perceived in me. The strategy that guided my decisions through prison opened opportunities to build my career upon release.

Remember my pledge to all participants of this course: I never ask anyone to follow any strategy I am not using. The Straight-A Guide strategy powered me through prison. It enhances prospects for me to succeed in society, as evidenced by the fact that you can access this course. Imagine the courage it takes for prison administrators to contract with me—a man that served 26 years in prison.

By living this guide's values-based, goal-oriented strategy, I open business relationships and income opportunities. I can open deals that few would think are possible for someone with my background. I've received purchase orders from federal judges, probation officers, US attorneys, and leaders of prison systems. Business leaders purchase products or services from companies I build. By keeping myself aware, I always keep my head in the game. And others are aware of the efforts I'm making to succeed. They invest alongside me, allowing me to create new opportunities.

The assets I accumulated continue to grow. Yet despite the business opportunities around me, I continue to invest time and energy to share these lessons with people in jail and prison. I hope others will use these lessons to transform their lives. No one should work harder than you on your preparations for success—but all people need to stay aware and keep their heads in the game.

I finished serving my sentence in August of 2013. But I continue living by the same principles that powered me through confinement. I feel a duty to teach the strategies I learned from leaders and masterminds to people in prison.

At the beginning of this lesson on awareness, I wrote how I used this strategy to deal with probation. Remember, I began preparing for probation at the start of my prison term. I lived a values-based, goal-oriented life through all the years I served. My avatars influenced me to focus on education, contributing to society, and building a support network.

At the end of my sentence, I could show that I made a 100 percent commitment to preparing for success. I avoided problems in prison. I rejected advice from people that told me to forget about the world outside. Instead, I prepared for my return to society.

When I came to the end of my term, I could report my progress to the US Probation Department. By writing the monthly letters from prison, my probation officer became aware of my commitment to succeed. She authorized me to build the career I wanted. She allowed me to travel. I kept her in the loop with all my efforts.

After one year, my probation officer joined a US Attorney in submitting a motion to a federal judge. They asked the judge to terminate my seven-year term of Supervised Release. The judge granted the order, allowing me to begin serving my 19-year term on Parole. After one year, my probation officer urged the US Parole Commission to terminate the remainder of my parole. I then began serving my three-year term on Special Parole. After another year, I received notice that the US Parole Commission had set me free—as I'll reveal more about in the next module.

This strategy of adhering to the Straight-A Guide has helped other justice-impacted people we feature on our podcasts and webinars. I am convinced that it can help anyone in prison.

Be aware of opportunities. Understand and accept that the decisions you make in prison directly influence your prospects for success.

Keep your head in the game of success—through prison and beyond!

Lesson 14: Celebrating Achievements

Great achievement is born of great sacrifice. Happiness comes from the achievement of a difficult task that demanded our best.
—Napoleon Hill

Routinely, I revise the lessons and modules that constitute our Preparing for Success after Prison series. The more I create outside, the more I can show the authenticity of this message. To succeed, we must adhere to a disciplined, deliberate path. With the Straight-A Guide, I've tried to outline the compass I used to navigate the labyrinthine world of confinement.

- » It starts with defining success,
- » Create a plan that will take you from where you are to where you want to go,
- » Put your priorities in place,
- » Develop your tools, tactics, and resources,
- » Execute your plan and hold yourself accountable.

These principled steps show our authenticity. To stay on the plan for extended lengths of time, we've got to train ourselves to celebrate every achievement, no matter how small.

That's a concept that remains clear to me each time I revise. I wrote the original version of this course on February 22, 2017—several years ago, during my fourth year of liberty.

After my release, I began working to advance ideas on prison and sentence reform. Specifically, I wanted to persuade judges, prosecutors, and prison administrators to **unite** in a call for reforms. I worked with law schools and published in law reviews, arguing that we could improve outcomes of America's criminal justice system if we incentivized people serving sentences. Those incentives should encourage people to participate in programs that would help them:

- » Prepare self-directed pathways to success,
- » Build release plans, and
- » **Obliterate** the toxic message that "the best way to serve time was to forget about the world outside and focus on time inside."

Through those efforts, speaking opportunities opened. After I gave a keynote speech at a judicial conference that the Ninth Circuit Court of Appeals sponsored, opportunities opened to build relationships with prison systems, the federal courts, and even with the Department of Justice.

The seeds we sow early can lead to new opportunities many years later.

Being able to contribute to prison systems feels like a real achievement. Yet had I not set a release plan at the start of my journey, and worked toward incremental achievements along the way, I would not have opened so many opportunities after release.

A great deal has transpired since I wrote the first version of the Preparing for Success after Prison series. In revising this edition, I still recall the monumental importance of February 22, 2017, the day I wrote the first version of this lesson. I celebrated a significant achievement that day, and in this module, we emphasize the importance of celebrating our incremental achievements. I had to work through several decades to make the achievement possible. More than anyone else, I wanted to share the achievement with people in prison—I thought it might help illustrate the importance of celebrating incremental achievements.

We all make daily decisions that influence prospects for success. By developing the mindset of success, we avoid bad choices, such as those I made as a young man. Through this series, I've tried to show how all decisions influence the future we create. The Straight-A Guide may lead people to better decisions than I made during that **reckless** transition between adolescence and adulthood.

People in prison need hope, and I've aspired to provide them with hope. People who work through these courses have months, years, or decades to serve. We can build safer communities if more people in prison find pathways to success. To **convert** that vision into a reality, we need to plant, nurture, and work to help the seeds we sow mature into strong trees that bear fruit.

A person's daily decisions influences life and opportunities that open. Sometimes the **monotony** of prison makes it difficult to make that connection. For that reason, I produce content daily, and I publish it on our various websites. I hope to spread that information into as many prisons as possible. I want people to see this connection between today's choices and tomorrow's success. They should connect their responsibility to prepare for success, regardless of what's happening in the institution—every decision matters.

To stay motivated, celebrate every small success along the way. Each success builds upon previous success, bringing higher levels of achievement. Like a snowball gathers size when it rolls downhill, success grows in geometric proportions. Start with small achievements. Keep feeding those achievements, and they will grow into more significant achievements.

Let me elaborate with an example of how small and early achievements brought me a reason to celebrate when I wrote the original version of this module in February of 2017.

In the previous lesson, I described the many layers of my sentence. Besides a lengthy prison term, my judge imposed 29 years of supervision. First, the judge ordered that I would have to complete seven years of Supervised Release. Then 19 years of Parole. Then three years of Special Parole.

US District Court Susan Judge Illston, from San Francisco, agreed that Supervised Release no longer served a purpose in my case.

One year after I finished with the Bureau of Prisons, the judge signed an order to free me, saving me six years. I transitioned to my term on Parole.

A year later, the US Parole Commission terminated my Parole, saving me 18 more years. And on February 22, 2017, at 10:33 a.m., an intern at US Federal Probation called to tell me he had good news. The US Parole Commission granted early termination of my Special Parole term.

If I didn't start sowing seeds in 1987, when I began my prison term, I might have had a different outcome. The seeds I planted at the start of my journey influenced the US Parole Commission to liberate me. On February 22, 2017—instead of 2033, I began living without supervision.

The early seeds led me to influence people I've never met. In fewer than four years from the day I finished with the BOP, people on the Parole Commission let me off.

As I frequently do, I reflect on the pivotal moments that made this possible. I would have been under supervision for decades. I'm free because an officer gave me a book that told me the story about Socrates. That story inspired me. Reading that book in 1987 helped me to develop the mindset of success in a solitary cell in the Pierce County Jail.

Socrates changed the way I thought. When I changed the way I thought, I changed my life.

Then, by reading the story of Frederick Douglass, I got further inspiration. He taught me that if a person could learn how to read better, and how to write better, a person could change the world. When I read his biography, I learned that after he escaped the bondage of slavery, he published biographies and became an influential speaker. Instead of going on to enjoy his liberty, Frederick Douglass used his personal story of living in slavery to persuade others to abolish laws that allowed slavery.

We all can use stories to change the world.

Take 20 Minutes

» 14-1: In what ways can a story change your life?

_____

_____

_____

_____

_____

_____

» 14-2: When meeting a person who could influence your prospects for success, what story would you tell about your adjustment in prison?

» 14-3: What pivotal moment caused you to commit to living as a law-abiding, contributing citizen?

» 14-4: How would you describe the incremental steps you took to prepare for success after prison?

Celebrate Small Achievements:

I remember reading the story of Socrates for the first time. I set the heavy book on my chest to think. As a young man in a jail cell, I didn't know what I would face ahead. But I knew my early decisions led to the friends I chose. Along with my friends, I made choices that led to my predicament instead of making choices that would bring a better life. I broke the law, authorities arrested me, and I pled not guilty—despite knowing of my guilt. Then I went to trial, lying on the stand, saying I wasn't guilty. Then a judge sentenced me.

Making the connection between my earlier decisions and my life in a jail cell got me started on the path to changing my thinking. I also accepted that I could make better decisions from a jail cell. I could map a plan for a new life by changing how I thought. It's never too early and never too late to begin building a pathway to success.

Reading Socrates' story helped me think about the people I would meet in the future, my avatars. Some of those people could change my life.

>   How could I use my time in prison to prepare?
>   How could I persuade avatars to help me?
>   What steps could I begin taking then, from inside a jail cell?

Setting clear values and goals led to the principled course of action of the Preparing for Success after Prison course. That strategy made all the difference for me throughout my decades in prison.

In the beginning, I could not see the end of the journey. Since I didn't know how to contemplate 26 years, I focused on the first ten. Before ten years passed, I wanted a college degree, publishing credentials, and a support network that would include at least ten influential people. Each of those achievements would be a milestone. To reach them, I would need to make many small achievements.

>   I would need to write letters to find a school,
>   I would need to get into school even though I didn't have money,
>   I would need to avoid problems in prison so that others would join my support network,
>   I would need to use all that I learned from school and people in my support network,
>   I would need to read books to learn from masterminds.

If I kept taking small steps, I would reach those small achievements. Together, they would put me in a different position after ten years. If I stayed the course, I believed that staff would transfer me from a high-security penitentiary to medium-security prison. Later I might get to a low-security prison. I trusted that if I stuck to the plan, I would persuade staff members to reclassify me and allow me to serve the last part of my sentence in a minimum-security prison.

With my sentence length, I had to start in the Special Housing Unit of a high-security prison. To serve my sentence in lower-security prisons, I needed to avoid problems with staff

members and other prisoners. I needed to make small achievements. Every decision would influence my journey through the decades I served. And my journey through decades of imprisonment would affect my prospects for success after release.

I had to celebrate small achievements to sustain a high level of energy and discipline. Reading a book or a story may be a small achievement. But if the story caused me to change the way I thought, it would change my life. If I acted in ways to reflect that I thought differently, I would make measurable achievements. Others would notice. Later, I could look back. I could see how each decision in jail influenced each opportunity.

Decisions from the day I read Socrates precipitated a step-by-step path. Each decision and each step aligned with my values and goals. By celebrating the small achievements, I stayed focused. I didn't need to think about serving 26 years. Instead, I thought about the small goals I needed to achieve. I knew I could open more significant opportunities by achieving those small goals.

Freedom from the government is one reward. There are more. In the previous lesson, I wrote about investors. By making a record of every success in prison, I had a solid case study. I could show people the tiny steps that I took. When I could show people how I worked through prison, they were willing to write checks to support projects I wanted to create. That support allowed me to build a new career. I'll describe that career in more detail in the next module.

As a participant of the Preparing for Success after Prison series, consider how you can develop a release plan that will lead to a series of incremental achievements.

> » Track those achievements with accountability tools.
> » Then, use those achievements to open new opportunities.

Build a string of small achievements. Those achievements will open new options, creating your path to success. If a release date is too far away, celebrate the small accomplishments, just like the people we profiled in the videos that accompany this course. This strategy will motivate you, building hope along the way as you develop the power within to influence a better future.

Those who want to continue working independently through the Preparing for Success after Prison series may invite their family members to visit our website PrisonProfessors.com to see the supporting self-directed books and workbooks. If they're not available in the prison's library, we recommend the following books or self-directed courses:

Earning Freedom: Conquering a 45-Year Prison Term

This lengthy book reveals the journey from the day that I came into prison, facing life without parole. It takes readers through the day that I transitioned into a halfway house. Each year I update the book to apprise readers of how a solid release plan helped to prepare for the journey.

Prison! My 8,344th Day Workbook

This self-directed workbook shows readers the importance of making intentional decisions each day. The exercises help participants see how they use their time inside to prepare for success upon release.

Success after Prison Workbook

This self-directed workbook shows the results after I returned to society. Readers will see how decisions inside opened opportunities to build a career in real estate investments, and how revenues from those decisions provided resources I could use to advance my work in advocacy for prison and sentence reform.

Perseverance Workbook

*This self-directed workbook offers insight participants can use to overcome the challenges that accompany confinement. By learning to think differently, and to adjust intentionally, people position themselves for **resilience**.*

Release Plan Workbook

This self-directed workbook offers insight into how participants can build an intentional release plan. It should put them on a pathway to argue for higher levels of liberty, at the soonest possible time.

Each workbook in our Preparing for Success after Prison series provides participants with a clear picture showing the importance of celebrating small achievements. If those achievements happened in one prison, we could dismiss them as luck. Yet the books and workbooks offer story after story, showing how small achievements accumulate from one prison to the next.

Regardless of what decisions administrators make, or what laws pass, people can always work to:

- » Develop a more robust vocabulary,
- » Develop better writing skills,
- » Develop better verbal communication skills,
- » Develop better critical thinking,
- » Develop a self-directed work ethic,
- » Develop a comprehensive release plan, and
- » Develop accountability logs that highlight incremental achievements.

Through all the coursework, readers get to learn about people from every background. They all show one ***coherent*** message: The decisions a person makes today influences the opportunities that open in the weeks, months, years, and decades ahead.

If this strategy only worked for me, some may say I was lucky. I agree that I've been fortunate, and I am grateful. Yet I urge students to pay close attention to the people I profile in the accompanying books and the supplemental videos that we make available in our Preparing for Success after Prison series. Participants will find interviews with many people who once served life

sentences, yet now they're free. Each person ***validates*** the concept that I'm striving to convey. They describe how each decision in prison put them on a path to new opportunities and, eventually, freedom.

Every person who transforms while in prison inspires me.

Deliberateness:

You may have seen the award-winning movie *Training Day* with Denzel Washington. Denzel plays the role of Alonzo, a corrupt police officer that trains a rookie. Alonzo tells the rookie, "This is chess, not checkers."

The memorable line from *Training Day* describes a complicated challenge with many moving parts. Everything can change in an instant. To succeed, we've got to see the big picture. Winners anticipate what will happen many moves in advance. They are deliberate with every choice. They know how to celebrate small wins. Those small wins lead to significant gains. Never forget that without a steady flow of small achievements, big wins are not possible.

In an earlier lesson, I wrote how Suzy Welch, an author, inspired me. She wrote a book about making good decisions, calling her strategy ten-ten-ten. Think of how every decision will influence your life.

Take 15 Minutes

» 14-5: How will your decision influence your life in the next ten minutes?

_____

_____

_____

_____

_____

_____

_____

_____

» 14-6: How will your decision influence your life in the next ten months?

_____

_____

_____

_____

_____

_____

_____

» 14-7: How will your decision influence your life in the next ten years?

_____

_____

_____

_____

_____

_____

_____

Make decisions in ways that can lead you to a series of small achievements. Together, those achievements build hope. You will see how yesterday's choices led you to overcome struggles and launched you to higher levels of success.

Leaders know how to get out of a bad situation and climb to a better position. Since the end is sometimes too far away, they focus on small steps they can take today. Those small steps make it more likely to achieve outcomes.

Make a 100% commitment to putting yourself in the best possible position to succeed. Celebrate small, incremental achievements along the way. If those achievements align with your values and goals, each success will bring more success. You will be able to say:

"I am the person I am today because of the decisions I made yesterday."

Written Word:
When I began my self-directed personal development journey, I didn't know how to use my time effectively. What could I do while locked in a solitary cell to prepare for a better future? I took an inventory of resources that I could get.

» I could get books.
» I could get paper.
» I could get pencils.

What else could I do?

> » I could read, write, sleep, run in place, do pushups, leg lifts, and squats in my cell.

I had to use the resources in my cell to prepare for success. By reading about Socrates, I knew what I wanted. I set goals that would lead to success. I would need to stay fit, and I would need to improve my skills. I could improve my fitness. I could build better reading and writing skills and improve my critical thinking to understand every decision's opportunity costs.

I believed the staff would transfer me into better conditions if I did well. In better conditions, I thought I could do more. Such a mindset inspired me to work toward doing well.

When I began serving my sentence, I did not know how to write a grammatically correct sentence. I would empower myself if I could learn how to write persuasively and confidently. To improve, I put a plan in place of writing 1,000-word essays each day.

What would I write?

It didn't matter. I wrote with one purpose in mind, wanting to become more confident in turning words into sentences. From a jail cell, I read books to learn how others wrote. I trained myself to think and write in sentences and paragraphs, believing the skill would help me prepare for success after release. I learned to structure writing:

> » I'd write openings to introduce the idea of an essay.
> » I'd write supporting paragraphs in the essay's body to help make a persuasive case.
> » I'd write a compelling close to present a message with force.

I trained myself to think like a writer. I prepared to earn more support from the types of people who could advance my prospect for success—my avatars.

Each letter, sentence, and paragraph I wrote felt like a small achievement I could celebrate. Like a runner who counts his laps, I calculated the words I wrote, pushing myself to exceed the explicit daily goal to write 10,000 words weekly.

> » What stops you from pursuing a similar goal of writing 1,000 words a day?
> » How would writing 1,000 words each day influence your critical-thinking skills?
> » How would writing 1,000 words each day affect your ability to create a life of meaning and relevance upon release?

Book Reports:
Reading represented an essential strategy for my commitment. We all had 24 hours on any given day. Even while we're incarcerated, to some extent, we could choose how we spent those 24 hours.

Looking for opportunities to advance my plan, I read books that aligned with my values and goals. The strategy, I hoped, would make favorable impressions on the people I anticipated meeting later. To memorialize the books I read, I wrote book reports that would serve as a kind of accountability log, tracking the systematic preparations for success after prison. Each book report followed a templated pattern:

- » Author's name:
  - ◊ Here, I'd write the author's name.

- » Book title:
  - ◊ Here, I'd write the book's title.

- » Date read:
  - ◊ I'd write the date I finished reading the book.

- » Why I read (title):
  - ◊ Here, I'd write why I chose to read this book.

- » What I learned from reading (title):
  - ◊ Here I'd write the impressions or takeaways I received from the book.

- » How reading (title) will contribute to my success upon release:
  - ◊ Here, I'd write my thoughts on how this book would influence my prospects for success.

Each book report gave me a cause to celebrate, making me feel like I'd created another tool, tactic, or resource to help. Those achievements felt like purposeful steps, leading me out of confinement.

Achievements:

Success is an ongoing journey of incremental achievements. Our mindset shows our commitment to success every day. When we make choices, those choices lead to our next opportunity.

Never forget how the decisions you make today will influence your future. Regardless of where you are in your journey, you can start sowing seeds that will lead to a better outcome. There is an old saying that I frequently quote. You may read the quote in some of my other work.

- » The question: When is the best time to plant an oak tree?
- » The answer: 20 years ago.
- » The second-best time is today!

None of us can change the past. But all of us can sow sees that will lead to a better future. Develop the mindset to success and start planting seeds that will allow you to build a better life.

Take 15 Minutes

» 14-8: Describe a book that influenced your life.

_____

_____

_____

_____

_____

_____

_____

» 14-9: What prompted you to read that book?

_____

_____

_____

_____

_____

» 14-10: What lessons did you learn from reading that book?

_____

_____

_____

_____

_____

» 14-11: In what ways will reading that book influence your prospects for success upon release?

_____

_____

_____

_____

_____

_____

_____

Lesson 15: Appreciation and Authenticity

As we express our gratitude, we must never forget that the highest appreciation is not to utter words but to live by them. Self-acknowledgement and appreciation are what give you the insights and awareness to move forward toward higher goals and accomplishments.
—John F. Kennedy

In earlier lessons, I wrote about how I would've liked to have received this message of self-directed learning as an adolescent. I would've made better decisions, choosing friends and role models that would have inspired me to make better decisions. I would've made decisions that led to success rather than decades in prison.

I offer that personal insight because I am determined to be authentic. I will never ask anyone to do or say anything I did not do or say while serving my sentence. To move from struggling to better times, we must live authentically.

I would not be authentic if I didn't disclose my many failures as an adolescent and student. Ironically, I didn't develop the mindset of success until a jury returned a guilty verdict and a federal judge sentenced me to serve a 45-year prison term.

As this course reveals, it's never too early and never too late to develop a success mindset. If you're living in challenging times, think **contemplate** steps you can take to be authentic. And think about how those steps reflect an appreciation for the blessings that have come your way.

Learn From Masterminds:

World leaders like Mahatma Gandhi inspired me, and I'm confident his message can encourage anyone. Regardless of where we are, Gandhi tells us that we can create our happiness. To create happiness, we must keep our thoughts, words, and actions in harmony. As I learned from Gandhi, we should make decisions showing that we're the change we want to see in the world.

I strive to be the change I want to see in the world. To earn trust, I live authentically. That isn't to imply that I don't make bad decisions. I am a human being, conditioned by having served 26 years in prison. I've made good decisions, and I've made bad decisions. Those decisions have led to great experiences and challenging experiences.

In 2018, for example, I made an investment that led me into a civil lawsuit. Settling that suit wiped out $3 million in equity I had built since getting out of prison. Rather than being angry at what I perceived as a great injustice, **sangfroid** helped me accept that I must live in the world as it exists and not as I want it to be. With a commitment to transparency, I published records from that lawsuit on my personal website, at MichaelSantos.com.

We will always face more challenges and we must always be ready to overcome those challenges. I felt grateful to have the confidence to rebuild. Lessons from masterminds helped me to develop that self-assurance.

Lessons in this course will help participants develop self-actualization. We ***self-actualize*** when we know that we're making progress. Our success becomes self-***evident***, as everyone knows we've conquered a challenge. When we're successful, we show appreciation for the lessons we learned. We share those lessons with others so they can become successful, too.

Why Pursue this Path?

I want people to avoid prison, and I want people in prison to leave that environment as success stories. A success story means someone isn't running from the law or anyone else. A success story implies an individual can keep his head high with dignity intact.

Those who pursue success realize the influence of every decision, seeing the opportunities and threats, the strengths and weaknesses in every choice they make. Strategic thinking—or the mindset of success—may help a person from the time they enter jail. It may guide adjustment strategies as days turn into weeks, weeks turn into months, months turn into years, and years turn into decades. A person's plan may lead to a more fulfilling outcome, regardless of where or when an individual begins.

Steve Jobs paraphrased the famous artist Picasso, who said:

Good artists copy ideas. Great artists steal ideas.

To write the Straight-A Guide, I stole ideas from masterminds. Participants that want to develop the mindset of success may use the same strategies of stealing ideas from masterminds.

Masterminds always:

» Identify values.
» Set clear goals.
» Pursue success with the right attitude.
» Have aspirations for the success they want to become.
» Take action steps.
» Hold themselves accountable.
» Stay aware of options, and make others aware of their commitment to success.
» Live authentically, developing tools, tactics, and resources.
» Celebrate every achievement along the way.
» Show appreciation for the blessings that have come their way.

Take 20 Minutes

» 15-1: How would you describe the steps that led to your current predicament?

_____

_____

_____

_____

_____

_____

» 15-2: What differentiates your preparation for success from others?

_____

_____

_____

_____

_____

_____

» 15-3: In what ways does your adjustment strategy resemple the way of masterminds?

_____

_____

_____

_____

_____

_____

Live authentically

Participants that adhere to the Straight-A Guide path become authentic. They don't talk about wanting to be successful. Instead, they pursue a path they designed with their values and goals. They understand how a documented strategy would advance their prospects for success in all areas.

Since writing the earlier version of this course, I've built many businesses requiring me to work closely with companies' leaders. I'm grateful for each lesson that I learn from leaders.

Like the ten principles identified above, the CEOs with whom I work teach that building a great company requires leaders to:

> » Identify a problem to solve,
> » Define the best possible outcome,
> » Document a strategy that will resolve the problem,
> » Create tools, tactics, and resources to succeed,
> » Execute the strategy every day, and
> » Measure progress and adjust as necessary.

We all can follow such principles to become the CEO of our life!

Anyone can self-actualize, making success self-evident. We don't need anyone else to say we're thriving. Living by our values and goals, we experience success every day.

Each of us has made bad decisions and good decisions in the past. At any given time, we can choose to learn from those decisions. We can choose how we define success. Then we can begin to make deliberate decisions. Our choices and actions reflect our values and goals. They take us from where we are to where we want to go. We know we're successful when we're living a values-based, goal-oriented life that keeps everything we say in harmony with everything we think and do.

Define your life with thoughts, words, and actions. Let those thoughts, words, and actions reflect your commitment to success.

Being Authentic:
The supplemental books and videos to the Preparing for Success after Prison series share stories about other people that conquered struggles. They may have made bad at different stages of their life. But they all chose to become better. They all decided to draw a line in the sand and work toward conquering the struggle. They began by defining success.

People that succeed define success with their values. They set clear goals to show their commitment to success:

> » They had the right attitude.
> » Their aspirations helped them to visualize success.
> » They took incremental action steps and held themselves accountable.
> » They became aware of opportunities to seize, and others became aware of them.
> » They celebrated small achievements.
> » And they were authentic.

Shon Hopwood:

You can see an example of someone who adhered to the Straight-A guide's principles by reading the story of my former partner in Prison Professors, Shon Hopwood. Shon authored *Law Man: My Story of Robbing Banks, Winning Supreme Court Cases, and Finding Redemption*. His story shows that regardless of bad decisions a person has made in the past, it's never too late to build a better future.

Shon's book reveals how he made terrible decisions as a student, choosing friends that led him into trouble. While in his late teens, Shon experimented with drugs and robbed banks, and he served ten years in federal prison after he pleaded guilty.

While in prison, however, Shon made a choice. He chose to learn and to become more than his past. Because of Shon defining success differently, he learned the law. Then he started to help other people in prison. He made a 100% commitment to learning how to read the law and research the law. Shon acted, learning how to write persuasive legal arguments. He held himself accountable by devoting time daily to improving his skill. Anyone could choose to follow Shon's path.

Shon kept his head in the game. He stayed aware of opportunities in the law that he could use to help others. Shon celebrated achievements when others won victories in court. Through his work, he contributed to winning cases in district courts, appellate courts, and the United States Supreme Court—all while he served his prison term.

Because of Shon's commitment to success, while serving ten years, opportunities opened for him. When he got out, Shon finished college. The Bill and Melinda Gates Foundation awarded him a full scholarship to attend law school, and the University of Washington awarded him a law degree. He accepted his first job as a clerk for the DC Circuit Court of Appeals, then Georgetown Law School made him a full-time associate law professor.

Shon's story shows how a person could choose to build a better life. He is authentic, and his success is self-evident. He shows his appreciation for the blessings that have come into his life. Others become aware of his commitment to volunteer hundreds of hours of community service. President Trump invited Shon to work with the White House on prison reform, and he became instrumental in passing the First Step Act, which applied to all people in federal prison.

Like Shon, everyone on our team at Prison Professors strives to bring systemic improvements to social justice issues, including sentence reform and reforms to our prison system that will lead to better outcomes. With the courses we offer, we ask each person in prison to join this effort to build safer communities and more effective systems.

First, however, we ask participants to invest in themselves. Learn to document a strategy for personal development and show appreciation by helping others along the way. Develop a personal release plan that will lead from struggle to success and create accountability logs that define the daily progress you're making.

To improve the outcomes of our nation's criminal justice system, we must persuade leaders that all justice-impacted people can use their time inside to prepare for success. Our team at Prison Professors will strive to push for the following reforms:

» More incentives that will encourage all people to work toward higher levels of liberty,
» Access to social furloughs to maintain community ties,
» Access to work-release programs that will prepare people to live as contributing, tax-paying citizens,
» Broader access to compassionate release or commutations of sentence, and
» Reinstatement of the U.S. Parole Commission.

To accomplish those goals, we need to influence leaders and legislators. If we can show how people in prison are building effective release plans that help them prepare for success upon release, we advance advocacy efforts.

Some may feel cynically about the possibility of succeeding with these efforts. We faced that same cynicism when I wrote *Earning Freedom*, which encouraged reforms that would lead to "Earned Time" credits, as we see in the First Step Act.

Incremental steps lead to successful outcomes.

Take 20 Minutes

» 15-4: What reforms would you like to see in the system?

_____
_____
_____
_____
_____
_____
_____

» 15-5: What challenges do you see in bringing these reforms

_____
_____
_____
_____
_____
_____
_____

»   15-6: In what ways can you contribute to advancing these reforms?

_____

_____

_____

_____

_____

_____

Walk The Way:

Anyone that adheres to the Straight-A Guide can go from struggle to success. But, it's one thing to know the way. It's quite another thing to walk the way.

While in prison, neither Shon Hopwood nor the people I profiled in earlier lessons knew what challenges they would face after release. They needed to prepare, to get ready to overcome challenges. They needed to define success with values and set clear goals.

Time in prison taught many lessons to people like Halim Flowers, Tommy Walker, Shon Hopwood, and others. All of us can learn from those lessons. By sharing lessons, we hope to inspire others. To overcome the challenges of our life, we must walk the way of masterminds.

Not for Everyone:

As I write these lessons, I remember reading about an interview with James Patterson. Mr. Patterson has authored dozens of novels and sold millions of books. During an interview, a journalist asked Patterson to respond to critics. Some of those critics accused Patterson of not being a very good literary stylist. The journalist asked Patterson how he would respond:

"I'm not a very good literary stylist. There are millions of people that don't like how I write. Fortunately, a few million do."

As one of the best-selling authors of all time, Patterson didn't need other people to define his success. Sales made his success self-evident. But there would always be people who disagreed with his approach. Those disagreements didn't matter because he defined success and pursued it with a 100% commitment.

Similarly, not everyone will agree with the Straight-A Guide's message of hope and self-reliance. Likewise, not everyone agrees with the efforts we make to advance more pathways for people in prison to earn freedom through merit. That's okay. We all must carve our own path.

We want our participants to define their path to success, and we're confident that anyone can reach a higher potential by following a principled approach.

Getting Out of Prison:

I will never forget the day my wife drove me from the prison in Atwater to the halfway house in San Francisco. With 25 years of prison behind me, I had to serve six more months in a halfway house, followed by six months of home confinement. After 9,500 days, I would conclude my obligation to the Bureau of Prisons. Then I would start my term of Supervised Release. My wife and I talked about the career I wanted to build. I told her a message that I've lived by since I first read about Frederick Douglass:

I want to make an impact on the world by helping people who live in struggle. Leaders taught me how to create meaning and relevance, and I want to share those lessons. It doesn't matter if they're in school, in prison, or struggling in other areas of their lives. We can reform systems to create better outcomes for people.

To earn trust from people, I needed proof. People had to believe the strategies would lead to their success. I told my wife I committed to building assets worth at least $1 million within five years of release. By achieving that goal, I believed people would be more inclined to accept my message's potency. They would accept that they could become more successful if they pursued this path. I've been on this path—with a mindset of success—since I began my prison term. I'm still on it today.

I connect with participants through words, photographs, and videos. Through those efforts, I strive to show my authenticity. But neither the digital assets nor the live presentations show how many hours I must devote to this daily effort. No one can see the incremental progress—or investment I must make to create courses. I could not complete any of this work if I did not begin in prison and follow the Straight-A Guide path daily.

Think it through.

On the day that I left prison, I was behind with technology. When I went to jail, the internet didn't exist. I never sent or received an email. I did not know how to create a video or publish it online. I didn't know how to use technology that would allow me to develop products. I had to purchase computer equipment and software. Once I had the equipment, I needed to invest thousands of hours learning how to use it. Each day I had to invest time to learn; a deliberate adjustment in prison prepared me to accelerate progress.

I create products. Then I must find a market for those products. Judges, US Attorneys, and Prison leaders are not so willing to purchase products from a man that served multiple decades in prison. After all, until February 23, 2017, I was still on Special Parole.

Participants who have access to the books I wrote will see that I did not begin this path on a whim. I've been committed to sharing this message for decades. If you do not have access to the

books, your family members can easily find them at PrisonProfessors.com. Those books will show my decisions through prison. They also will show strategies I used to overcome challenges since my release.

I hope you will see that by adhering to the Straight-A Guide principles, I'm authentic.

Authenticity and Appreciation:

When we're authentic, it's easy to appreciate the blessings that have come our way. Living in gratitude brings more blessings, empowering others along the way.

Every day opens an opportunity for further growth and fulfillment. Masterminds plant seeds and they nurture gardens. Consider the metaphor. By enriching the soil, caring for plants, removing weeds, and caring for details, we allow gardens to thrive.

Masterminds invest energy in building great gardens. They see the value of creating strong networks. To build more robust networks, they invest in others that prove worthy. Those investments bear fruit, bringing more value. People can show appreciation for blessings that come their way. They give time, energy, or resources, making their commitment to success full circle. They create more success for more people and live more fulfilling lives.

Map of Success:

Masterminds give us their map. Observe and learn from the principled approach to life that leaders show us. We see how to chart our course to success as we define success—with our values and goals.

Arriving at our success begins with our preparation. Commit by following the map. Think of this concept as preparing for a transatlantic journey. Years may pass before we reach our destination. Yet, we know the value of the choices we make every day. Choices will either bring us closer or lead us farther away.

If we're beginning our journey on the other side of the world and want to come home, we need to consult this map. The map helps us stay the course. We know that we'll face storms of adversity along the way, but by staying the course, we also know that we will reach our destination.

Each lesson has value, including this final lesson on "appreciation."

Concept of Appreciation:

Struggles anywhere can lead to a culture of negativity. Negativity can pull a person under the current. At any given moment, storms threaten to sink spirits. Accept the principled path of masterminds to triumph over the pull that drags down so many. Use the strategy as a compass. To reach your destination, anticipate darkness. You'll face rough seas, even hurricanes. Use the

strategy as your map and your compass. The concepts will lead you to calmer seas and advance you along your course.

» Stay true to the values by which you profess to live.
» Always set short- and long-term goals.
» Proceed with your 100% commitment to success.
» Never lose sight of your aspiration.
» Pursue aspiration as the days turn into weeks, the weeks into months, and the months into years.
» Seize every opportunity for productive actions that align with your definition of success.
» Your action steps will open further opportunities for growth.
» Hold yourself accountable.
» Live transparently, inviting others to hold you accountable.
» Keep your head in the game.
» Become aware of new and exciting ways to accelerate your progress.
» Others will become aware of your pursuit of excellence. They will invest in you.
» Celebrate every achievement.
» Be authentic.
» Express gratitude and appreciation for the blessings that come your way.
» Invest in community renewal, helping those around you to reach their highest potential.

This strategy will influence:

» The friends you choose,
» The activities you pursue,
» The mentors you bring into your life,
» The way that people in authority treat you,
» The gradual improvements in your living conditions,
» The employment opportunities you open,
» The language you use to communicate,
» The time you devote to your fitness,
» The books that you read,
» The skills that you develop,
» The relationship you build with your family and loved ones,
» The resources you can draw upon,
» The way that you use those resources,
» The support network that believes in you,
» Your access to credit and investors,
» Your access to business opportunities,
» Your reputation.

Gambler or Investor:

Living in struggle may influence your perspective. I encourage you to introspect. Consider whether you want to live as a gambler or as an investor. Either way, you make a choice.

A gambler may play the odds and live by chance, while an investor thinks more strategically. An investor assesses the landscape and surroundings, then determines the best way to deploy resources. Both gamblers and investors have opportunities to win, but those who think strategically succeed at a far higher level.

The greatest gamblers operate more like investors and minimize chance by training to read signs and clues. They place their bets using a skill set that they develop over time.

» What factors influence their decisions?

They look at every data point that comes their way. With sports betting, they want to know big-picture issues like weather patterns and soil conditions. They also want to know minute issues, like rosters and injury lists, and statistics of personal athletes. The more they know, the better they can place their bets.

Investors take the same approach, considering as many data points as possible when making decisions. They evaluate price-earnings multiples, and they look at year-over-year sales growth. Investors want insight into equity returns and assess the organization's overall competency. Data points make investors more confident to put money on the line.

Whether you live as a gambler or an investor, make good decisions. Always acknowledge the stakes. With your life, liberty, and future at stake, take a big-picture view and assess what you can do now. Then set priorities that are consistent with your values and goals. Remember that the right decision at the wrong time is the wrong decision.

Big Picture Perspective:

The big-picture perspective for people in prison is ugly. Statistics show that seven out of every ten people in prison face challenges when they get out. They struggle to find employment and face challenges in finding permanent housing. Some have trouble with substance abuse.

Strategies in this course helped me overcome my problems, and I'm convinced the techniques can help others.

But each must decide.

We wish you success!

Take 10 Minutes

» 15-7: In what ways would living in gratitude influence your prospects for success upon release?

_____

_____

_____

_____

_____

_____

_____

_____

_____

_____

_____

_____

_____

_____

_____

_____

_____

_____

_____

_____

_____

_____

_____

_____

_____

_____

_____

_____

SECTION III

In this third section of Preparing for Success after Prison, we invite participants to join our coalition for reforms that would expand the concept of "earning freedom" by incentivizing excellence.

In Section I, the first five hours of our Preparing for Success after Prison course, we provided the construct for living a values-based, goal-oriented adjustment.

In Section II, we endeavored to show a practical application for the next ten hours of the course. I used the Straight-A Guide as a compass to prepare for success upon release.

In Section III, we offer an additional 15 exercises on personal development. These final 15 lessons involve more writing and critical thinking; participants should use critical thinking to memorialize their personal growth and preparations for success.

Purpose:

Throughout this course, I've written that I would offer guidance that I learned from leaders. Those leaders taught me the importance of life-long learning. If we're always preparing, we're living more intentionally.

We must identify strengths, weaknesses, opportunities, and threats. I pledge transparency and would never ask anyone to do anything I'm not doing. Subsequent lessons will show how I'm still using these strategies today.

Since completing my prison term, in August of 2013, working toward prison reform and sentence reform has been like a ministry for me. Every day, I advocate for reforms that include:

» Expansion of incentives that would allow all people in prison to earn higher levels of liberty through merit and reconciliation.
» Access to work release for people in federal prison who qualify.
» Meaningful access to commutations and compassionate release.
» Reinstatement of the US Parole Commission.

To succeed with such efforts, I need help from people in prison. When more people show that they're building release plans and using those plans to guide their preparations for success, we become more successful at persuading administrators, business leaders, and citizens on the need to expand the use of incentives in prison.

We invite participants to subscribe to our newsletter. If you haven't done so already, consider becoming a part of our community:

Prison Professors Talent
32565 Golden Lantern Street, B-1026
Dana Point, CA 92629

Corrlinks:
Interns@PrisonProfessorsTalent.com

Subject line: Requesting a Scholarship

LESSON 16: VENI, VIDI, VICI

Some participants may have heard the Latin phrase *"Veni, vidi, vici."*

Scholars attribute that phrase to Julius Caesar, a Roman general, and statesman. He lived during the first century BCE (Before the Common Era). We can translate the phrase into English as follows:

Veni:

> *This word translates to "I came" or "I arrived." It refers to the act of arriving at a particular place or situation.*

Vidi:

> *This word means "I saw." It represents observing or perceiving something with one's own eyes.*

Vici:

> *The word Vici says "I conquered" or "I overcame." This word signifies achieving victory or triumph over a challenge or opponent.*

History tells us that Julius Caesar used this phrase when he wrote a letter to the Roman Senate around 47 BCE. He wanted to describe his swift and decisive victory against another king **succinctly**. Over the following centuries, others have used the *Veni, Vidi, Vici* phrase to express a concise statement of a successful accomplishment or a display of confidence.

I used *Veni, Vidi, Vici* when drafting the **manuscript** for *Earning Freedom: Conquering a 45-Year Prison Term*. The book would become **cornerstone** content for the career I wanted to build upon release: I aspired to persuade leaders of the need for reforms that would allow people to earn freedom through merit rather than turning calendar pages. Since the book would have to cover multiple decades in confinement, I needed a logical section to engage readers.

Veni: The first section of the manuscript shows a young man going in to serve a multi-decade term.

Vidi: The **penultimate** section shows what he saw and how preparations for success led to an effective release plan that focused on results rather than the process of serving time.

Vici: The final section shows how an effective release plan could open opportunities and deliver a higher potential for people who return to society.

As I learned from the life story of Frederick Douglass, I started with a plan:

» A book, or series of books, would help me tell the story of how preparing for success after prison led to an effective release plan. Writing that book became a priority and a part of an overall plan.

» With the book, I hoped to open opportunities and persuade citizens that incentives would lead to improved outcomes of America's criminal justice system.

» The book led to invitations to teach in a university, publishing in peer-reviewed journals, and creating advocacy campaigns to advance the plan's next steps.

» We would need to collect data to influence people to join a coalition for reform.

» Collecting data could show how preparing for success upon release improves outcomes. That data would counter opposing voices with a vested interest in repealing laws that encouraged people to work toward milestone credits or earn-time credits.

» We developed resources to hire a social scientist from UCLA. With her data, she could profile how incentives lead to hope and that hope leads to more effective release plans, and more effective release plans lead to lower recidivism rates, lower costs, improved cultures, and better outcomes for citizens.

To spread the program further, we would need to expand our coalition to include prison administrators, employers, and people in prison. Together, we anticipated that we could build more support for reforms that would include:

» Expansion of incentives for all people in prison,
» Access to work-release programs,
» Opportunities to pursue compassionate release, furloughs, or sentence commutations when appropriate.

As a personal-development exercise, write responses to the following questions.

Please allow yourself a total of one hour to respond to the following questions:

» What does the phrase "seek first to understand, then to be understood mean to you?"

_____

_____

_____

_____

_____

_____

» What did you observe when you came to prison?

» What thoughts did you have about preparing for higher levels of liberty while you served your sentence?

» How would you have defined success at the start of your sentence?

_____

_____

_____

_____

_____

_____

_____

_____

_____

_____

_____

_____

_____

_____

» What goals did you put in place to advance prospects for success?

_____

_____

_____

_____

_____

_____

_____

_____

_____

_____

_____

_____

_____

_____

_____

_____

Lesson 17: Accountability for Growth

Vocabulary Word:

Accountability - Taking responsibility for one's actions, decisions, and their consequences.

Lesson Content:

In the pursuit of personal growth, accountability plays a crucial role. It requires a person to take ownership of:

» choices,

» actions, and

» outcomes.

Embracing the concept of accountability allows us to develop self-awareness, learn from our mistakes, and make positive life changes.

During my time in prison, I realized the significance of accountability in shaping my future. I acknowledged that the decisions I made and the actions I took had led me to this point. By embracing accountability, I began to see opportunities for growth and transformation. I understood that by taking responsibility for my choices, I could move forward with purpose and create a better life for myself.

In Earning Freedom: Conquering a 45-Year Prison Term, I wrote about the steps I took to persuade universities to admit me, even though I had been a terrible high school student and did not have financial resources. By holding myself accountable, I could create a clear plan that would lead to more opportunities.

Start creating your personalized accountability plan to prepare for your success after release. To embrace accountability for personal growth, follow these steps:

Reflect on Your Actions:

Take time to reflect on the choices you have made and their consequences. Recognize the impact they have had on your life and the lives of others. Honest self-reflection is the first step toward accountability.

Accept Responsibility:

Acknowledge that you have the power to change your circumstances. Accepting responsibility for your actions empowers you to make different choices and take positive steps toward personal growth.

Learn from Mistakes:

View mistakes as learning opportunities. When you misstep, analyze what went wrong and identify the lessons you can take from the experience. Use these insights to make wiser decisions in the future.

Set Clear Goals:

Establish clear and measurable goals for your personal growth. These goals will serve as a roadmap, guiding your actions and holding you accountable for making progress.

Seek Support:

Surround yourself with individuals who encourage and support your journey toward personal growth. Seek mentors, counselors, or fellow students who can provide guidance and hold you accountable to your goals.

Questions and Activities: In one hour, answer as you deem appropriate

» How do you define accountability and its importance in personal growth?

_____

_____

_____

_____

_____

_____

_____

_____

_____

» Share an experience where embracing accountability helped you overcome a challenge or make positive changes in prison.

_____

_____

_____

_____

_____

_____

_____

»   How does taking responsibility for your actions contribute to personal development?

»   How can accountability help you prepare for a successful life after release?

»   What goals have you set that require accountability during the time you serve?

Activities for personal development:

» Reflect on a recent situation where you could have taken more accountability.

» Write how you could have approached the situation differently and the potential positive outcomes that could have resulted from taking responsibility.

» Identify one action you will take to hold yourself accountable and foster personal growth moving forward.

» Remember, embracing accountability is not about dwelling on past mistakes. It's about taking control of your future. By holding yourself accountable, you can make positive changes, grow as an individual, and lay the foundation for a successful life beyond prison walls.

» Stay committed to your personal growth journey and embrace the power of accountability!

LESSON 18: HARNESSING AMBITION

Vocabulary Word:

Ambition - A strong desire to do or to achieve something, typically requiring determination and hard work.

Lesson Content:

In what ways are you working toward your ambitions?

At the start of my prison journey, I set high ambitions of what I wanted to achieve during the time I served. I visualized the career I wanted to build. The more clarity I could bring to that vision, the better I could use the decades I served inside to prepare.

If I didn't prepare well, I anticipated facing many more challenges after I got out. But if I prepared, I could open opportunities.

My ambitions required that I set a three-part strategy. Every day, I would work to:

» educate myself,
» build a support network, and
» contribute to society.

The three-part clarity guided my steps. I hoped to get out with my dignity intact and opportunities to prosper.

Ambition is the fuel that can drive us toward achieving our goals. A strong desire to improve, achieve, and maximize our potential can make all the difference. In personal development, especially for those serving time, harnessing ambition can be a powerful tool for growth and change.

Follow these steps to build ambition for personal development:

Set High Goals:

Ambition starts with setting goals that challenge you. These should be things that you truly desire to achieve that will require determination and hard work. The danger isn't in setting goals that are too high but in setting minimal goals and failing to make further progress.

Plan Your Path:

Once you know where you want to go, the next step is to plan how you will get there. Learn new skills and build a stronger mindset.

Stay Committed:

Ambition requires commitment. It means sticking with your goals even when progress slows, or obstacles arise.

Seek Growth:

Always look for opportunities to learn and grow. Ambition requires us to work toward becoming a better version of ourselves along the way.

Celebrate Progress:

Recognize and celebrate progress. We should acknowledge each small step toward our goals because they set us on a path to new opportunities.

Questions and Activities: In one hour, answer as you deem appropriate

» How do you understand the concept of ambition?

_____

_____

_____

_____

_____

_____

_____

_____

_____

_____

_____

_____

» How does ambition relate to personal development?

_____

_____

_____

_____

_____

_____

_____

_____

_____

» When did your ambition help you overcome a challenge or achieve a goal in prison?

» How did this experience contribute to your personal development/

» How can harnessing your ambition help you prepare for a successful life after release?

_____
_____
_____
_____
_____
_____

» What ambitious goals are you working toward during your time in prison?

_____
_____
_____
_____
_____
_____
_____
_____
_____
_____
_____

Activity:

» Reflect on an ambitious goal you have set for yourself. Write down why this goal is important to you and your steps to achieve it.

» Identify one new strategy you could use to harness your ambition and drive you closer to your goal.

» Remember, ambition is more than just the desire to achieve—it's about the determination and hard work you're willing to put in to reach your goals. As you continue your journey of personal development in prison, your ambition will be a powerful driving force toward your success upon release. Keep dreaming, keep striving, and keep pushing your limits!

LESSON 19: EFFECTIVE COMMUNICATION

Vocabulary Word:
Communication - Exchanging information, thoughts, and feelings through verbal and non-verbal means.

Lesson Content:
Effective communication is a vital skill. When it comes to personal development, communications play a crucial role.

When I walked into a US Penitentiary at the start of my sentence, I couldn't see anything beyond the 40-foot walls surrounding me. I was 23 years old and anticipated that decades would pass before I got out. If I didn't learn to communicate differently, I expected that my long prison term would minimize opportunities to succeed when I got out.

Leaders taught me that I would have more opportunities to succeed if I could become a better communicator. To become a better communicator, I had to rely upon myself—not the prison system. But opportunities would open to transcend the walls around me if I could become a better communicator.

Strong communication skills involve expressing oneself clearly, listening actively, and connecting with others on a deeper level. By honing our communication skills, we enhance our interpersonal interactions and foster stronger relationships inside and outside the prison environment. By working to develop communication skills, I grew more confident. Those skills helped me recalibrate and rebuild after I returned to society.

Understanding the concept of communication is essential for personal development:

Clear Verbal Expression:
Effective communication begins with the ability to express oneself clearly and articulately. It involves using appropriate language, organizing thoughts coherently, and conveying messages with clarity and precision.

Active Listening:
Communication is not only about speaking; it also involves actively listening to others. Active listening means paying attention, seeking to understand, and responding appropriately. By practicing active listening, we show respect and empathy toward others' perspectives and foster meaningful connections.

Non-Verbal Communication:
Non-verbal cues, such as body language, facial expressions, and gestures, are an integral part of effective communication. Being aware of and using non-verbal signals effectively can enhance the understanding and impact of our messages.

Empathy and Understanding:
Communication is not just about transmitting information; it's about connecting with others on an emotional level. Empathy and understanding enable us to recognize and validate others' feelings, creating a sense of trust and rapport.

Conflict Resolution:
Effective communication skills are crucial for resolving conflicts and managing disagreements constructively. By employing active listening, respectful dialogue, and problem-solving strategies, we can navigate conflicts in a productive and peaceful manner.

Questions and Activities: In one hour, answer as you deem appropriate.

» In what ways are you working to improve your communication skills?

_____

_____

_____

_____

_____

_____

_____

_____

_____

_____

_____

» Why is effective communication important for personal development, particularly during imprisonment?

_____

_____

_____

_____

_____

_____

_____

_____

» Share an example of a time when effective communication helped you resolve a conflict or improve a relationship in prison. How did your communication skills contribute to your personal growth?

» How can honing your communication skills help you prepare for successful interactions and relationships after release?

» What strategies can you implement to enhance your communication skills during your time in prison?

_____

_____

_____

_____

_____

_____

_____

_____

_____

_____

_____

_____

Activity:
   » Reflect on a recent conversation or interaction where your communication could have been more effective.
   » Describe what could have been improved regarding clarity, active listening, or non-verbal cues.
   » How would these improvements have changed the outcome?
   » Identify one aspect of your communication skills that you would like to develop further. Write down specific actions you can take to enhance that skill, such as practicing active listening or seeking feedback from others.
   » Remember, effective communication is a powerful tool for personal growth and meaningful connections. By honing your communication skills during your time in prison, you equip yourself with the ability to express yourself, understand others, and build stronger relationships. These skills will serve you well in your journey towards post-release success.

LESSON 20: UNLEASHING CREATIVITY

Vocabulary Word:
Creativity - The ability to generate original and innovative ideas, solutions, and expressions.

Lesson Content:
Creativity is a powerful force for personal development, particularly during confinement. It involves tapping into our imagination, thinking outside the box, and expressing ourselves uniquely and innovatively. By embracing and nurturing our creativity, we unlock our potential for self-expression, problem-solving, and personal growth.

Through all our courses, I write about the amazing people who inspired me through the journey. People that served time effectively helped me to become more creative. Frederick Douglas helped me believe that even though I served multiple decades in prison, I could become productive and play a positive role in society—even though a jury convicted me of serious drug crimes.

If I could learn to communicate better, I could develop effective advocacy skills. I would need to build credibility to become the change I wanted to see in the world. Pursuing academic credentials and then publishing became the strategy that worked for me.

» Leaders such as Halim Flowers, who once served a life sentence, became a painter.
» Tommy Walker worked out of a life sentence by building an extraordinary and compelling record.
  ◊ In what ways are you being creative?

Anyone can develop creativity, but it starts with attitude.

Embracing Imagination:
Creativity begins with embracing our imagination and allowing ourselves to dream and envision new possibilities. It involves breaking free from conventional thinking and exploring alternative perspectives.

Cultivating Curiosity:
Curiosity fuels creativity. By maintaining a sense of wonder and a thirst for knowledge, we open ourselves to new experiences, ideas, and inspirations. Cultivating curiosity allows us to explore different paths and discover innovative solutions.

Overcoming Fear of Failure:
Fear of failure can hinder creativity. Embracing creativity involves letting go of perfectionism and the fear of making mistakes. It means taking risks, learning from setbacks, and viewing failures as opportunities for growth and learning.

Thinking Outside the Box:

Creativity thrives when we think outside the box and challenge traditional norms and assumptions. It involves seeking alternative perspectives, considering multiple solutions, and embracing unconventional approaches.

Self-Expression:

Creativity provides a means for personal expression. Through various artistic mediums, writing, or any form of creative outlet, we can express our emotions, thoughts, and experiences. We foster self-discovery and develop a deeper understanding of ourselves by sharing our unique voice.

Questions and Activities: In one hour, answer as you deem appropriate.

» How do you understand the concept of creativity?

_____

_____

_____

_____

_____

_____

_____

_____

_____

_____

_____

_____

_____

_____

» Why is creativity important for personal development, particularly during imprisonment?

_____

_____

_____

_____

_____

_____

» Share an example of a time when embracing creativity helped you solve a problem or express yourself in prison. How did it contribute to your personal growth?

» How can nurturing your creativity help you prepare for a fulfilling life after release?

» What strategies can you employ to enhance your creativity during your time in prison?

_____

_____

_____

_____

_____

_____

_____

_____

_____

_____

_____

_____

Activity:
   » Reflect on a recent situation in which you used creativity to overcome a challenge or express yourself. Describe the creative process you went through and how it impacted the outcome. What did you learn from this experience?
   » Identify one area where you would like to foster more creativity. Write down specific actions you can take to nurture your creativity in that area, such as exploring new hobbies or engaging in brainstorming exercises.
   » Creativity is a powerful tool for self-expression, problem-solving, and personal growth. By embracing and nurturing your creativity during prison, you open up a world of possibilities for self-discovery, innovation, and post-release success.

LESSON 21: DEVELOPING CRITICAL THINKING

Vocabulary Word:

Critical thinking - The ability to analyze, evaluate, and interpret information objectively and logically in order to form well-reasoned judgments and make sound decisions.

Lesson Content:

Critical thinking involves thinking independently, assessing information objectively, and making thoughtful decisions based on evidence and logical reasoning. It involves questioning and challenging assumptions, biases, and preconceived notions. With critical thinking, a person thinks deeper and tries to get the logical coherence of arguments. It goes beyond accepting information at face value.

In prison, it's crucial to develop critical thinking. People spread rumors, or cling to fantasy rather than reality.

Developing critical thinking skills enhances our problem-solving abilities, increases our understanding of complex issues, and makes us more self-reliant decision-makers.

Our course offers many examples to show how critical thinking influences prospects for higher success levels. We should always grasp how today's decisions influence opportunities for tomorrow.

I've written about many people who developed strong critical thinking during their time in prison. For example, consider Weldon Long. Drug abuse led him to commit violent crimes. A judge sentenced him to prison when he was 19. While Weldon served his sentence, he allowed other people to influence him. Bad adjustment decisions led to further problems when he got out. Within a couple of years, authorities charged Weldon with new criminal conduct. He returned to prison. Again, a failure to prepare for success during his second term in prison brought consequences. He got out and found more problems. Within a couple of years, Weldon returned to prison a third time. During his third term in prison, however, Weldon exercised will power. He rejected the bad advice of people around him and developed himself. Those skills helped him leave prison the third time with exceptional critical thinking. That commitment to personal development led to a massively successful career in corporate training.

We feature Weldon's story in one of our supplemental DVD recordings. If you listen to Weldon, you'll hear him talk about his regret that he didn't develop critical thinking during his first or second terms. But it's never too late to work on personal development.

Each person in prison uses critical thinking every day. To the extent that we consider the opportunity costs that accompany every decision, we make better decisions. We want participants in our course to make better decisions. For that reason, we emphasize the importance of critical thinking for personal development:

To make the best progress:

Analyze Information:

Critical thinking begins with the skill of analyzing information. It involves breaking down complex ideas or situations into their parts, examining evidence, and identifying relevant factors.

Evaluate Arguments:

Critical thinking requires assessing the strengths and weaknesses of arguments or claims. It involves questioning assumptions, considering alternative viewpoints, and distinguishing between valid reasoning and logical fallacies.

Consider Objectivity and Open-Mindedness:

Critical thinking necessitates approaching information and ideas with objectivity and open-mindedness. It means being willing to challenge our beliefs and biases, considering different perspectives, and being receptive to new evidence or viewpoints.

Be a Problem-Solver and Decision-Maker:

Critical thinking enhances our problem-solving and decision-making skills. It involves systematically analyzing a situation, considering multiple options, and selecting the most viable solution based on logical reasoning and evidence.

Communicate Ideas Effectively:

Critical thinking aligns with effective communication. It involves articulating our thoughts clearly, supporting our arguments with evidence, and engaging in thoughtful discussions to refine our ideas.

Questions and Activities: In one hour, answer as you deem appropriate.

» How do you understand the concept of critical thinking?

_____

_____

_____

_____

_____

_____

» Why is critical thinking important for personal development, particularly during imprisonment?

_____

_____

_____

_____

_____

_____

» Share an example of a time when critical thinking helped you make a sound decision or solve a problem in prison. How did it contribute to your personal growth?

_____

_____

_____

_____

_____

_____

» How can developing your critical thinking skills help you prepare for making informed choices and solving complex problems after release?

_____

_____

_____

_____

_____

_____

» What strategies can you employ to enhance your critical thinking during your time in prison?

_____

_____

_____

_____

_____

_____

Activity:

» Reflect on a recent decision and describe how you used critical thinking to arrive at that decision. Analyze the steps, the information you considered, and the reasoning behind your choice. What could you have done differently to improve your critical thinking process?

» Identify one area where you would like to apply critical thinking more effectively. Write down specific actions you can take to develop and enhance your critical thinking skills, such as seeking out diverse perspectives or conducting research on the topic.

» Remember, critical thinking is a powerful personal development, problem-solving, and decision-making tool. By developing and honing your critical thinking skills during your time in prison, you equip yourself with the ability to analyze information objectively, make sound judgments, and confidently navigate complex situations. These skills will serve you well in your journey towards post-release success.

LESSON 22: EMBRACING DILIGENCE

Vocabulary Word:

Diligence - Careful and persistent work or effort.

Lesson Content:

Diligence is a virtue that speaks to the quality of our work and our commitment to carrying tasks through to completion. For most people in prison, a time will come when the gates open. Even people who serve life sentences have an opportunity may argue for a higher level of liberty at some point.

For that reason, each person should be diligent about preparing for success after prison.

A lack of diligence can lead to cascading problems after release. Consider the example of James and Juan, people with contrasting stories. At one point, they were on a similar path. But they took vastly different approaches to their circumstances.

Both James and Juan served time in prison for similar offenses. During their incarceration, they each had the opportunity to access self-study programs to enhance their knowledge and skills. However, their reactions to this chance set them on contrasting journeys. One chose to be diligent in his preparations for success, and the other didn't care about preparing.

Juan, an optimistic and determined individual, recognized the importance of diligent self-improvement, and took full advantage of available resources. He didn't wait for the system to offer courses or credits. Juan immersed himself in various self-directed study materials. He learned to communicate better, and he learned better math skills. Those efforts led to studies ranging from entrepreneurship to finance. Juan dreamed of creating a brighter future for himself and others.

After he got out, Juan had a solid foundation of knowledge and skills. He combined his newfound understanding of business with his passion and creativity, eventually founding a successful company. Juan created a thriving business through hard work, dedication, and the ability to adapt. He also became an inspiration to others who faced similar challenges.

On the other hand, James held a more cynical perspective during his time behind bars. Rather than engineering a diligent adjustment strategy, he complained. He argued that the system didn't allow him to improve his situation. He dismissed the idea of self-study programs, believing they were a waste of time.

Upon his release, James faced a series of difficulties. Without the skills and knowledge necessary to secure stable employment, he struggled to find suitable work. His lack of preparation during his time in prison left him ill-equipped to reintegrate into society. His failure to prepare diligently led to further problems, such as homelessness and brushes with the law, which only compounded his challenges.

The divergent paths of Juan and James highlight the significance of personal initiative and diligent self-improvement, even in the face of adversity. While Juan embraced the opportunity to grow and acquire valuable knowledge and skills, neglect perpetuated problems for James.

The story of James and Juan reminds us that, regardless of circumstances, we make daily choices. Our actions can profoundly impact our lives. It is a testament to the transformative power of determination, resilience, and personal growth.

Consider the valuable lessons contained within this tale. Just as Juan built a successful future through his diligent preparation and perseverance, so can you overcome challenges and create a path toward prosperity.

If you're diligent, you'll do things carefully, consistently, and to the best of your ability. In personal development, particularly while incarcerated, embracing diligence can be transformative.

The following steps may foster diligence for personal development:

Set Clear Goals:

Start by outlining what you want to achieve. Master a new skill, improve physical fitness, or nurture emotional well-being.

Create a Plan:

Once you set your goals, create a plan to achieve them. Break down each goal into smaller, manageable tasks, and commit to completing these tasks diligently.

Set Priorities:

As Stephen Covey wrote in The Seven Habits, ensure you put first things first. You've got to take little steps to open new opportunities later.

Consistency:

Be consistent in your efforts. Diligence isn't about making one significant effort; it's about the small, regular steps that lead to substantial change over time.

Focus:

Concentrate on the task at hand. Maintaining focus in an environment full of distractions is an act of diligence that can significantly enhance your personal development.

Patience:

Practice patience. Achieving goals takes time, and diligence means persisting despite slow progress.

If you follow this path and memorialize your efforts, others will notice when you begin to self-advocate in the future.

Questions and Activities: In one hour, answer as you deem appropriate.

» How do you understand the concept of diligence?

_____

_____

_____

_____

_____

_____

_____

_____

» Why do you think diligence can lead to personal development?

_____

_____

_____

_____

_____

_____

_____

_____

_____

» Share a recent example when you demonstrated diligence in accomplishing a task or pursuing a goal.

_____

_____

_____

_____

_____

_____
_____
_____
_____

» How did your diligence contribute to your personal growth?

_____
_____
_____
_____
_____
_____
_____
_____

» How can practicing diligence help you prepare for a successful life after release?

_____
_____
_____
_____
_____
_____
_____
_____
_____

» What specific tasks or goals are you pursuing diligently during your time in prison?

Activity:
   » Reflect on a recent task or goal you've worked on. Write down how you demonstrated diligence in this process and what you learned from it. Identify one new approach you could adopt to enhance your diligence further.
   » Remember, diligence is about the journey, not just the destination. It's about embracing the process, being committed to your tasks, and doing them to the best of your ability. As you continue to grow and develop in prison, the diligence you cultivate now will form a strong foundation for your success upon release.

LESSON 23: EMOTIONAL INTELLIGENCE

Vocabulary Word:

Emotional intelligence - The ability to recognize, understand, and manage one's own emotions and the emotions of others, and to use this awareness to guide thinking and behavior in social interactions.

Lesson Content:

Emotional intelligence involves being aware of and effectively managing our own emotions. It also leads to better understanding and empathy with the feelings of others. By developing our emotional intelligence, we cultivate healthier relationships, improve communication, and navigate conflicts with compassion and resilience.

I'll offer a scenario from my memories of living in a high-security federal prison. Tensions often run high in those environments, and conflicts arise frequently.

Jake, a person with high emotional intelligence, was in a precarious situation. Two others, Alex and Ryan, engaged in a heated argument. Jake, recognizing the importance of emotional intelligence in diffusing the situation, took the following actions:

1. Self-awareness: Jake acknowledged his emotions. He tried to remain calm and composed despite the tense environment of the pen. He understood that his emotional state could influence the outcome of the situation.

2. Empathy: Both Alex and Ryan had their own frustrations and challenges. Jake approached the situation with empathy, attempting to grasp their underlying emotions and perspectives.

3. Active Listening: Jake listened to Alex and Ryan without judging them. He encouraged them to express their concerns and frustrations. They all had an equal opportunity to express themselves, fostering a sense of understanding.

4. Mediation: Jake could mediate, facilitating an open and respectful dialogue between Alex and Ryan. He encouraged them to express their grievances but helped them see each other's point of view.

5. Emotion Regulation: Jake demonstrated emotional stability and self-control. He managed his own emotions, avoiding personal biases and remaining neutral. His composed demeanor created an environment conducive to conflict resolution.

6. Problem-solving: Jake guided the conversation toward identifying solutions to the underlying issues. He helpd Alex and Ryan find common ground and encouraged them

to brainstorm mutually beneficial resolutions. Jake promoted cooperation and a shift away from confrontation by focusing on problem-solving.

7. Follow-up and Support: After mediating the dispute, Jake followed up with Alex and Ryan individually to ensure that tensions had eased and that they had resolved the conflict.

Jake's emotional intelligence helped to de-escalate a problem, and that skill would prove highly valuable to a person in prison or after release. It requires practice, understanding, and patience.

Self-Awareness:

Emotional intelligence starts with self-awareness. It involves recognizing and understanding our emotions, including their triggers, patterns, and impact on our thoughts and behavior. By becoming more self-aware, we can better regulate our emotions and make conscious responses.

Empathy:

Empathy is a key component of emotional intelligence. It is the ability to understand and share the feelings of others. By empathizing with others, we develop deeper connections, enhance communication, and build trust and rapport.

Emotional Regulation:

Emotional intelligence includes the skill of effectively managing and regulating our emotions. It involves recognizing and acknowledging our emotions without being overwhelmed by them, and finding healthy ways to express and cope with them.

Social Awareness:

Emotional intelligence extends to social awareness, which is the ability to perceive and understand the emotions and needs of others. By being attentive to non-verbal cues and actively listening, we can better understand and respond to the emotions of those around us.

Relationship Management:

Emotional intelligence encompasses the skill of managing relationships effectively. It involves communicating assertively, resolving conflicts constructively, and fostering positive connections based on empathy, understanding, and respect.

Questions and Activities: In one hour, answer as you deem appropriate.

» How do you understand the concept of emotional intelligence?

_____

_____

_____

_____
_____
_____
_____
_____
_____
_____
_____

» Why is emotional intelligence important for personal development, particularly during imprisonment?

_____
_____
_____
_____
_____
_____
_____

» Share an example of a time when emotional intelligence helped you navigate a challenging relationship or conflict in prison. How did it contribute to your personal growth?

_____
_____
_____
_____
_____
_____

» How can developing your emotional intelligence help you prepare for building healthy relationships and resolving conflicts after release?

_____

_____
_____
_____
_____
_____
_____
_____
_____
_____

» What strategies can you employ to enhance your emotional intelligence during your time in prison?

_____
_____
_____
_____
_____
_____
_____
_____
_____
_____
_____

Activity:
» Reflect on a recent interaction or conflict where you could have demonstrated more emotional intelligence. Describe the emotions involved, how you responded, and the outcome of the situation. What could you have done differently to handle the situation with more emotional intelligence?
» Identify one aspect of emotional intelligence that you would like to develop further. Write down specific actions you can take to enhance that aspect, such as practicing active listening, seeking feedback from others, or practicing self-reflection.
» Remember, emotional intelligence is a powerful tool for personal development, building positive relationships, and resolving conflicts. By developing and nurturing your emotional intelligence during your time in prison, you equip yourself with the ability to understand and manage emotions, empathize with others, and foster healthy and fulfilling connections. These skills will serve you well in your journey towards post-release success.

LESSON 24: CULTIVATING EMPATHY

Vocabulary Word:
Empathy - The ability to understand and share the feelings, perspectives, and experiences of others, and to respond with compassion and sensitivity.

Lesson Content:
Empathy is a vital skill for personal development. It involves stepping into the shoes of others, understanding their emotions, and responding with compassion and understanding. By cultivating empathy, we foster deeper connections, build stronger relationships, and create a more supportive and harmonious environment.

If we develop empathy, we simultaneously develop skills that lead to higher success upon release. On the flip side, we can ignore empathy's value and adjust to a prison setting with apathy. That means we don't care about others or adapt in ways that make us comfortable in prison—but incapable of functioning in society.

We must think about the challenges that follow for all people who leave prison. People who serve time in prison may face challenges with:

» Finding employment,
» Obtaining credit,
» Opening business relationships.

Those who develop empathy will have a higher skill set they can draw upon to overcome those challenges. For example, had I not developed empathy while serving 26 years in prison, I would have faced more challenges after release. I trained myself to think as if I'd always be unemployable. When I walked out, I felt as if I would have to create my own income streams.

Empathy plays a crucial role for people who choose to live an entrepreneurial life. We must connect with customers, understanding their needs. We listen so we can solve their problems, then we create products and services around their needs.

By empathizing with the end users, an entrepreneur engages in active listening. He must research markets to learn more about pain points he wants to resolve. An empathetic approach will help an entrepreneur understand the nuances of the market.

As a former prisoner who strives to create products and services for the prison system, I listen to the market and strive to understand the needs of people who are very cynical of me—because of my background.

Develop empathy while serving a prison term, and a person will advance prospects for success upon release.

Perspective-Taking:

Empathy begins with perspective-taking. It involves putting ourselves in the position of others, imagining their experiences, and seeing the world through their eyes. By considering different viewpoints, we gain a broader understanding of the human experience.

Active Listening:

Empathy is closely tied to active listening. It means attentively and non-judgmentally listening to others, seeking to understand their emotions and concerns. By fully engaging in the conversation and showing genuine interest, we create a safe space for people to share their thoughts and feelings.

Emotional Recognition:

Empathy requires recognizing and acknowledging the emotions of others. It involves being attuned to verbal and non-verbal cues, and validating their feelings. By acknowledging and accepting their emotions, we demonstrate empathy and support.

Cultivating Compassion:

Empathy is connected to compassion, which is the genuine concern for the well-being of others. It involves responding with kindness, empathy, and a willingness to help. Cultivating compassion fosters a sense of connectedness and promotes positive relationships.

Respecting Diversity:

Empathy encompasses respecting diversity and appreciating the unique experiences and backgrounds of others. It involves recognizing and valuing different perspectives and cultural differences. By embracing diversity, we create an inclusive and empathetic environment.

Questions and Activities: In one hour, answer as you deem appropriate.

» How do you understand the concept of empathy?

_____

_____

_____

_____

_____

_____

_____

_____

_____

_____

» Why is empathy important for personal development, particularly during imprisonment?

_____

_____

_____

_____

_____

_____

_____

_____

_____

» Share an example of a time when empathy helped you understand someone's perspective or support them in prison. How did it contribute to your personal growth?

_____

_____

_____

_____

_____

_____

_____

_____

_____

_____

_____

» How can cultivating empathy help you prepare for building meaningful relationships and resolving conflicts after release?

_____

_____

_____

_____

_____
_____
_____
_____
_____
_____
_____

» What strategies can you employ to enhance your empathy during prison?

_____
_____
_____
_____
_____
_____
_____
_____
_____
_____
_____

Activity:

» Think of a recent interaction where you could have demonstrated more empathy. Reflect on the situation and describe how you could have better understood the other person's feelings and responded with empathy. What steps can you take in the future to cultivate empathy in similar situations?

» Identify one area where you would like to develop greater empathy. Write down specific actions you can take to enhance your empathy in that area, such as practicing active listening, engaging in perspective-taking exercises, or seeking opportunities to learn about different cultures and experiences.

» Remember, empathy is a powerful tool for personal development, fostering connections, and creating a compassionate environment. By cultivating and practicing empathy during prison, you develop a deeper understanding of others, build stronger relationships, and contribute to a more empathetic society. These skills will serve you well in your journey towards post-release success.

LESSON 25: EMPOWERMENT

Vocabulary Word:

Empowerment - The process of gaining the knowledge, skills, confidence, and autonomy to take control of one's life, make informed decisions, and achieve personal goals.

Lesson Content:

When a federal judge says "I sentence you to the custody of the attorney general," we lose personal autonomy.

While we serve the sanction, other people enforce policies that influence our lives. Those policies will tell us:

> » Where to sleep,
> » With whom we share small spaces,
> » When we eat,
> » What we eat,
> » How we communicate, and
> » How we spend our time.

All of us will have to make it through 24 hours every day and roughly 365 days every year. What we choose to do with our time will determine whether we empower ourselves or allow the institution to govern our lives completely.

If we learn to empower ourselves, we take a giant step toward our preparation for success upon release.

To empower ourselves, we acquire the necessary tools, knowledge, and confidence to take control of our life, make informed choices, and work toward achieving personal goals. The daily lessons in our course Preparing for Success after Prison put considerable emphasis on showing the value of developing the following skills:

> » Building a more robust vocabulary,
> » Becoming better writers,
> » Improving our communication skills,
> » Critical thinking,
> » Being self-directed.

By working toward personal development in those areas, we can overcome obstacles, build resilience, and create a brighter future. They empower us. On a personal level, I can attest to how those skills opened higher levels of liberty and success after I completed 9,500 days in federal prison.

For that reason, I consider empowerment crucial for personal development:

Self-Awareness:

Empowerment starts with self-awareness. It involves recognizing your strengths, weaknesses, values, and aspirations. By understanding yourself better, you can identify areas for growth, set meaningful goals, and take ownership of your journey.

Knowledge Acquisition:

The more we learn, the more we empower ourselves. It requires actively seeking information, learning new skills, and expanding our understanding. You become better equipped to make informed decisions and navigate challenges by continuously acquiring knowledge.

Building Confidence:

Empowerment and confidence go together. As we empower ourselves, we believe in our abilities, embrace a positive mindset, and challenge self-limiting beliefs. By building self-confidence, we can overcome self-doubt, take risks, and persevere through setbacks.

Taking Action:

Empowerment involves taking action toward goals. It requires setting clear objectives, breaking them into manageable steps, and creating action plans. By taking consistent action, we can make progress and realize our potential.

Seeking Support:

Empowerment is not a solitary journey. It involves seeking support from others, building a network of positive influences, and surrounding yourself with individuals who uplift and inspire you. Connecting with others allows us to access valuable resources, gain insights, and cultivate community.

Questions and Activities: In one hour, answer as you deem appropriate.

» How do you understand the concept of empowerment?

_____
_____
_____
_____
_____
_____
_____
_____
_____

» Why is empowerment important for personal development, particularly during imprisonment?

» Share an example of when empowerment helped you overcome a significant obstacle or achieve a goal in prison. How did it contribute to your personal growth?

» How can embracing empowerment help you prepare for a successful life after release?

_____

_____

_____

_____

_____

_____

_____

» What strategies can you employ to enhance your sense of empowerment during prison?

_____

_____

_____

_____

_____

_____

_____

_____

_____

_____

Activity:

» Think about a goal or aspiration you have for your future. Write it down and describe how achieving that goal would empower you. Reflect on the knowledge, skills, and actions you need to develop to make progress toward that goal.

» Identify one area in your life where you want to experience greater empowerment. Write down specific actions to empower yourself in that area, such as seeking relevant educational opportunities, connecting with supportive mentors, or setting small achievable goals to build confidence.

» Remember, empowerment catalyzes personal development, resilience, and positive change. By embracing empowerment during prison, you can tap into your inner potential, make informed choices, and create a fulfilling future. Your journey towards post-release success begins with empowering yourself today.

LESSON 26: PERSONAL EXCELLENCE

Vocabulary Word:
Excellence - The quality of being outstanding.

Lesson Content:
I began serving my federal prison sentence in the late 1980s. I didn't know what challenges I would face once I got out. A mentor sent me a copy of *In Search of Excellence*, a book by Thomas Peters, suggesting I might learn some lessons from the book.

My mentor helped me a great deal. By learning from him, I understood that we could always work to pursue excellence personally. Our pursuit of excellence didn't have anything to do with the decisions that others made. It had everything to do with our commitment to excellence.

First, we need to define excellence.

Those who've read *Earning Freedom: Conquering a 45-Year Prison Term* may recall how the same author, Tom Peters, wrote a separate book that included a profile about a federal prison warden, Dennis Luther. Warden Luther pursued excellence. I interviewed him for the master's thesis I wrote about preparing for success after prison. Although Warden couldn't change sentencing laws, he could build incentive-based programs that allowed people to work toward achieving their highest potential.

Striving for personal excellence helps us improve and work toward becoming the best version of ourselves. It involves setting and consistently meeting personal standards, being accountable for our actions, and always trying to exceed our previous best.

The path to personal excellence might seem challenging in prison, but a person can always work toward excellence with patience, persistence, and a positive mindset.

We develop confidence when we focus on:

» personal growth,
» learning new skills, and
» making the best use of the time available to prepare for a successful life after release.

In defining personal excellence, leaders teach us that it's essential to consider the following:

Self-awareness:
Understand our strengths, weaknesses, passions, and values. This knowledge forms the basis for setting personal goals and standards.

Goal-setting:

Define clear, achievable goals for ourselves. These goals should challenge us and be realistic, contributing to our personal growth and development.

Persistence:

We should consistently strive to meet our goals and standards, no matter the obstacles. Persistence is vital to achieving personal excellence.

Continuous learning:

Seek to learn something new every day. Learning is a lifelong process, especially crucial in a challenging environment like prison.

Positive Mindset:

Maintain a positive attitude. See every difficulty as an opportunity for growth and every failure as a chance to learn and improve.

Questions and Activities: In one hour, answer as you deem appropriate.

» In your own words, how would you define personal excellence?

_____

_____

_____

_____

_____

_____

_____

_____

_____

_____

_____

_____

» What does personal excellence look like for you?

_____

_____

_____

_____

» What personal goals can you set to strive for excellence while in prison?

» How can achieving these goals prepare you for success after release?

» Can you identify a recent situation in which you demonstrated persistence despite facing a challenge?

_____

_____

_____

_____

_____

_____

_____

_____

_____

» How did this experience contribute to your journey toward personal excellence?

_____

_____

_____

_____

_____

_____

_____

_____

_____

_____

Activity:

» Reflect on your definition of personal excellence and write it down. Then, set at least three personal goals that align with this definition. These goals should be specific, measurable, achievable, relevant, and time-bound (SMART).

» Remember, personal excellence is a journey, not a destination. It's about self-improvement and becoming the best version of yourself. It's not about comparing yourself with others but surpassing your past performance. Personal excellence will prepare you for success upon your release from prison. So, strive for excellence, not perfection!

LESSON 27: GOAL SETTING

Vocabulary Word:

Goal Setting - The process of identifying specific, measurable, achievable, relevant, and time-bound objectives that guide and motivate individuals towards desired outcomes.

Lesson Content:

Rudy and I met during the final five years of my sentence. Rudy had already served 15 years when we met, and he anticipated release within two years. We worked together on the farm at a minimum-security camp in Lompoc, California. Like Rudy, I was in the final years of my prison term.

While we were on the job, we met Lee. Lee owned a large business, employing more than 500 people. He served a relatively short sentence for a tax-related offense.

While the three of us worked together on the farm, Lee offered career advice to us both. He recommended that each of us begin to write our goals. If we wrote specific goals and put clear timelines on those goals, we'd be more effective at making progress that would help us succeed upon release.

Recognizing that Lee had a lot of wisdom, I embraced the advice he offered. I showed him my goals, describing the accomplishments I intended to make during the final five years of my imprisonment. On the other hand, Rudy said he didn't need to write down his goals. He said he would figure out the steps to take once he got out. He didn't see any value in writing down goals.

Later, when I got out, I began building advocacy campaigns. Through that work, I had to profile people who faced challenges after their release from prison. By working with community groups, I saw Rudy again. As a homeless man, Rudy said he participated in the group because he had so many challenges trying to get on his feet.

After we parted ways, I remembered that conversation the three of us had during the time we spent working on that prison farm at Lompoc. Had Rudy listened to guidance from Lee, he could have set goals. Those goals may have led to better outcomes.

The salient point is that regardless of where we are, we can always work to set Specific, measurable, action-oriented, realistic, time-bound goals.

Goal setting is a fundamental skill for personal development. It involves defining and planning objectives that serve as guideposts for our actions and motivate us to achieve desired outcomes. By mastering the art of goal setting, we can create a clear roadmap toward success and maximize our potential.

Understanding the concept of goal setting is essential for personal development:

Specificity:

Goals should be specific and well-defined. By clearly articulating what you want to achieve, you create a target to focus your efforts and actions upon. Specific goals provide clarity and serve as a compass for your journey.

Measurability:

Goals should be measurable, allowing you to track progress and determine success. Establishing quantifiable criteria ensures that you can assess whether you are moving closer to your desired outcome or if adjustments are necessary. Measurable goals enable you to celebrate milestones along the way.

Achievability:

Goals should be realistic and attainable. While it's important to set ambitious goals that challenge you, they should also be within the realm of possibility. By setting achievable goals, you build confidence and maintain motivation throughout the process.

Relevance:

Goals should align with your values, aspirations, and overall vision for personal development. They should be meaningful and relevant to your individual circumstances and desires. Relevance ensures that you stay engaged and committed to pursuing your goals.

Time-bound:

Goals should have a defined timeframe or deadline. Setting specific timelines creates a sense of urgency and helps prioritize tasks. Time-bound goals enable you to manage your efforts effectively and prevent procrastination.

Questions and Activities: In one hour, answer as you deem appropriate.

» How do you understand the concept of goal setting?

_____

_____

_____

_____

_____

_____

_____

_____

» Why is goal setting important for personal development, particularly during imprisonment?

» Share an example of a goal you set for yourself in prison. How did goal setting contribute to your personal growth and progress?

» How can effective goal setting help you prepare for a successful life after release?

_____
_____
_____
_____
_____
_____
_____
_____
_____

» What strategies can you employ to enhance your goal-setting skills during your time in prison?

_____
_____
_____
_____
_____
_____
_____
_____
_____
_____

Activity:

» Think about a long-term goal you want to achieve after your release. Write it down and break it down into smaller, actionable steps. Consider the specific, measurable, achievable, relevant, and time-bound aspects of each step. Create a timeline for achieving each milestone.

» Reflect on a goal you set in the past and achieved. Write down the steps you took to accomplish it and how goal setting played a role in your success. Identify any challenges you faced and how you overcame them. Share your experience with the class to inspire others.

» Remember, goal setting is a powerful tool for personal development and progress. By setting clear, actionable goals and applying the principles of specificity, measurability, achievability, relevance, and time-bound aspects, you can pave the way for success. Embrace goal setting during your time in prison as a pathway to a brighter future.

LESSON 28: GRATITUDE AND APPRECIATION

Vocabulary Word:

Gratitude - The quality of being thankful and showing appreciation for the positive aspects of life, acknowledging the goodness in oneself, others, and the world around.

Lesson Content:

I'll always feel grateful to Officer Wilson, who presided over the housing unit during my time in pretrial detention. After a jury convicted me of every count, I faced a life sentence. Since I was only 23, I didn't know how to process that possibility.

Officer Wilson stood outside my cell. Through the locked door, he spoke with me, offering encouragement. He recommended a book that he thought would help my spirits. The book was about Nelson Mandela.

I did not know Nelson Mandela. But when I began reading his story, I learned that he was an active anti-apartheid activist who had been in prison for decades. In his writing, Nelson Mandela emphasized the importance of gratitude in various aspects of life. A quote from his work:

"Let us rise up and be thankful, for if we didn't learn a lot today, at least we learned a little, and if we didn't learn a little, at least we didn't get sick, and if we got sick, at least we didn't die; so, let us all be thankful."

The quote reflected Mr. Mandela's ability to find gratitude even in challenging circumstances. It conveys his belief in acknowledging and appreciating the positive aspects of life, no matter how small they may seem.

Mandela's remarkable life and ability to maintain resilience and optimism even during his 27-year imprisonment serve as a testament to his embodiment of gratitude in practice. It helped me climb through the 26 years I lived as number 16377-004.

Nelson Mandela taught me that gratitude is a powerful practice that can transform our perspective and contribute to personal development, even in challenging circumstances like imprisonment. It involves recognizing and appreciating the positive aspects of life, fostering a sense of contentment, and cultivating a mindset of abundance. By embracing gratitude, we can enhance our well-being, resilience, and overall outlook on life.

Understanding the concept of gratitude is essential for personal growth:

Appreciation:

Gratitude begins with appreciating our blessings and positive experiences, no matter how small they may seem. It involves recognizing the goodness in oneself, others, and the world around us. By acknowledging and valuing these aspects, we cultivate a sense of gratitude.

Mindfulness:

Gratitude requires being present and mindful of the present moment. It involves paying attention to the beauty, kindness, and opportunities in everyday life. Practicing mindfulness makes us more attuned to the positive aspects that often go unnoticed.

Perspective Shift:

Gratitude involves shifting our perspective from focusing on what we lack to acknowledging what we have. It requires reframing challenges as opportunities for growth and finding silver linings in difficult situations. By adopting a grateful perspective, we cultivate resilience and optimism.

Gratitude Practices:

We can cultivate gratitude through various techniques. These include keeping a gratitude journal, expressing appreciation to others, reflecting on positive moments, and practicing acts of kindness. By engaging in these practices, we reinforce our gratitude mindset and strengthen our sense of appreciation.

Ripple Effect:

Gratitude has a ripple effect on our relationships and overall well-being. When we express gratitude, we enhance our happiness while simultaneously uplifting and strengthening our connections with others.

When we spread gratitude, we contribute to a positive and supportive environment.

Questions and Activities: In one hour, answer as you deem appropriate.

» How do you understand the concept of gratitude?

_____

_____

_____

_____

_____

_____

_____

» Why is cultivating gratitude important for personal development, particularly during imprisonment?

» Share an example of a situation in prison where practicing gratitude helped you maintain a positive mindset and enhance your personal growth.

» How can embracing gratitude help you prepare for a successful life after release?

_____
_____
_____
_____
_____
_____
_____
_____

» What strategies can you employ to cultivate gratitude during your time in prison?

_____
_____
_____
_____
_____
_____
_____
_____
_____
_____
_____
_____

Activity:

» Take a few moments to reflect on three things you are grateful for today. Write them down in your journal and briefly explain why you appreciate them. Challenge yourself to identify both big and small aspects of your life to cultivate a broad perspective of gratitude.

» Think about someone in your life who has made a positive impact on you, whether it's a friend, family member, or staff member. Write a letter expressing your gratitude and appreciation for their presence in your life. If possible, consider sharing this letter with them or keeping it as a reminder of gratitude.

» Remember, gratitude is a practice that can transform your mindset and enhance your personal growth. By cultivating a grateful perspective, acknowledging the positive aspects of life, and expressing appreciation, you can find strength and resilience even in challenging circumstances. Embrace the power of gratitude during your time in prison and beyond.

LESSON 29: GROWTH MINDSET

Vocabulary Word:

Growth Mindset - The belief that abilities and intelligence can be developed through dedication, effort, and learning. It emphasizes the power of resilience, embracing challenges, and seeking opportunities for growth.

Lesson Content:

People in prison need a growth mindset. It can help us understand that we can improve through dedication and effort. When living in a prison setting, we must embrace challenges, persist in the face of setbacks, and seek opportunities for growth and learning.

While growing through my sentence, Thomas Edison, who invented the electric light bulb, inspired me. He's famous for saying:

"I have not failed. I've just found 10,000 ways that won't work."

His words reflect an extraordinary mindset. He didn't see setbacks and failures as signs of defeat. They were steppingstones on his path to success.

Edison's perseverance and willingness to learn from each attempt ultimately led to his groundbreaking invention.

Embracing a growth mindset can transform the way we approach challenges and setbacks. It involves understanding that setbacks are not indicative of our intelligence or worth but rather opportunities for learning and improvement.

With a growth mindset, we become more resilient, adaptable, and open to new possibilities. Although I had to climb through a 45-year sentence, leaders like Thomas Edison helped me prepare for the journey and to emerge successfully.

Understanding the concept of a growth mindset is essential for personal development:

Belief in Development:

A growth mindset starts with believing we can develop our abilities through effort and learning. It challenges the notion that intelligence or talent is fixed and encourages individuals to view their potential as limitless. By embracing this belief, we become more motivated to pursue growth and strive for improvement.

Embracing Challenges:

Having a growth mindset means actively seeking out challenges and seeing them as opportunities for growth. Instead of avoiding difficulties, individuals with a growth mindset embrace them, knowing that challenges provide valuable experiences and avenues for learning. They understand that effort and perseverance are necessary to overcome obstacles.

Persistence and Resilience:

A growth mindset encourages us to persist despite setbacks and failures. Rather than being discouraged by setbacks, individuals with a growth mindset view them as temporary setbacks and opportunities to learn, adjust, and try again. This resilience helps individuals bounce back stronger and continue their journey toward personal growth.

Learning from Feedback:

Instead of feeling threatened or defensive, we welcome feedback, even if it's critical. Feedback provides insights and areas for development. We should use feedback as a guide to refine our skills and make progress.

Cultivating a Passion for Learning:

A growth mindset fosters a love for learning and continuous improvement. It encourages individuals to explore new ideas, expand their knowledge, and seek new experiences. By nurturing a passion for learning, individuals with a growth mindset stay curious and engaged, continually pushing their boundaries.

Cultivating a growth mindset involves specific strategies:

Embrace Challenges:

Seek out opportunities to challenge yourself and step outside your comfort zone. Embrace tasks that may seem difficult initially, knowing they offer growth chances.

Practice Positive Self-Talk:

Challenge negative self-talk and replace it with positive and encouraging statements. Remind yourself that you can learn and improve with effort.

Set Goals:

Set specific and realistic goals that stretch your abilities. Break them down into manageable steps, and celebrate milestones along the way.

Learn from Failures:

View failures as learning experiences rather than personal shortcomings. Analyze what went wrong, identify lessons, and use them to adjust your approach and improve.

Seek Feedback:

Actively seek feedback from others and be open to constructive criticism. Use feedback Certainly! Here's a section with self-directed questions and activities to accompany the lesson on the importance of having a growth mindset:

Questions and Activities: In one hour, answer as you deem appropriate.

Interns@PrisonProfessorsTalent.com / Page 258

» How would you describe your current mindset?

_____

_____

_____

_____

_____

_____

_____

_____

_____

_____

» Do you tend to have a growth or fixed mindset in different areas of your life?

_____

_____

_____

_____

_____

_____

_____

_____

_____

_____

_____

_____

» What situations or challenges trigger a fixed mindset for you?

_____

_____

_____

_____

_____

_____

_____

» How do you typically respond in those situations?

_____

_____

_____

_____

_____

_____

_____

_____

_____

_____

_____

_____

_____

_____

_____

Activity:

Growth Mindset Journal:
Create a growth mindset journal where you can reflect on your experiences, challenges, and progress. Take a few minutes each day to write about a situation or encounter where you applied a growth mindset. Describe how you approached the situation, what you learned, and how you plan to continue growing in that area.

Interview with a Growth Mindset Role Model:
Identify someone who embodies a growth mindset, such as a successful entrepreneur, athlete, or artist. Research their journey and accomplishments, and if possible, arrange an interview or find existing interviews or articles about them. Take note of their mindset, how they approach challenges, and the strategies they use to foster growth. Reflect on what you can learn from their example and how you can apply those insights to your own life.

Visualization Exercise:
Find a quiet and comfortable space where you can relax. Close your eyes and visualize yourself fully embracing a growth mindset. Imagine approaching challenges with enthusiasm and resilience, seeking out opportunities for growth, and celebrating your progress along the way. Engage all your senses to make the visualization vivid and powerful. Afterward, journal about your experience and the emotions it evoked.

Lesson 30: Integrity and Building Trust

Vocabulary Word:

Integrity - The quality of honesty, having strong moral principles, and adhering to ethical standards in one's actions and decisions.

Lesson Content:

Viktor Frankl exemplified remarkable integrity during his time as a prisoner in German concentration camps during World War II. Despite enduring immense suffering and witnessing unimaginable atrocities, Frankl demonstrated an unwavering commitment to his principles and values, serving as a beacon of integrity in the darkest circumstances.

Officer Wilson passed me a book about Viktor Frankl when I was locked in solitary before sentencing. I had been confined in solitary for several months while I awaited judicial proceedings. Since it was my first experience in prison, the solitude saddened me. When I read the book about Viktor Frankl, a renowned psychiatrist, I remember feeling as if I had a model for how I wanted to emerge from prison —regardless of the sentence length I would receive.

Dr. Frankl refused to compromise his beliefs or distort the truth, even when faced with extreme coercion or threats. His integrity, manifested through his unwavering honesty and authenticity, inspired anyone who read his story. His honesty extended to his interactions with anyone he met. Regardless of what atrocities he endured, he remained steadfast in upholding the dignity and humanity of others, offering support and compassion amidst the dehumanizing conditions.

Dr. Frankl wrote about the importance of developing meaning and purpose in life, regardless of external circumstances. Despite the immense despair and hopelessness surrounding him, he refused to succumb to despair. Instead, he dedicated himself to finding meaning while going through unimaginable suffering. His pursuit of purpose provided solace and encouraged others to hold onto their humanity and strive for something greater.

Dr. Frankl's integrity shone through his resilience and determination to remain faithful to his values. He refused to participate in or condone acts of cruelty, even if it meant endangering his life. In the face of dehumanization and the constant threat of death, he maintained his ethical stance, refusing to compromise his integrity for personal gain or survival.

Understanding the concept of integrity is essential for personal development, particularly for people in prison.

Honesty and Authenticity:

Integrity begins with being honest with oneself and others. It involves living aligned with our values and principles, being true to who we are, and representing ourselves honestly to the world. We build trust and credibility in our interactions by embracing honesty and authenticity.

Dr. Viktor Frankl's writing is one of the reasons we begin our course with the module on defining success—we have to know who we are and what we aspire to become if we want to succeed.

Ethical Decision Making:

Integrity guides ethical decision-making processes. It involves considering the moral implications of our choices and striving to do what is right, even when faced with difficult situations or temptations. Individuals with integrity prioritize ethical behavior and uphold moral standards.

Consistency and Reliability:

We demonstrate integrity through consistency and reliability in our words and actions. As Gandhi wrote, we must keep everything we think, say, and do in harmony. We must follow through on commitments, keep promises, and be dependable. By practicing consistency and reliability, we build a reputation of trustworthiness and earn the respect of others.

Accountability and Responsibility:

Integrity involves taking accountability for our actions and accepting responsibility for the consequences they may bring. It means owning up to mistakes, learning from them, and making amends when necessary. Individuals with integrity understand the impact of their choices and strive to make things right.

Building Trust and Character:

Integrity plays a vital role in building trust and character. It fosters healthy and meaningful relationships, both personally and professionally. By embodying integrity, we inspire others and create an environment of respect, openness, and trust.

Questions and Activities: In one hour, answer as you deem appropriate.

» How do you understand the concept of integrity?

_____

_____

_____

_____

_____

_____

_____

_____

_____

_____

_____

» Why is integrity important for personal growth and development, particularly during imprisonment?

_____

_____

_____

_____

_____

_____

_____

_____

_____

_____

_____

_____

» Share an example of a situation in prison where acting with integrity helped you maintain your values and contributed to your personal growth.

_____

_____

_____

_____

_____

_____

_____

_____

_____

_____

_____

» How can living with integrity help you prepare for a successful life after release?

_____

_____

_____

_____

_____

_____

_____

_____
_____
_____
_____
_____
_____

» What strategies can you employ to cultivate and demonstrate integrity during your imprisonment?

_____
_____
_____
_____
_____
_____
_____
_____
_____
_____
_____

Activity:
   » Reflect on a situation in which you faced a moral dilemma or had to make a difficult decision. Write about how acting with integrity influenced your choices and the outcomes that followed.
   » Discuss the lessons you learned and how they contribute to your personal growth.
   » Identify three personal values that are important to you. Describe how you align your actions with these values to live with integrity. Consider possible challenges and strategies to overcome them.
   » Remember, integrity is the foundation of personal growth and character development. By living with honesty, ethical principles, and accountability, you build trust, strengthen relationships, and pave the way for success. Embrace the power of integrity during your time in prison and carry it as a guiding principle in all areas of your life.

APPENDIX / VOCABULARY

#	Word	Definition	Type of word
1	abdicate	renounce a position, or fail to fulfill	verb
2	aberration	departure from the norm	noun
3	abolish	put an end to something	verb
4	abolition	stop	noun
5	abound	exist in large numbers	verb
6	absolve	set or declare (someone) free from blame, guilt, or responsibility.	verb
7	abundance	a very large quantity of something	noun
8	academia	environment of learning	noun
9	accompany	go somewhere with someone	verb
10	according	in a way that is appropriate to the particular circumstances.	adjective
11	accountability	being responsible and keeping track	noun
12	accumulate	in a way that is appropriate to the particular circumstances.	verb
13	acquisition	an asset or object bought or obtained, typically by a library or museum.	noun
14	acronym	an abbreviation formed from the initial letters of other words and pronounced as a word	noun
15	adapt	make suitable	verb
16	adhere	stick fast to, or believe in and follow	verb
17	adjunct	supplemental, or extra	adjective
18	admonish	an act or action of admonishing; authoritative counsel or warning.	verb
19	adolescence	after puberty, or when a young person develops from a child into an adult.	noun
20	adolescent	a young person	adjective
21	adversary	an opponent in a contest, or conflict	noun
22	advocate	public support, or pleading for something or on behalf of someone	noun or verb
23	alchemy	trasnformation of something from one form to another	noun
24	align	place or arrange in a straight line	verb
25	altercation	a noisy argument or disagreement, especially in public.	noun

#	Word	Definition	Type of word
26	amends	make minor changes in (a text) in order to make it fairer, more accurate, or more up-to-date	verb
27	analogy	a comparison between two things, typically for the purpose of explanation or clarification.	noun
28	anthology	a published collection of writing	noun
29	anticipate	regard as probable; expect or predict.	verb
30	antidote	a medicine taken or given to counteract poison	noun
31	apartheid	segregation on grounds of race	noun
32	apex	the top or highest part of something, especially one forming a point.	adjective
33	apply	make a formal applicatin or request	verb
34	ascertain	find (something) out for certain; make sure of.	noun
35	aspire	direct one's hopes or ambitions towards achieving something.	verb
36	assess	evaluate or estimate the nature, ability, or quality of.	verb
37	asset	something useful or valuable	noun
38	asylum	shelter or protection from danger, an institution	noun
39	atone	make amends or reparation.	verb
40	audacity	a willingness to take bold risks	noun
41	audaucious	showing willingness to take risks	adjective
42	author	someone who writes books, or writing books	noun or verb
43	autobiography	an account of a person's life written by that person	noun
44	autodidactic	self taught	noun
45	avatars	an incarnation, embodiment, or manifestation of a person or idea.	noun
46	axis	an line that supports something that rotates, a structure that supports a rotating object	noun
47	behalf	In the interest of	noun
48	bestow	To give something	verb
49	bi-partisan	supported by or consisting of two parties	adjective
50	biography	the life story of someone	noun
51	bleak	empty and not welcoming	adjective
52	bondage	slave	noun
53	burdensome	difficult to carry out or fulfill; taxing.	adjective

#	Word	Definition	Type of word
54	bureacracy	complex organization with many layers	noun
55	candidate	a person or thing regarded as suitable for or likely to receive a particular fate, treatment	noun
56	capacity	the maximum amount that something can contain.	noun
57	capital	money or other assets for a particular purpose such as starting a company or investing.	noun
58	caption	Short text that describes a picture, book, or video	noun
59	career	a type of job or profession	noun
60	catalyst	something that spawns change	verb
61	catapult	jumping over something	verb
62	catastrophic	really bad event	adjective
63	characterize	describe the distinctive nature or features of.	verb
64	charlatan	a fake, or imposter	noun
65	coalition	a group of people that come together in a common cause	noun
66	cog	a part of a larger mechanism	noun
67	collateral	someting pledged to support something else, or as an adjectice, connected to something	noun or adjective
68	colossal	extremely large	adjective
69	commute	the distance between two places	noun
70	compass	an instrument that shows direction	noun
71	comprehend	grasp mentally; understand.	verb
72	concentric	a pattern of circles and rings with the same center	adjective
73	concept	an idea or feeling or opinion	noun
74	conclude	to bring to an end	verb
75	condemn	to punish	verb
76	condition	a particular state of existence.	noun
77	configure	to put together	verb
78	confront	meet (someone) face to face with hostile or argumentative intent.	verb
79	conclusion	the end of something	noun
80	consent	to be okay with something or agree	verb or noun
81	consequence	the result of something	noun
82	constant	always going	adjective
83	consumer	a person who buys something	noun

#	Word	Definition	Type of word
84	contemplate	look thoughtfully for a long time at.	verb
85	contend	struggle to surmount (a difficulty or danger).	verb
86	context	the situation that can explain something	noun
87	convalescent	a place to rest	noun or adjective
88	converse	to talk	verb
89	convert	cause to change in form, character, or function.	verb
90	convey	to give something or communicate	verb
91	cope	adjusting to difficulty	verb
92	correspondence	to communicate through text or writing	noun
93	crabs in a bucket	theory that losers want to pull others down	phrase
94	credential	some type of authority or validation	noun
95	credibility	authority	noun
96	critical thinking	considering the opportunity cost of every decision	noun
97	culpable	responsible for something	noun
98	cultivate	develop something to a higher potential	verb
99	cynical	insincere and not trustworthy	adjective
100	debt	an obligation or something owed	noun
101	decipher	to understand or untangle	verb
102	differentiate	to show why someone or something is unique	verb
103	deficient	weaknesses in something	adjective
104	deliberate	with a thorough and clear intent	adjective
105	delude	to hide or deceive	verb
106	delusion	a belief in something that isn't true	noun
107	demise	the end or failure of something	noun
108	derail	to take off track	verb
109	despite	without being affected by, or inspite of	preposition
110	determinate	fixed and not changeable	adjective
111	determine	cause (something) to occur in a particular way; be the decisive factor in.	verb
112	detest	to hate	verb
113	devote	to be faithful	verb
114	devour	to consume	verb
115	disk	a round flat surface	noun
116	dismal	poor performance	adjective

#	Word	Definition	Type of word
117	disparate	something utterly different	adjective
118	dubious	questionable, hestitating, doubtful	adjective
119	dupe	to misrepresent and scam	verb
120	duress	under difficulty	noun
121	dwell	to spend too much time on	verb
122	ecosystem	all the things that work together in common	noun
123	elect	to get results through a democratic vote	verb
124	eligible	a possible contender	adjective
125	embark	to start	verb
126	embody	to make up something entirely	verb
127	embrace	to hold	verb
128	emerge	to get out of	verb
129	empower	to strengthen	verb
130	emulate	to be like something else	verb
131	encounter	to meet	verb
132	engineer	to plan	verb
133	enhance	to improve	verb
134	entangle	to get trapped up in	verb
135	epoch	a particular period of time	noun
136	equinimity	balanced in tough times	noun
137	era	a particular time	noun
138	erupt	to blow up	verb
139	esoteric	unusual and not easily understood	adjective
140	eternity	forever	noun
141	ethnic	different or distinct from others, with a shared culture	adjective
142	ethnicity	the culture of someone	noun
143	evolve	to grow and mature	verb
144	exemplary	a great example	adjective
145	exhaustion	to be tired	noun
146	existential	the life force of something	noun
147	expose	to show	verb
148	external	something outside	adjective
149	facilitate	to help	verb
150	faze	to surprise or worry someone	verb
151	fluent	to become comfortable with something, like language	adjective

#	Word	Definition	Type of word
152	formative	the start of something	adjective
153	fortitude	to strengthen	noun
154	foster	to make or promote something	verb
155	fragile	delicate	adjective
156	fraud	inauthentic and fake	noun
157	fund	to provide resources or a pot of money	verb or noun
158	gender	a group of people that share characteristics, like male or female	noun
159	generate	to create	verb
160	govern	to rule over	verb
161	graze	to eat in a field	verb
162	harmonize	to make consistent	verb
163	Hellenic	Relating to the ancient Greeks	adjective
164	hence	as a consequence	adverb
165	herd	a group of animals as a noun, or to move together as a verb	noun or verb
166	highlight	to bring attention to something	verb
167	hinder	to put a block on	verb
168	immense	large	adjective
169	immigrate	to move to another area	verb
170	imminent	to happen soon	adjective
171	immutable	not capable of change	adjective
172	impact	the force or action of one thing hitting another, or a powerful effect	verb or noun
173	implicate	to bring into trouble	verb
174	impose	to put upon or to insert	verb
175	impression	an idea or feeling or opinion	noun
176	incentivize	to reward	verb
177	incipient	the start	adjective
178	inclination	a likely outcome	noun
179	incline	going up	verb
180	incremental	in small steps	adjective
181	indefatigable	never get tired	adjective
182	indelible	stays permanently	adjective
183	indeterminate	not set in stone	adjective
184	indict	to formally charge	verb
185	infinite	never ends	adjective
186	inflict	to cause harm	verb

#	Word	Definition	Type of word
187	influence	to persuade or push toward a particular position	verb
188	infuse	to put inside of something	verb
189	initial	the first	noun
190	innovate	begin something	verb
191	insight	to gain awareness	noun
192	integral	part of the whole	adjective
193	integrate	to bring together	verb
194	integrity	being consistent with the whole, honorable	noun
195	intend	to want to do something	verb
196	intention	showing a commitment to do something	noun
197	intentional	showing a commitment to do something	adjective
198	interactive	working together in a dynamic way	adjective
199	intergeneration	spanning different generations	noun
200	interlude	something in between	noun
201	intermediate	something in between	adjective
202	intervene	to get in the middle of, or to become involved	verb
203	intricate	something precise and essential	adjective
204	introspect	to think back	verb
205	irony	normally signifying the opposite, typically for humorous or emphatic effect.	noun
206	journey	a trip or a voyage	noun or verb
207	judicial	having to do with the courts	noun
208	jurisdiction	having to do with the authority over a person or area	noun
209	justice-impacted	someone that has a relationship to the courts	adjective
210	keynote	a presentation or speech for an event	noun or verb
211	labyrinth	a maze	noun
212	languish	to wait for a long time	verb
213	legislate	to vote or create laws	verb
214	lens	a prism or perspective through which a person sees	noun
215	lethal	deadly	adjective
216	leverage	the action of using a lever to gain power over	noun or verb
217	lexicon	a dictionary or body of words	noun
218	manifest	to make clear	noun or verb

#	Word	Definition	Type of word
219	market	a place to shop or a way to gain customers	noun or verb
220	marketing	to bring attention to something	noun
221	matriculate	to enroll in an academic institution	verb
222	maxim	a known fact	noun
223	mediate	to bring into accord	verb
224	medieval	relating to a period of time around the 16th century	adjective
225	mediocre	bland and undistinguished	adjective
226	meditate	to make better	verb
227	mentor	to train or advise	noun
228	merge	to bring together	verb
229	merit	something earned	noun or verb
230	metaphor	something that relates or alludes to something else	noun
231	methodical	in a systemic way	adjective
232	metric	something to measure	adjective
233	ministry	a devotional purpose	noun
234	minotaur	a mythological beast	noun
235	modify	to change	verb
236	momentum	to gain traction or force	noun
237	moniker	a nickname	noun
238	monotony	the same thing over and over	noun
239	monumental	large and important	adjective
240	myth	something not true, but believed to be true	noun
241	mythological	existing as a work of fiction	adjective
242	nadir	the bottom of something, or lowest point	noun
243	naïve	gullible and unwise	adjective
244	navigate	to find the way	verb
245	necessitate	Essential to something	verb
246	neither	not either of two things	adverb or conjunction
247	network	a group of things or to bring a group of things together	verb or noun
248	neutral	not partial to one way or another	adjective
249	niche	a specific place	noun
250	obligate	to make responsible to do	verb
251	obliterate	to wipe out	verb
252	obsess	to dwell on something	verb
253	obstruct	to get in the way of	verb

#	Word	Definition	Type of word
254	odyssey	a long journey	noun
255	onerous	very hard	adjective
256	onus	a burden or responsibility	noun
257	ooze	to come out of	verb
258	optional	a choice	adjective
259	opus	a distinguished body of work, usually related to art	noun
260	oration	a speech	noun
261	orator	a speaker	noun
262	orchestrate	to make things happen	verb
263	ordinary	not unusual	adjective
264	paraphrase	to say something similar, but not exact	verb
265	pasture	a field	noun
266	perceive	to think about	verb
267	perception	the way a person thinks	noun
268	permeate	to spread throughout	verb
269	perpetuate	to keep going	verb
270	perseverance	to have strength to continue	noun
271	perseverate	to dwell on something	verb
272	persist	to stick with something	verb
273	perspective	a way of looking at things	noun
274	persuade	to bring people to your point of view	verb
275	pervasive	to spread throughout	adjective
276	phase	a stage of something	noun
277	philosophy	a way of thinking	noun
278	pitch	to state a point of view, or to throw	verb or a noun
279	pivot	to switch direction	verb
280	pledge	to make a commitment	verb
281	plethora	an abundance	adjective
282	plight	a difficult circumstance	noun
283	plural	more than one	adjective
284	poise	composure and dignity of manner.	noun
285	potency	powerful	adjective
286	potent	powerful	adjective
287	potential	possible	adjective
288	precipitate	to come before	verb
289	predator	something that preys on others	noun

#	Word	Definition	Type of word
290	predicament	a difficult circumstance	noun
291	perjure	to lie under oath	noun
292	presence	to have state of mind, or be in a place	noun
293	preside	to oversee something	verb
294	prevalent	widespread in a particular area or at a particular time	adjective
295	principle	a fundamental truth	noun
296	pristine	to be clean and without blemish	adjective
297	pro se	on one's own	adjective
298	proclamation	to state affirmatively	noun
299	profane	of a person or their behavior) not respectful of orthodox religious practice; irreverent	adjective
300	project	To look forward	verb
301	prolong	to keep going over time	verb
302	prompt	To get started	verb
303	prong	each of the separate parts of an attack or operation	noun
304	pronoun	a word that is used instead of a noun, like he or she	noun
305	prospect	a possibility, trying to make something happen	verb
306	protagonist	the hero of the story	noun
307	proximity	something close	noun
308	prudent	to use good sense	adjective
309	pursue	to go after or follow for a purpose	verb
310	quadrant	having four parts	noun or an adjective
311	quasi	almost but not quite	adjective
312	quest	a logn search for something	noun
313	rear	the back of something as a noun, or to raise as a verb	noun or verb
314	recalibrate	to reset and go again	verb
315	recidivate	to fail and return to the starting point	verb
316	recidivism	to happen over and over	noun
317	recidivist	someone who returns to the same problem	noun
318	reckless	without care or deliberateness	adjective
319	reconcile	to make amends	verb
320	reconfigure	to make over again	verb
321	redeem	to make right	verb

#	Word	Definition	Type of word
322	reflect	to think back	verb
323	refrain	to hold back	verb
324	relentless	to be persistent and keep going	adjective
325	relevance	to be of importance to the situation	noun
326	relevant	with meaning and purpose	adjective
327	remedial	to bring up to speed	adjective
328	remorse	to feel sad for poor behavior	adjective
329	render	to provide or give service or deliver	verb
330	resilient	the capacity to recuperate or recover	noun
331	resourceful	capable of self generating solutions to difficulties	adjective
332	restore	to make whole again	verb
333	retaliate	to take revenge	verb
334	reveal	to show	verb
335	revere	to show respect and admiration	verb
336	revert	to go back to the old way	verb
337	rife	filled and in abundance, plentiful	adjective
338	robust	big and powerful	adjective
339	salient	important and relevant to something	adjective
340	sanctions	punishment	noun
341	sanctuary	a place of rest	noun
342	sangfroid	calm and eaze in difficult circumstances	noun
343	scholar	Studious of a specific subject	adjective
344	scholarship	a body of work, or a reward	noun
345	sector	a division of something	noun
346	seize	To take	verb
347	self-actualization	to reach the highest potential, conscientiously	verb
348	self-advocate	to argue for a cause that applies to a person	verb
349	self-directed	to make things happen independently	adjective
350	self-empower	to build force through intrinsic motivation	verb
351	series	going in order	noun
352	Smart goals	goals that are specific, measurable, realistic, and time bound	noun
353	Socratic questioning	open ended questions, that lead to other questions in search of truth	verb
354	solicit	to sell, to try to obtain something from someone	verb

#	Word	Definition	Type of word
355	solitude	alone	noun
356	spawn	to make things	verb
357	speculate	to gamble	verb
358	spindle	a part of a machine that turns	noun
359	statute	a law	noun
360	statutory	relating to a law	adjective
361	stigma	something awful that sticks	noun
362	stint	a short time at something	noun
363	stoic	relating to the philosophy of ancient Greeks who taught that people should be objective.	noun
364	strategy	a plan or method or series of maneuvers	noun
365	strive	to go after something	verb
366	structure	something solid or permanent, like a building	noun
367	succumb	to give into something	verb
368	sufficient	enough	adjective
369	surmise	to think or infer without certain or strong evidence	verb
370	surreal	something unbelieveable	adjective
371	susceptible	vulnerable to something else	noun
372	swindle	to cheat or deceive	verb
373	systematic	in a methodical order	adjective
374	systemic	in a methodical order	noun
375	tacit	understood but not written out	adjective
376	tactic	a design that will lead to an end result	noun
377	task	something to do	noun
378	template	a formulaic way or model	noun or verb
379	The Enlightenment	an era	noun
380	theory	something more substantial than a guess, but not necessarily a fact	noun
381	thrive	to prosper	verb
382	titan	a leader or authority figure	noun
383	tolerant	kind and understanding	adjective
384	trait	a characteristic	noun
385	trajectory	on a path to something	noun
386	transcend	to overcome and get beyond	verb
387	transform	to change in form or appearance	verb
388	transition	movement, passage, or change	noun

#	Word	Definition	Type of word
389	transitional	an interim stage of something	adjective
390	trauma	a suffering or difficulty	noun
391	treacherous	evil and bad	adjective
392	trilogy	a three part thing	noun
393	tripart	having three parts	adjective
394	trivial	little and insignificant	adjective
395	typical	something normal or to be expected	adjective
396	tyranny	ruling over something unfairly	noun
397	undergrad- uate	not yet graduating from college	noun
398	unscathed	not harmed, injured, or changed	adjective
399	unsolicited	without asking or being asked	adjective
400	vacate	to do away with something	verb
401	variable	an optional thing	noun
402	vehement	strenous and with force	adjective
403	venture	to offer something	verb
404	verdict	a finding of fact	noun
405	virtual	relating to something but not existing	adjective
406	vocabulary	a body of words	noun
407	volatile	quick to change	adjective
408	vulnerable	weaknesses in something	adjective
409	wither	to die or fade away	verb
410	yield	to pause or give way	verb

Made in the USA
Columbia, SC
25 September 2024

42874068R00152